Childhood and Youth in African History

SE Duff

Childhood and Youth in African History

palgrave
macmillan

SE Duff
Colby College
Waterville, ME, USA

ISBN 978-3-031-11096-2   ISBN 978-3-031-11097-9 (eBook)
https://doi.org/10.1007/978-3-031-11097-9

© The Editor(s) (if applicable) and The Author(s), under exclusive licence to Springer Nature Switzerland AG 2022

This work is subject to copyright. All rights are solely and exclusively licensed by the Publisher, whether the whole or part of the material is concerned, specifically the rights of translation, reprinting, reuse of illustrations, recitation, broadcasting, reproduction on microfilms or in any other physical way, and transmission or information storage and retrieval, electronic adaptation, computer software, or by similar or dissimilar methodology now known or hereafter developed.

The use of general descriptive names, registered names, trademarks, service marks, etc. in this publication does not imply, even in the absence of a specific statement, that such names are exempt from the relevant protective laws and regulations and therefore free for general use.

The publisher, the authors, and the editors are safe to assume that the advice and information in this book are believed to be true and accurate at the date of publication. Neither the publisher nor the authors or the editors give a warranty, expressed or implied, with respect to the material contained herein or for any errors or omissions that may have been made. The publisher remains neutral with regard to jurisdictional claims in published maps and institutional affiliations.

Cover illustration: REUTERS / Alamy Stock Photo

This Palgrave Macmillan imprint is published by the registered company Springer Nature Switzerland AG.
The registered company address is: Gewerbestrasse 11, 6330 Cham, Switzerland

Acknowledgements

This book was commissioned and written under pandemic conditions and, as a result, there are many people to whom I owe profound thanks for their help, patience, and kindness. At Colby College, I am lucky to be in a department which supports, enthusiastically, research and writing, and so my thanks to Rob Weisbrot, Raffael Scheck, Paul Josephson, Larissa Taylor, and, especially, John Turner, Arnout van der Meer, and Danae Jacobson. I am particularly grateful to Danae, Jesse Meredith, Lauren Parker, Viktor Schmagin, Mary Ellis Gibson, Charles Orzech, and Chris Walker, who provided fantastically useful commentary on the early chapters of the manuscript. I am grateful that these colleagues are friends too, alongside Denise Bruesewitz, Thom Klepach, Mo Shabangu, Annie Hikido, Justin Becknell, Kate Sartoris, Sonja Thomas, Dean Allbritton, Masi Ngidi-Brown, Kerill O'Neil, Valerie Dionne, Nikky Singh, Dan Cohen, Winifred Tate, Jin Goh, Laura Seay, Luke Parker, Ray Grant, and Ellen Richmond and the ladies of the book group.

Kristine Alexander, Stephanie Olsen, and Karen Vallgårda are some of my best and most challenging intellectual interlocutors. I am thankful, too, to Divya Kannan and Anandini Dar, whose wonderful conference, 'Childhood, Youth, and Identity', at Shiv Nadar University in January 2020 shaped many of the ideas in this book. Tom Spear commissioned an entry for the *Oxford Research Encyclopedia of African History* which formed the basis of this book. All mistakes and omissions are very much my own.

I completed this book in South Africa in the months before my father's death and am especially indebted to supportive friends there and correspondents abroad: Saskia Beranek, Jane McGaughey (and Eric), Megan Jones, Elizabeth de Stadler, Ester Levinrad, Claudia Gastrow and Chris Ouma (and, of course, Nava), Shireen Hassim, Stephen Sparks, Nafisa Essop Sheikh, Lucy Allais, Catherine Burns, Sharad Chari and Ismail Jazbhay, Kate Hollander, Sandra Swart, Claire Loveday, Natasha Erlank, and Isabel Hofmeyr. Profound thanks to my family—Elizabeth Duff, Anton Barguirdjian, Francois van Schalkwyk, and Samantha Masters—my parents, and especially and above all, my mother, Denni Duff, who knows this book better than I do. My gratitude to her is unending. Christopher Lee made all things feel possible.

Colby made available sabbatical funding, without which this book would not exist. My great thanks to Margaret McFadden for her stalwart institutional support, and Teresa Van Deventer's exceptional kindness and efficiency. At Palgrave, I thank Emily Russell, who commissioned this book, as well as the eternally helpful and patient Joseph Johnson and Eliana Rangel. I appreciate the care and enthusiasm with which Alison D. Ollivierre of Tombolo Maps and Design drew the maps.

I am grateful to the following archives, libraries, and photographers for permission to reproduce photographs: the National Library of Scotland, the Yale Divinity School Library, the Leipzig Mission Picture Archive, the Basel Mission Archive, the Moravian Archives Herrnhut, the Melville J. Herskovits Library of African Studies Winterton Collection at Northwestern University Libraries, Omar Badsha, and the University of Cape Town Libraries.

Contents

1 Introduction 1
2 Age and Generation 17
3 Enslavement and Unfreedom 45
4 Race and Childhood 79
5 Schooling and Education 101
6 Work and Play 131
7 Politics and Violence 155
8 Conclusion 191

Bibliography 197

Index 209

List of Maps

Map 1.1 Africa in 2022   5
Map 4.1 Africa in 1914   92

List of Photographs

Photograph 1.1	Young girls doing laundry in Rungwe District, Tanzania, observed by the anthropologist Monica Wilson, c.1935–1937, Monica and Godfrey Wilson Collection, University of Cape Town Libraries	8
Photograph 2.1	A mother and baby in Pondoland, South Africa, 1931, Monica and Godfrey Wilson Collection, University of Cape Town Libraries	34
Photograph 2.2	A group of boys in Gonja, Tanzania, described by the German missionary Wilhelm Guth as being 'newly circumcised', c. 1913–1938, the Leipzig Mission Picture Archive	41
Photograph 3.1	Two girls (named Mumbi on the left, Mwabura on the right), described as 'freed slaves' and employed at a mission station in Rungwe, Tanzania, c. 1894, the Moravian Archives Herrnhut	72
Photograph 5.1	A Quran school in Tabora, Tanzania, the Moravian Archives Herrnhut	107
Photograph 5.2	A sewing school at a mission, Ghana, c.1885–1895, Special Collections, Yale Divinity School Library	113
Photograph 5.3	Boys working in the garden of the Livingstonia Mission in Malawi, 1903, The National Library of Scotland	117
Photograph 5.4	Pupils at the main entrance of the Marist Brothers College, Kisangani, Democratic Republic of Congo, c.1920–1940, Special Collections, Yale Divinity School Library	122
Photograph 5.5	Pupils at a school in Tsévié, Togo, c.1920–1940, Special Collections, Yale Divinity School Library	126
Photograph 5.6	A kindergarten in Blantyre, Malawi, staffed by African converts and a British missionary, 1926, The National Library of Scotland	129
Photograph 5.7	A Roman Catholic mission school in Bailundo, Angola, c.1920–1940, Special Collections, Yale Divinity School Library	130

Photograph 6.1	Boys cooking outdoors, Malawi, c.1910, The National Library of Scotland	135
Photograph 6.2	Children described as 'Matabelle' by the photographer, but probably in Matabeleland, Zimbabwe, c.1910–1920s, image courtesy of the Melville J. Herskovits Library of African Studies Winterton Collection, Northwestern University Libraries	137
Photograph 6.3	Girls doing laundry work, Bali Nyonga, Cameroon, c.1908–1911, Basel Mission Archive	141
Photograph 6.4	A group of porters, including children, in the Belgian Congo, now the Democratic Republic of Congo, c.1920–1940, Special Collections, Yale Divinity School Library	142
Photograph 7.1	The son of a district chief in Pondoland, South Africa, dressed for a beer party, 1931, Monica and Godfrey Wilson Collection, University of Cape Town Libraries	164
Photograph 7.2	Student Protest, Durban, 1986, Omar Badsha, University of Cape Town Libraries	180

CHAPTER 1

Introduction

In 1985, nineteen-year-old Andrew Zondo planted a bomb in Amanzimtoti, a popular beach resort town for white South Africans on the south coast of what is now KwaZulu-Natal. The explosion killed five people. Zondo, a soldier in Umkhonto we Sizwe (MK), the armed wing of the African National Congress (ANC), was arrested, tried, and hanged for murder the following year. The sociologist and anti-apartheid activist Fatima Meer interviewed Zondo in his prison cell and provided expert testimony at his trial. In her account of Zondo's brief life, published as *The Trial of Andrew Zondo* (1987, 1989) and *The (mis) Trial of Andrew Zondo* (1998), Meer describes with care and sympathy Zondo's dawning political awareness, even as a very young child. Increasingly unwilling to tolerate the poor-quality education provided to him and other black youth,[1] and the brutality with which student protesters were met by the police, Zondo became active in local politics in what was then the province of Natal in his early teens. Deeply religious—his parents were committed Christians—and an excellent student, he was able to keep his organising quiet from his family.

Meer spoke to his parents and asked if they were aware of Andrew's life beyond their household, which included friends and leisure activities, and not only politics. His father, Aiken Zondo, explained that 'he did not know about Andrew having girlfriends or going to the cinema. ... even if Andrew had any [girlfriends], decorum demanded that he did not discuss them with his parents.' He added: '"That is cultural. African children don't talk about such things to their parents. You don't get an African youth coming home and saying 'Mummy,

---

[1] I use the category 'black' here and elsewhere in this book as defined by the Black Consciousness Movement, encompassing everyone who was discriminated against by the colonial and apartheid states on the grounds of race. As a result, 'black' refers to Africans, as well as to those who might be described as Indian, multiracial, or 'coloured' (meaning of multiracial ancestry, in South Africa and some other parts of Southern Africa).

I've got a new girlfriend.""[2] But Meer demonstrates that the kind of 'normal' childhood and youth described here by Aiken Zondo was very far from the experiences of most young black people in 1980s South Africa: the apartheid system itself had rendered this impossible, with even very young children caught up in protests against apartheid education and drawn into the struggle. In her testimony to the court, Meer argued that apartheid had produced the circumstances to which black youth could only respond with political organising. She explained: 'these children grow up in an environment where they learn almost from the time they are born that they will get nothing out of the system unless enormous pressures are exerted and they themselves are prepared to make enormous sacrifices for their personal freedoms.'[3] In this light, Andrew Zondo's decision eventually to join the ANC in exile and to participate in the attack in Amanzimtoti was a reasonable response to an intolerable context.

Age is crucial for understanding Andrew Zondo's actions and motivations. Not only was his perception of apartheid shaped specifically by his youth, but his response to the system was also informed by interactions with people as young as he. His experiences of being young help us to explain how the nature of, and expectations associated with, childhood and youth change over time. Under apartheid, what constituted a 'normal' childhood changed, meaning that what his father might have described as normal youthful behaviour was no longer the case for him and his generation.

Children figure prominently in media depictions of Africa. Coverage of the Biafran War (1967–1970) and the devastating 1983–1985 Ethiopian famine focused on haunting images of desperate childhood: young children with distended bellies and wide, frightened eyes. Kevin Carter's well-known and controversial photograph, 'The Struggling Girl' (1993), depicts an emaciated Sudanese child, doubled over, while a vulture waits in the distance. Although intended to raise international awareness of appalling human rights abuses and the scale of suffering experienced by the innocent, these images have had the effect of associating African childhood and youth with permanent crisis. While accurate, nuanced reporting on children's involvement in violence and conflict in Africa remains profoundly important—the plight of the Chibok girls kidnapped by Boko Haram in Nigeria in 2014, for instance, or the experiences of children in the war which began in Tigray, Ethiopia, in 2020—these examples are not representative of all childhoods across the continent. They feed into stereotypes of African childhood which belie not only the complexity of life for children and young people on the continent, but also the normality—the mundanity—of everyday existence for the majority of people who live in Africa. Babies have been born and raised, children have played and learned, adolescents have been awkwardly incorporated into adult society, for as long as their counterparts in other regions of the globe. The history of childhood and youth in Africa is one which should be familiar to all readers, regardless of their depth of knowledge about the continent.

Yet African childhoods have also been influenced by events and forces which, if not all of them specific to Africa, certainly shaped the continent's societies

---

[2] Fatima Meer, 'From *The (mis)Trial of Andrew Zondo*,' in *Fatima Meer: A Free Mind*, ed. Shireen Hassim (Cape Town: HSRC Press, 2019), p. 479.
[3] Meer, 'From *The (mis)Trial of Andrew Zondo*,' p. 490.

and states profoundly: West and Central Africa's involvement in the trans-Atlantic slave trade transformed states and societies in those regions as millions of people, most of them young, were taken against their will across the ocean; although some European empires had established footholds, mainly on the coast, in West, Southern, and East Africa by the early nineteenth century, the conquest of Africa occurred quickly from the 1870s and 1880s and massively altered African societies. Slightly more than half a century later, decolonisation again caused significant social, political, and economic rupture. Historians have explored how—like Andrew Zondo—children and young people understood, adapted to, challenged, and navigated often unpredictable contexts, which were by no means of their own choosing.

Scholars of Africa have long been interested in how youth responded to colonial conquest and postcolonial freedom. In the early twentieth century, anthropologists considered the impact of urbanisation, particularly on young African men in Africa's growing cities. From the 1980s, historians began to study how inter-generational conflict fuelled anti-colonial movements in the middle of the century, for example. Since the 1990s—and reflecting a trend in the field of the history of childhood and youth more broadly—they have been especially attentive to how definitions of 'childhood' and 'youth' have changed over time: who counted as a child or a young person, and who did not, and why. How have Africans conceptualised, debated, and remade age categories? As a result of this, scholars have turned, too, to younger children and others who, because of their gender or status, were less capable of acting to shape their worlds. In so doing, research on the history of childhood and youth has begun to paint a nuanced portrait of the complexity of the lives of children and young people on the continent, including, for instance, babies and toddlers as well as those in their twenties, both girls and boys, and those who were free and unfree.

The purpose of this book is to introduce readers to the major themes in the scholarship on children and youth in African history. Moving through the precolonial, colonial, and postcolonial eras, the book pays attention to how definitions of 'childhood' and 'youth' changed over both time and space, and how the experience of being a 'child' or a 'youth' also changed, often in intersection with questions of race, class, and gender. The book touches on the questions which have interested historians as they have studied children and young people: how does the inclusion of children in histories of labour (both free and unfree) and migration, for instance, change how we think about work and movement? How are histories of play and education important for thinking about the constitution of colonial and postcolonial states? And how do we approach young people's involvement in politics? These questions demand that historians not only insert children and young people into existing accounts of the history of the continent, but also that they are alert to how age itself serves to shape people's positions within African societies. The remainder of this chapter delves into how age is a useful category of historical analysis for historians and then discusses how historians have approached childhood and youth in their scholarship since about the 1960s, paying attention to the particular challenges that scholars of the continent face when working on children, especially in relation to the sources available to them.

AGE AS A CATEGORY FOR HISTORICAL ANALYSIS: WRITING CHILDREN AND YOUTH INTO AFRICAN HISTORY

Age is an important category for historical analysis. By this, historians mean that like race, class, and gender, age is one of the factors which determines how power is exercised within societies. Or, put another way, age is a vector of power: it allows and denies certain kinds of people particular forms of power at specific moments. As historians Corinne T. Field and Nicholas L. Syrett observe, the significance of age to the working of the modern, bureaucratic nation-state is now so normalised that it is difficult to imagine how the state would function without it: chronological age determines who must attend school, who may have sexual intercourse and enter into marriage, who may open a bank account and own property, and who may work and who may retire from employment. Citizenship and the right to vote are decided by age. But the use of chronological age in regulating individuals' access to and relationship with the state has a history. There is nothing inherent to the ages of eighteen or twenty-one which render them particularly significant for marking the attainment of adulthood or citizenship. It is the meanings attached to them by human societies which render them so powerful.

The use of age for deciding who accesses the state—and when and how—emerged in Western Europe in the eighteenth century and was globalised in the following two hundred years with the expansion of European empires and the acceleration of processes of globalisation. One of the features of global modernity has been the standardisation of the life course: increasingly, across the world, the same ages are used to demarcate the same phases of life. It is now common in most places for children to attend school between, roughly, the ages of five and eighteen and to enter the workforce after this, or, less frequently, to enrol at college or university. The age of retirement falls somewhere between sixty and seventy, and, generally speaking, we peg middle age at fifty. The reasons why this collection of ages—five, eighteen, fifty, and sixty, for instance—carry such significance are varied: including the influence of the early twentieth-century child study movement which framed childhood as a series of developmental stages, feminist and social reform movements which lobbied, globally, for the raising of the age of consent for women, and the labour movement's campaign to provide all workers with pensions. So even if chronological or calendar age—the time that has elapsed since birth—might feel like a neutral or even natural metric, which can be easily applied universally, it is clearly the product of specific historical forces. Moreover, these age boundaries have been used to discriminate against particular groups of people. Perhaps most obviously, these systems allow more power to people defined as adults. In its intersection with categories of gender and race, so age can work to marginalise some, installing them perpetually in the same category as children.[4]

---

[4] Corinne T. Field and Nicholas L. Syrett, 'Introduction: Chronological Age: A Useful Category of Historical Analysis,' *The American Historical Review*, vol. 125, no. 2 (April 2020), pp. 371–379.

Map 1.1 Africa in 2022. Alison D. Ollivierre, Tombolo Maps & Design

Age carries with it multiple meanings, which are subject to change over both time and place. To be sure, age is located in a biological truth: there are obvious physical, intellectual, and psychological differences between a two year-old, a thirteen year-old, a thirty-five year-old, and a sixty-five year-old. But the ideas and expectations associated with those ages are constructed socially, culturally, and politically. As historians of childhood and youth have pointed out, while age categories like 'childhood' and 'youth' may describe a biological reality, how societies define who counts as a child or a young person is a process, and one which is inflected by considerations of race, class, and gender, and which changes and is contested over time and place. As a result, even despite the relative homogenisation of the life course around the world, often multiple definitions of an age exist within a society. In the case of Andrew Zondo, for instance, the facts of his African-ness and political organising rendered him an adult in the eyes of the apartheid state, while white young people of the same age were regarded as teenagers and, thus, potentially less culpable for their actions.

For historians of childhood and youth, revealing the processes by which age categories are created, imposed, experienced, and contested is an important part of their work. However, it is only one facet of their scholarship, which is as interested in pulling children into accounts of the past. In much the same way that historians of women and of gender have from the 1960s insisted that any interpretation of the past which does not include women is incomplete and runs the risk of re-enforcing patriarchal politics which position women as powerless and insignificant, so historians of childhood argue for a 'child's eye view' of the past. How does including children and young people in our analysis of the past shift more conventional histories? Is it possible for us to capture the degree to which children had the capacity to shape their own contexts? Perhaps unsurprisingly, then, the field of the history of childhood first emerged during the youth rebellion of the 1960s. The founding text of the field is *L'enfant et la vie familiale sous l'Ancien Régime* published in 1960, and translated as *Centuries of Childhood* in 1962, by Annales School historian Philippe Ariès. In this book, Ariès, a medievalist by training, suggested that the contemporary, twentieth-century understanding of 'childhood' as a period located in the care of the family and the school did not exist in Europe before the Enlightenment. Although historians have since vigorously debated Ariès's arguments and methodology, as Hugh Cunningham has noted, the real significance of *Centuries of Childhood* is the convincing case it makes for the fact that childhood—as a category and as a set of experiences—has a history.[5]

Reinvigorated by the cultural turn of the 1990s, the field of the history of childhood and youth has developed a range of key sites of inquiry, including schools and education, international institutions interested in childhood (from the Red Cross to the Girl Guides), theories and ideologies of childrearing and development, the intersections of categories of childhood and race, the making of the categories of 'girlhood' and 'boyhood', the material cultures of youth, children and labour, youth sexuality, childhood and the history of the emotions, and migration and young people. While the field's first professional organisations and major journals remain based in the West, much of the recent scholarship is focused beyond the United States and Europe and grapples with questions of colonial conquest and empire building.

---

[5] Hugh Cunningham, 'Histories of Childhood,' *The American Historical Review*, vol. 103, no. 4 (Oct. 1998), p. 1187.

If there is a unifying theme across this research, it is a particular sensitivity to the unstable, historically and culturally contingent definition of age categories. Acknowledging, as noted above, the biological and legal 'truths' of age, historians have, nonetheless, pointed to its flexibility, particularly in contexts where it works alongside race, gender, class, and other factors, in determining how power is distributed and wielded.

Scholars of Africa have long paid attention to youth on the continent. Some of the earliest scholarship on children and young people was produced by anthropologists during the first half of the twentieth century. To a certain degree, this research was informed by interwar colonial anxiety about a phenomenon which anthropologist Godfrey Wilson described as 'detribalisation': a process during which Africans learned to negotiate modernity beyond the cultural frameworks available to them in 'traditional' society. While colonial administrators—drawing on racist conceptions of Africans as inherently 'backward'—were apt to blame detribalisation for what they construed to be social problems in African cities, Wilson was attempting to describe the emergence of an African proletariat in the interwar period. Although scholars have since criticised Wilson for presenting African societies as being closed to change,[6] his work was important for a number of anthropologists—like Godfrey Pitje, Jean la Fontaine, and Philip and Iona Mayer, for instance—interested in how young men and women negotiated urbanisation: the move from the countryside into the continent's growing cities in the interwar period. How did they adapt to life in what were often slum conditions, to waged employment, and to shifting social and cultural mores? How did they learn to think about themselves as they moved from a world structured by age grades to one where they might be regarded fully as adults or as 'juvenile delinquents'? Anthropologists like E. Evans-Pritchard and Monica Wilson may not have been interested in youth specifically, but in their research on the structure of African societies, their identification of the significance of age grades to those communities had the effect of emphasising the lives of young people. The socialisation of children into age groups and the processes of initiation they underwent to signal their entry into youth and adulthood were of particular interest to anthropologists describing social reproduction in Africa.[7]

Among the first historians to be interested in children's experiences were those working on slavery in both the Atlantic and Indian Ocean worlds. Much of this scholarship demonstrated not only that children were implicated in both of these trades—and, in the case of the trans-Atlantic trade, the enslavement of children intensified as the trade was increasingly restricted, particularly by the British government—but also that they experienced enslavement differently

---

[6] John L. Comaroff, 'The Closed Society and Its Critics: Historical Transformations in African Ethnography,' *American Ethnologist*,' vol. 11, no. 3 (Aug. 1984), pp. 572–573.

[7] Deborah Durham, 'Youth and the Social Imagination in Africa: Introduction to Parts 1 and 2,' *Anthropological Quarterly*, vol. 73, no. 3, Youth and the Social Imagination in Africa, Part 1 (Jul. 2000), pp. 113–120.

Photograph 1.1 Young girls doing laundry in Rungwe District, Tanzania, observed by the anthropologist Monica Wilson, c.1935–1937, Monica and Godfrey Wilson Collection, University of Cape Town Libraries

from adults. Systems of pawnship elaborated with the ending of slavery over the course of the nineteenth and twentieth centuries, and children worked—under various degrees of exploitation—under colonial rule.[8] From the mid-1970s, historical interest in questions of age and generation began to grow, often in overlap with the anthropological research. Historians recognised that membership of age groups was one of the systems which structured many pre- and colonial societies, determining who had access to political and economic power. Generation became, then, a useful lens for understanding change within African societies under colonial rule, and one which emphasised African agency. Echoing anthropological research, for historians, rituals and ceremonies marking men and women's transition to youth and to adulthood became key sites for understanding ideas about the functioning of African societies: about gender roles, sex and sexuality, marriage and the transmission of wealth, as well as the division of labour. Much of this scholarship was centred on questions of resistance to colonial conquest. Not only were young people—particularly young men—at the forefront of anti-colonial movements, not for nothing

---

[8] Abosede George, *Making Modern Girls: A History of Girlhood, Labour, and Social Development in Colonial Lagos* (Athens, OH: Ohio University Press, 2015), p. 13.

were the most stridently nationalist political parties often youth leagues, but the effects of colonial rule were also often felt most sharply in generational terms. To generalise, young men's ability to achieve full adulthood—which usually included access to land and other forms of wealth, and the ability to marry and to establish a family—was frequently hindered by colonial policies which favoured African (adult) elites. Generational crisis could not be disentangled from colonial crisis.

Perhaps unsurprisingly, then, another strand of research on youth in African societies has focused on questions of violence and trauma, examining young people's involvement in conflict, as victims of various forms of violence, as well as perpetrators of that violence. Since the beginning of the twenty-first century, there has been a significant increase in historical scholarship on children and youth in Africa, echoing similar developments in the field of the history of childhood and youth more broadly. A difference between this and earlier research has been a greater attentiveness to the shifting, contextual meanings of age categories. This is particularly important for the study of colonial societies, where multiple definitions of childhood and youth existed simultaneously. Under colonial rule, pre-existing notions of childhood and youth—themselves subject to change even before conquest—were overlaid with new ways of defining age categories (which included people across the age spectrum, from babies to the elderly). As historian Saheed Aderinto observes as regards Nigeria, 'modern childhood did not simply replace the preexisting or precolonial/"traditional" one', instead these modes 'coexisted, creating often opposing and contradictory results'.[9] While it might be tempting to identify a monolithic 'European' understanding of 'childhood' and 'youth', this would be misleading, and particularly because the use of age in the management of colonised populations was elaborated only after 1919, with the expansion of colonial states during the interwar era. It is certainly true that childhoods were increasingly uniform in the West towards the end of the nineteenth century, informed by a powerful ideology of the innocent child, but, equally, other conceptualisations of childhood still circulated. Indeed, new ideas about childhood and youth were generated in the colonial encounter, particularly as regards questions of race.

This careful awareness of the pitfalls of generalising age categories across African societies exists in a tension with historians' research on youth resistance to colonial rule. One of the key debates among both historians and anthropologists of Africa has been over the implications of scholars' long focus on young people's opposition to colonial states and the African elites who worked alongside colonial administrators. With a few notable exceptions, the 'youth' who feature in those studies tend to be African, male, and in their teens and twenties. While it is entirely appropriate that this particular group of young

---

[9] Saheed Aderinto, 'Colonialism and the Invention of Modern Nigerian Childhood,' in *Children and Childhood in Colonial Nigerian Histories*, ed. Saheed Aderinto (New York: Basingstoke, 2015), p. 2.

people receive the scholarly attention that they do—after all, they were often the agents of significant change within African societies—scholars have also questioned the implications of this focus. Firstly, it has the potential to rehearse and to reinforce some of the most pernicious stereotypes about the continent. In both media and academic reporting and analysis of the continent, 'youth' has often invoked racist anxieties about violence and disorder, implying that all young African men are threatening to social stability. In this way, 'youth' no longer refers to an age category, but rather to a perception of threat, encompassing all those men—not necessarily even those who are young—who might be politically active, engaged in criminal activity, or seen in other ways as being dangerous (they might be students or workers).[10]

Secondly, this focus is exclusive. As historian Abosede George has observed: 'The overwhelmingly male focus of the study of youth in the African history field raises the question: Where are the girls?' She argues for the 'girling' of the subject of the history of childhood and youth in Africa, not simply to add 'girls to the picture of the problem of youth history in Africa, or African girls to the study of girlhood in comparative perspective', but, rather, to understand 'gendered ideologies of childhood' and to historicise 'changes in the ideology of childhood over time'.[11] Put another way, while including a greater range of children and young people in an account of the past will always produce a richer understanding of human experience, it also demands that historians think more carefully about how ideas about children, childhood, youth, and age changed over time.

Thirdly, one of the consequences of including a greater range of children in the writing of African history is a demand that historians address the question of agency in their research. The emergence of the field of African history in the 1960s at the same time as the decolonisation of much of the continent produced a body of work written often in sympathy with nationalist politics, as well as with a heavy emphasis on African resistance. Partly in an effort to counter narratives of African victimhood, historians often went in search of African resistance in the archive, producing a rich body of work which reveals, particularly, grassroots organising against colonial conquest. However, historians have, too, pointed out that resistance in these terms—active, sometimes violent, always formulated in direct antagonism to the colonial state—represents only some forms of African responses to colonial rule. As Frederick Cooper has noted, for instance, that in working with a simple resistor/oppressor binary, 'the texture of people's lives is lost; and complex strategies of coping, of seizing niches within changing economies, of multi-sided engagement with forces inside and outside the community, are narrowed into a single framework'.[12] In

---

[10] Jean and John Comaroff, 'Reflections on Youth: From the Past to the Postcolony,' in *Frontiers of Capital: Ethnographic Reflections on the New Economy*, eds. Melissa S. Fisher and Greg Downey (Durham, NC: Duke University Press, 2006), pp. 268, 274.

[11] George, *Making Modern Girls*, pp. 14–15.

[12] Frederick Cooper, 'Conflict and Connection: Rethinking Colonial African History,' *The American Historical Review*, vol. 99, no. 5 (Dec. 1994), p. 1533.

addition to this, the emphasis on seeking out African agency has frequently been carried out in equally narrow terms. As Lynn Thomas observes, simply 'proving' the agency of Africans—demonstrating that Africans could exert change on their circumstances—is not an especially intellectually satisfying project. Everyone possesses some ability to create change in the contexts they inhabit, although, of course, to lesser and to greater degrees. Thomas argues, then, that historians should historicise questions of agency and understand 'that people in the past have defined and deployed [the concept] in quite different, and sometimes disorienting, ways'.[13] Historians of childhood have, too, pointed out that agency-as-resistence is a limiting framework of analysis. Echoing Cooper, Mona Gleason has argued that 'interpretive approaches to children's agency that rely on binaries (adult/child; good/bad; powerful/powerless)' can be 'very problematic' in how they ignore 'the messier "in between" of more nuanced and negotiated exchanges' between children, parents and grandparents and children, and relationships outside the family.[14] She notes that agency is not 'an undifferentiated, monolithic, and easily knowable phenomenon'.[15] Children's agency is usually limited, but it is clear that children do exert change in the world—and, often, simply by existing as *children*. A baby will cause its parents or other adults to react to it by crying, for example. Focusing on children's reactions to (adult) power also risks ignoring how children might negotiate the world on their own terms.

Historians of childhood and youth—both in Africa and elsewhere—have tended to foreground questions of agency and resistance to authority out of a laudable desire to recognise that children—far from being victims—can shape the worlds in which they live. However, an emphasis on using agency-as-resistance to seek out children in the archives can privilege particular kinds of youth—African young men being the obvious example, as noted above. The question, then, is how should historians go about locating children in the archive, aware of the fact that some of those children might leave faint traces?

VOICES AND SOURCES: FINDING CHILDREN IN THE ARCHIVES

Broadly speaking, historians of Africa have been particularly alert to the complexities of negotiating archives when attempting to reconstruct histories of the continent. Those scholars focusing on societies in the precolonial era which did not produce written documents have relied on a variety of methods to reach back into the very distant past, including the linguistic analysis of contemporary patterns of speech, collecting oral histories in the present, and relying on written accounts produced by visitors to those regions. Oral

---

[13] Lynn M. Thomas, 'Historicising Agency,' *Gender & History*, vol. 28, no. 2 (Aug. 2016), p. 335.
[14] Mona Gleason, 'Avoiding the Agency Trap: Caveats for Historians of Children, Youth, and Education,' *History of Education*, vol. 45, no. 4 (2016), p. 448.
[15] Gleason, 'Avoiding the Agency Trap,' p. 449.

tradition—the information passed purposefully between generations, transmitting history, law, and spiritual knowledge, for example—and oral histories—accounts of personal experience—are invaluable sources for historians working on more recent history. Scholars of colonial and postcolonial Africa have been careful to acknowledge the limitations of their sources, particularly when they were produced by colonial administrators and missionaries. Oral history and tradition—even with their limitations—offer historians Africans' own thoughts and accounts of experiences in their own words and on their own terms.

Scholars of childhood and youth have pointed, too, to the challenges of seeking out children in the archives. Perhaps most obviously, children's points of view are often missing from those records which tend to be preserved in archival collections. It is difficult—although not impossible—to write from children's perspectives and to produce detailed and granular accounts of all children's day-to-day lives. For historians of childhood and youth in Africa, these obstacles are compounded by the issues described above: how to access African children's voices in archives produced, frequently, by institutions and individuals allied to the colonial project? Historians have, though, found ways of addressing these and other questions.

Perhaps surprisingly, the colonial archive provides a great deal of information about children and young people, and often in recognisable terms, using age categories familiar to historians. Legal and police records, papers produced by colonial departments focused on children (particularly as regards education, labour, and welfare), and commissions of enquiry not only provide some understanding of how colonial states regarded young people, but also occasionally make available accounts from young people themselves or the adults who worked closely with them. In the twentieth century, liberation organisations and allied groups managed young members, established work forces, and opened schools and crèches in exile. Their records show how the project of decolonisation was linked to particular visions of the lives that young people should lead. Missionary and church sources and the archives of benevolent societies, schools, reformatories, and other similar institutions open up the worlds inhabited by children. Newspapers and periodicals describe popular culture.

It is no accident, then, that most scholarship on the history of childhood and youth in Africa is on these two centuries. However, despite their abundance, these sources allow some children to be heard far more loudly than others. The most insistent voices in the archive belong to middle-class youth. In settler colonies, these tend to be white and often female. Because bourgeois young men and women were encouraged to devote their leisure time to improving themselves, there are many diaries and collections of correspondence between members of this age category and class in public and private collections. Middle-class families loom large in the archive, providing often detailed descriptions of the care and rearing of infants and young children and insights into parental anxieties about the education and, later, employment of older children. Archival collections pertaining to middle-class families—who were often, but certainly not always, white—provide historians with the most rounded accounts of growing up on the continent, contrasting adult and children's points of view, and with accounts of youth from babyhood to late adolescence.

It is far more difficult to access the same kinds of rich accounts of children—most of whom were African—who were not middle class. While these children are often to be found missionary reports, legal documents, the records of philanthropic organisations, and newspaper articles, they often fall into the category of social problem to be solved or to be saved. Their voices and subjectivities are, usually, missing. As noted above, the large scholarship on 'African youth' often replicates precisely these problematic categories, equating all youth with young, African men, and assuming that 'youth' is, for instance, always politically active or delinquent. As noted above, the large scholarship on 'African youth' often replicates precisely these problematic categories, equating all youth with young African men, and assuming that 'youth' is always politically active or delinquent. As a result, scholars need to be especially careful to unpack precisely who documents mean by 'youth', for example. Historians do possess a range of skills which allow them to excavate to some degree what African children's points of view may have been. Cultivating historical empathy—an ability to empathise with subjects existing under very different kinds of social and cultural conditions—is a useful tool, as is working with a much wider array of sources beyond written documents (such as photographs, toys and games, and songs and rhymes) and reading sources 'against the grain' for the silences and absences in which children's voices might be present.

For historians of precolonial Africa, oral tradition—including folktales and stories for children—provides some sense of how age structured societies, how age categories were conceptualised, and how social norms were inculcated in children. Oral histories can also provide accounts of individuals' experiences as young children. In both cases, though, historians use these sources with care, acknowledging that oral tradition, for instance, provides little sense of change over time and may not necessarily represent with absolute accuracy the societies in which it was recounted; oral histories are complicated sources, shaped as much by failing memory, subjects' contemporary preoccupations, and the dialogue between interviewer and interviewee as much as anything else. Yet written sources from the pre-conquest period—and, indeed, later too—can be as unreliable. Records kept by slave traders and by slave ships, by sailors and early settlers in the Cape, for example, were produced by the prejudices and violent circumstances of the slavery and settlement in the seventeenth and eighteenth centuries.

Scholarly texts are useful to historians as primary sources too. Anthropological interest in African societies in the first half of the twentieth century produced rich and complex—albeit frequently flawed—accounts and their ethnographies describe the lives and activities of children and young people across the age spectrum in both rural and urban areas.

Historians must, though, be alert to the potential pitfalls of seeking out children's voices in the archive. Much of the debate over the question of agency among historians of childhood stems from many scholars' commitment to centring children's views and words in their scholarship. Sociologist Allison James has raised concerns about this approach. No voice emerges pure and 'authentic' from the archive. Certain children's voices are always privileged above others and for very specific reasons. Instead of using children's archival voices uncritically, historians must ask why particular points of view were preserved, and others not, and to what ends children's voices have been put. Moreover, no single child can be said to speak for all children. To suggest, in other words, that children's voices represent a kind of truth speaking from the distant past is not to take seriously the fact that all sources are produced in complex contexts which also need to be taken into account.[16]

THE STRUCTURE OF THIS BOOK AND NOTES ON TERMINOLOGY

While this book begins in the precolonial period and concludes in the present, its approach to the scholarship on children and youth in Africa is largely thematic, drawing attention to the questions and debates which have interested historians over the past few decades. This book aims to provide a broad understanding of this scholarship, meaning that there are some omissions. Perhaps most importantly, the book focuses on sub-Saharan Africa. Scholars of North Africa are at work on nuanced, complex histories of childhood in the region, paying attention to continuities with the Middle East. Also, the continent's extensive diaspora—based particularly around the Atlantic world—is beyond the scope of this book.

The second chapter focuses on the precolonial period, with a particular emphasis on how generation structured African societies. Children in precolonial societies occupied one position within bigger age-based systems, where age was a key vector for apportioning power. Alongside age, free or unfree status was one of the most significant factors shaping the status of people within precolonial societies—and this is the focus of the third chapter. Many precolonial and colonial African societies practised forms of enslavement and pawning (the latter referring to the loaning of individuals—often, but not always, women and children—in exchange for money or other goods), frequently to increase the size of kinship groups. Scholars of West and Central Africa developed the concept of 'wealth in people' as they sought to understand how Africans justified the enslavement of people—and their subsequent sale to traders on the coast, as those regions were drawn into the trans-Atlantic slave trade. Chapter 3 pays attention to the enslavement and pawning of children within African societies, as well as their experiences of the trade in enslaved people across the Atlantic and Indian Oceans. The numbers of children sent across, particularly, the Atlantic grew towards the end of the eighteenth century, as the abolitionist movement placed increasing pressure on slave traders. While

---

[16] Allison James, 'Giving Voice to Children's Voices: Practices and Problems, Pitfalls and Potentials,' *American Anthropologist*, vol. 109, no. 2 (2007), pp. 261–272.

scholars have documented the Middle Passage from the perspectives of adults, shifting to children's points of view requires new approaches to the forced dispersal of millions of Africans around the Atlantic world. Children were frequently the first to experience the transformation of forms of enslavement into pawning or other kinds of unfree status.

The fourth chapter moves on to colonial rule. As the previous two chapters demonstrate, African definitions of childhood and youth changed over time and space. Age functioned in specific, structuring ways in African societies. With the elaboration of colonial rule—which occurred, for the most part, in the early twentieth century—European ways of understanding age, tied to the functioning of the state and informed by evangelical Christian, Romantic, and Enlightenment notions of childhood innocence, overlaid those already existing in African societies. Perhaps most importantly, colonial rule also racialised African childhood, producing the 'African child' as a figure whose vulnerability justified the colonial and, later, humanitarian projects. This was complicated by the presence of white children in settler colonies, as notions of innocent childhood were increasingly associated with whiteness. Multiracial children occupied an even more ambivalent space, sometimes welcomed in colonies with pronatalist policies, while also held in suspicion by other administrators and colonial populations.

Chapters 5 and 6 are particularly interested in how childhood and youth changed under colonial rule and describe these shifts through the lenses of education, work, and play. All African societies developed systems by which children assimilated the knowledge and acquired the skills necessary to take up positions as adults within those communities. In Islamic states in West Africa, in particular, the education provided in religious schools would have been familiar to Europeans. However, when Christian missionaries opened schools in the nineteenth century—a project eventually and reluctantly taken over by colonial states especially after the First World War—schooling was seen as a tool for making 'civilised' colonised subjects. Children and their parents used education for their own ends, though, and often to access the colonial state. Similarly, and as discussed in Chap. 5, the organised leisure activities designed for African children and youth by philanthropic societies—like the Boy Scouts and Girl Guides, for instance—were frequently useful means for proving the loyalty of an African middle class to the colonial state. This noted, colonial states remained suspicious of African children not ostensibly involved in productive activity. However, what the colonial state read as 'idleness'—an accusation laced with anxiety about moral collapse—was, frequently, play intended to teach children skills they would need in adulthood, like cattle herding for boys and raising crops for girls (these activities differed across the continent).

Chapter 5 considers the boundaries between play and labour, as well as the colonial state and colonial elites' changing attitudes towards the employment of children and young people. On the one hand, while hawking in early twentieth-century Lagos might have been condemned as a form of abuse wrested on innocent girlhood, the presence of young domestic servants in middle-class African households in Zambia after decolonisation was tolerated by the state. With the introduction of cash economies and crops and systems of migrant labour, children—who had usually worked in precolonial societies—worked in different ways. However, in the twentieth century, this was in a context of a growing global backlash against children's wage earning. How could children be 'innocent' if they were labourers, asked social reformers?

The final chapter grapples, too, with this vexed notion of childhood innocence, in its focus on children's rebellions against power, and their involvement in violent conflicts across the continent. The chapter explores how colonial and postcolonial anxieties about youth delinquency shaped adult responses to young men and women's efforts to shape lives for themselves under changing and often challenging conditions. But the chapter emphasises—too—that young people have been, frequently, the victims of political violence, even as some have perpetrated it.

As social constructs, age categories carry with them a range of associations and meanings and change over both time and place. Historians need, then, to be careful in their deployment of these categories, avoiding both anachronism and being aware of the possibility of erasing or distorting past definitions of, for instance, childhood and youth. As a result, I have been careful in my use of terms which might feel familiar to contemporary readers—like teenager (a category produced in the 1930s) and, even, adolescent (popularised from 1904)—while using 'baby', 'child', and 'young person', and always acknowledging that it was never necessarily obvious who counted as a 'child' or a 'youth'.

CHAPTER 2

Age and Generation

The *Sundiata* is an epic which describes the upbringing, adventures, and triumph of Sundiata Keita, the founder of the Empire of Mali in the thirteenth century. One of the key moments at the beginning of the story is the birth of the hero, whose coming and glorious rule is foretold to his father—also a king, but a relatively minor one—by a passing hunter. When his mother, Sogolon, goes into labour, his father orders 'the nine greatest midwives of Mali' to attend her 'constantly'. He is 'worried and agitated', and nothing, not even music, can soothe his anxiety. At the end of an unseasonal thunderstorm, his new son's birth is announced triumphantly by one of the midwives. Although initially overwhelmed with emotion at the news, he soon goes to congratulate his wife. The story describes the rituals celebrating the newborn, and particularly the celebrations carried out eight days after his birth:

> The name was given the eighth day after his birth. It was a great feast day and people came from all the villages of Mali while each neighbouring people brought gifts to the king. ...
>
> In Sogolon's house the king's aunt cut off the baby's first crop of hair while the poetesses, equipped with large fans, cooled the mother who was nonchalantly stretched out on soft cushions.
>
> The king was in his antechamber but he came out followed by Doua [his griot]. The crowd fell silent and Doua cried, 'The child of Sogolon will be called Maghan after his father, and Mari Djata, a name which no Mandingo prince has ever borne. Sogolon's son will be the first of his name.'
>
> Straight away the griots shouted the name of the infant and the tam-tams [drums] sounded anew. The king's aunt, who had come out to hear the name of the child, went back into the house, and whispered the double name of Maghan and Mari Djata in the ear of the newly-born so that he would remember it.

> The festivity ended with the distribution of meat to the heads of families and everyone dispersed joyfully. The near relatives one by one went to admire the newly-born.[1]

Even if some of the rituals depicted here may be unfamiliar to many audiences, the emotions described by the teller of the tale would be recognisable to any new parent: fear, anxiety, relief, and elation. This is also an account of a newborn whose arrival is a cause for celebration, and one who is loved and accepted as an individual, with his own name. This is a description of the first few days of an elite child and a future king, one whose life would be quite different from his commoner peers. But, even so, the *Sundiata* offers us some insight not only into how children were welcomed into the world in Mandinka-speaking communities in West Africa in the eleventh and twelfth centuries, but also into how adults felt at their arrival.

The *Sundiata* is an ancient, living text. Although versions of the epic have been written down and published for wider reading, it is still told in the modern nation-state of Mali, as well as in other parts of West Africa, particularly where speakers of Mande languages have settled, like Guinea and Senegal. The people responsible for its transmission over generations are a class of professional musicians and storytellers, often called griots, who also feature in the *Sundiata*. As part of an oral tradition, the epic has limitations for what it offers historians: every iteration of its telling will differ, shaped by the interests of its speaker and listeners and the context in which it is transmitted; its primary purpose is not necessarily to provide a factually accurate account of the biography of the founder of the Empire of Mali; and it contains, thus, fabulous and magical elements (for instance, some characters, like Sogolon, transform into animals or other mythical beasts).

Yet, for all of this, it remains a remarkably valuable source. The protagonist, Sundiata Keita, was the first ruler—or *mansa*—of Mali, a wealthy polity encompassing much of the Sahel (a stretch of grassland to the south of the Sahara), governed by a Muslim elite, and deriving much of its power and influence from the cross-Sahara trade in gold. A significant portion of the *Sundiata* is devoted to the childhood and upbringing of its hero and a careful reading reveals much for the historian of childhood and youth. It includes descriptions of ceremonies marking stages in the life of the child and the young person, references to the normative behaviours associated with children at different developmental phases, and ideas about appropriate relationships between the young and old. As noted above, though, unlike the more conventional sources historians use, it opens up a world of affect—of feeling—which describes emotional responses to children and to childhood.

However, we cannot generalise the *Sundiata* beyond its particular context: it is not a source on African childhood broadly defined, let alone precolonial

---

[1] Djibril Tamsir Niane, *Sundiata: An Epic of Old Mali*, revised ed. (London: Pearson, 2006), pp. 14–15.

African childhood. It is not too much of a stretch to suggest that it is impossible to identify a single experience of 'African childhood' in the long period of time leading up to colonial conquest in the nineteenth century. Africa's deep history—it is, after all, the cradle of humankind—and the complexity and variety of the societies which populate the continent, along with the varied nature of their interactions with people from around the globe during this era, render it impossible to describe an essentialised 'African' way of life, or view of the world. The people who lived in Africa did not consider themselves to be 'African' and did not necessarily think of themselves as being fundamentally similar to one another, as they were in the eyes of the European nation-states which colonised them. A history of childhood and youth in Africa's precolonial past requires, then, attention to the specificity of particular historical and geographical contexts, and to change over time.

This chapter is on childhood in the era before colonial conquest. Considering that this period of time encompasses literally thousands of years, it would be impossible to provide a detailed description of the multiple and changing definitions and experiences of childhood and youth across such a diverse continent. In addition to this, precolonial African history represents a particular challenge to scholars because of the nature of the primary sources available to them. What this chapter aims to do is to convey a broad understanding of how childhood was conceived of, and how it was experienced, at different times and places across the continent. More specifically, this chapter pays particular attention to how ideas about generation were crucial to structuring African societies. Childhood and youth—or the range of similar age categories which existed across the continent—were important age stages in themselves, but part of a bigger, elaborate system in which age was a vector for apportioning social, political, and economic power. Put another way, alongside gender, for instance, age was a key determinant of an individual's position within African societies.

Understanding Precolonial Africa

Most historians, anthropologists, and other scholars of African societies tend to understand African history as being composed of three broad periods: the precolonial, colonial, and postcolonial. Like most attempts at periodisation, there are significant problems with folding long sweeps of time into these categories. In this case, the experience of colonial conquest becomes the defining moment in the history of the continent, when, in fact, colonial rule encompassed only slightly more than a century of most of Africa's past (although this does vary across the continent—European settlement of Southern Africa dates from the mid-seventeenth century, for example). Moreover, the term 'precolonial' does not describe the complexity of the continent's changing social forms, political and economic systems, and embeddedness in various global networks over many, many centuries. 'Precolonial' history for Africa begins with the origins of humanity, and concludes, for most of the continent, in the late nineteenth century. Why, then, proceed with a category which appears to hide more than it illuminates?

One compelling reason is linked to how historians access the past. While some precolonial African societies—particularly in West, Central, and East Africa—left written records at particular periods of time, most did not. This means that historians have resorted to a variety of methods to excavate this past, including the analysis of the objects produced by Africans over time; of archaeological evidence; of oral tradition, like the *Sundiata*; of oral histories collected from people with memory of worlds before colonial conquest; and of linguistic analysis: accessing the past through the languages spoken by Africans in the present. Precolonial history—despite its breadth and depth—is defined, then, by the methods scholars have developed to describe it.

Another reason for using this categorisation of time is the scale and profundity of the change wrought on the continent by colonisation. While Africans had contact with visitors from Europe and Asia long before conquest, the imposition and elaboration of European rule, especially from the second half of the nineteenth century, caused profound change across African societies. As a result, it is possible to argue that the colonial period represented a significant rupture with the precolonial past, meaning that the colonial period should be studied separately.

If we are to work with the idea of the 'precolonial'—fully acknowledging the limitations of the category—then we start at the origins of human life on earth, and the slow population of the continent. This era begins with the first hominins—bipedal ancestors of modern humans—who appear to have populated parts of Eastern, Western, and Southern Africa between six and eight million years ago. Archaeologists estimate that the first anatomically modern people originated on the continent between 200,000 and 150,000 years ago, and then migrated out of the continent, populating parts of Asia and Europe by 70,000 years ago. As the historian John Iliffe remarks, the defining challenge for early African societies was the settling of their own continent. The continent's landscape and what he describes as its 'hostile' environment—its 'poor soils, fickle rainfall, abundant insects, and unique prevalence of disease'—meant that the first humans to settle on the continent had to contend with 'innumerable local frontiers'.[2] Establishing settled human communities and societies in Africa was complicated by the challenges posed by finding productive land for agriculture and herding, avoiding or managing disease often borne by insects, and ensuring a steady water supply. But Africans learned how to adapt to these circumstances, developing ways of living which took into account the challenges posed by their environments.

Scholars of ancient Africa have identified four major language groups on the continent, and they trace the origins of those languages to the period between 22,000 and 12,000 BCE. These four language families are: Afro-Asiatic

---

[2] John Iliffe, *Africans: The History of a Continent*, second ed. (Cambridge: Cambridge University Press, 2007), pp. 1–4.

people, who originated along the Red Sea and eventually settled in the Horn of Africa; Nilo-Saharan speakers, who were from just south of the Nubian mountains, and who moved south and west, along with their cattle; the Niger-Congo language family that emerged in the interior of West Africa; and, finally, the Khoesan family in what is now Tanzania and who moved southwards. Archaeological evidence suggests that humans in Africa began to develop and adopt agricultural technologies, like grinding wild seeds to make flour for bread, in about 8000 BCE. Slowly, humans settled, domesticating animals, building more permanent settlements, and using more complicated tools and systems to grow and irrigate crops.[3]

The first evidence of metalworking on the continent was in what is now Southern Egypt, in about 5000 BCE. The first major empire on the continent originated along the banks of the Nile in c. 3100 BCE, when the Kingdom of Upper Egypt conquered the delta kingdom of Lower Egypt, beginning 3000 years of royal rule over the region. South of Egypt, the kingdom of Nubia was established at about the same time as the unification of Egypt. To the west of Egypt, along the coast of North Africa and in the slowly desiccating Sahara (the Sahara as we know it now was well irrigated until about 5000 BCE, when rainfall began to decrease), nomadic groups—such as Berbers—herded cattle and, where possible, grew crops. This region of the continent was pulled into the Mediterranean world through conquest by successive imperial powers: the Phoenicians and the Romans, perhaps most famously. After the death of the Prophet Muhammad in 632 CE, North Africa was drawn into the Islamic world, conquered by Arab armies over the following two centuries. Trade helped to bring Islam across the Sahara to West Africa, and across the Indian Ocean to the East African coast. Christianity was present in the regions of North Africa within the Roman Empire. In Egypt, the Coptic Church was founded in the first century CE, and it was Coptic Christians who took the religion southwards, to Nubia and, in the fourth century, into Aksum, the predecessor of Ethiopia.[4]

Iron appears to have been worked between 1000 and 600 BCE in Central Africa, specifically in the area between Lake Chad and the Great Lakes. This spread first westwards, and much later to the east. Iron pots and utensils, tools, and arrows and weapons gave communities an advantage in hunting, war, and agriculture. Knowledge of iron-working was spread by Bantu-speaking people, who originated roughly in what is now Cameroon. 'Bantu' refers to a family of languages within the Niger-Congo group, now spoken across much of sub-Saharan Africa (in fact, there are about 500 Bantu languages). The parent 'Bantu' language—the term 'Bantu' itself means 'people'—was spoken by groups of people who moved gradually across the continent, settling, and bringing with them iron-working technology, as well as skills in crop cultivation and pottery making. Their slow settling of Central, East, and

---

[3] Iliffe, *Africans*, pp. 10–14.
[4] Iliffe, *Africans*, pp. 17–49.

Southern Africa has been called the 'Bantu migrations' by historians. This migration took place between approximately 5000 and 1500 years ago, and was never a concerted project of expanding a frontier of human settlement. It was, rather, an incremental process by which Bantu speakers established new villages and cultivated land, starting families, and whose offspring later founded their own homesteads on new land. As they settled, they mingled with existing groups, introducing new languages and a way of life shaped by a set of technological innovations, particularly pottery making and metallurgy. It was these communities' working of iron which determined where they would move and settle, as they searched for deposits of iron ore and a reliable supply of wood for charcoal.[5]

These early Iron Age people were farmers, who learned to cultivate crops often under unforgiving circumstances, such as variable rainfall. Favoured crops differed from region to region, including sorghum, millet, yams, rice, and bananas. Some kept livestock, mainly for milk, and some hunted to supplement their diets. Their villages were usually small, with houses arranged around a central space where livestock were penned. Villages farmed and stored food together. Village life was based around the family and kinship networks; labour was divided between men and women and children; they traded; they engaged in forms of ancestor worship, and had rituals which marked important moments in the life course. This was a life that changed over time and space, precisely as Bantu speakers moved across the continent. Although everyday life tended to be organised on the level of the village, Bantu people and members of other language groups experimented with a range of political systems across the continent. In West Africa, some of the earliest empires located in the Sahel—Ghana (c. 400 and 1200 CE) and Mali (at the height of its power between the thirteenth and fifteenth centuries), for instance—accrued vast wealth by trading gold mined in the interior of the region, with merchants who crisscrossed the Sahara. These and other empires in this dry region, many of which embraced Islam, were governed from centralised courts, and frequently possessed standing armies.[6]

In the West African forest, though, states tended to be smaller—the Yoruba kingdoms, for instance, or the kingdom of Benin—or did not exist at all: 'stateless societies'—like the Igbo—were governed on the village level, which might be dominated by a Big Man, who had managed to accrue wealth and power through trade, family connections, or other means. Relatively independent villages or clusters of villages could be conquered and drawn into new states: in the Great Lakes region in East Africa, where predictable and generous rainfall made possible dense, settled populations dependent on banana cultivation, small and powerful states emerged as villages were absorbed into more centralised kingdoms: Bunyoro was founded in the late fifteenth century, Buganda 200 years later, and Rwanda and Burundi in the eighteenth century. While

---

[5] Iliffe, *Africans*, pp. 16, 34–36.
[6] Iliffe, *Africans*, pp. 36, 51, 52–53.

West African societies—stateless or otherwise—were drawn into a dense network of trade which connected village markets—usually dominated by women—to the Mediterranean and Atlantic worlds, trade in East Africa was limited largely to the coast, where the long stretch of coastline from contemporary Somalia in the north and Mozambique in the south was part of the monsoon-dependent Indian Ocean trade. A society incorporating African, Arab, South Asian, and other cultural, religious, and social influences established itself on this Indian Ocean shoreline.

Southern Africa was the last region to be settled by Bantu migrants—c.2000 years ago—although they were preceded by hunter-gatherer Khoesan speakers, whose language and ways of life Bantu speakers incorporated. Some groups established centralised kingdoms—the Zulu kingdom, which was centralised in the early nineteenth century, being, perhaps, the best known. Ample land meant that there was little incentive to settle under irksome rule, so the Xhosa, for instance—on South Africa's east coast—remained in a loose affiliation of clans. While most of these societies were organised around the ownership of cattle, gold was mined north of the Limpopo, and probably served to enrich the kingdom which appears to have been established at what is now known as Great Zimbabwe: a collection of high-walled buildings where a twelfth-century kingdom became wealthy trading in gold with merchants on the coast.[7]

This brief overview of the continent's very long human history demonstrates the emptiness of some of the most pernicious stereotypes of Africa: this was no 'dark continent'; its people have long been connected to other regions of the world; and its societies are complex, differ across space, and have changed over time. This slow peopling of Africa was done in the face of disease which attacked both animals and humans—sleeping sickness and malaria, for instance—shifting rainfall patterns, which dried out some regions and increased the watering of others, and a landscape which was not always conducive to agriculture and human settlement. Crop failures meant famines, and conflict—in the West African savannah, for example—could destroy fragile communities. Perhaps understandably, then, family and the accrual of large kinship networks became particularly important to precolonial societies. This is the focus of the following section.

Wealth in People: Generation, Lineage, and Precolonial Societies

One of the most profound challenges facing historians of precolonial Africa is understanding how Africans thought about themselves. How did parents conceptualise childhood? What constituted 'childhood'? Who was a 'child'? How did these categories and the normative behaviours associated with them change over time? In many societies, the categories and terminologies which people in

---

[7] Iliffe, *Africans*, pp. 63–88, 100–126.

the precolonial era developed to describe children have been lost, and often as a result of the social disruptions produced by colonial conquest. But there are strategies available to historians to help them to reconstruct the worlds inhabited by young people. One of these is to understand their position within a much bigger generational system. Or, put another way, it is difficult to write histories of childhood and youth in precolonial Africa without thinking about the overarching systems which placed all people within societies into age categories.

Across the continent, generation—or age—was one of the most important systems for structuring societies. Writing about East Africa, G. Thomas Burgess and Andrew Burton observe, 'no concept or social category surpassed generation both in terms of its importance and governing relations and as a source of values and sensibilities.'[8] Put simply, this generational system of ordering societies placed all people into age cohorts, who moved through life together, marking significant transitions—from childhood into youth, for instance, or marriage—together, in ceremonies and rituals. In this way, although children certainly constituted an important age category within African societies, they were at the bottom of a social scale which used age to apportion more power to those at its top than to those lower down. But generation was about more than power: it was the basis for the norms governing social relations, determining how people related to and interacted with one another. Younger people owed older people respect; movement into adult age categories demanded new kinds of behaviour of young men and women. As Burgess and Burton explain: generation was 'also a world of social expectations, of ideas of duty, honour, and virtue'.[9]

How did societies structured according to generation function? Broadly speaking, many age-based societies tended to divide generations into age-sets, usually segregated by sex: these were groups of peers of roughly similar age, who would progress from one life stage to the next at about the same time. Historians and anthropologists have also called these life stages 'age grades' to indicate how ageing was conceptualised as a series of steps through which people moved, usually having participated in a ceremony or ritual, or sworn an oath.[10] Age-sets created generational solidarity and, in some societies, replicated the functions of kinship groups: the members of the sets regarded one another as siblings, even if they were not closely related. For example, in the early twentieth century, anthropologist Monica Wilson described the age villages of the Nyakyusa people of Southern Tanzania. Within this society, villages

---

[8] G. Thomas Burgess and Andrew Burton, 'Introduction,' in *Generations Past: Youth in East African History*, eds. Andrew Burton and Helene Charton-Bigot (Athens, OH: Ohio University Press, 2010), p. 1.
[9] Burgess and Burton, 'Introduction,' p. 8.
[10] Paul Spencer, *Youth and Experiences of Aging among Maa: Models of Society Evoked by the Maasai, Samburu, and Chamus of Kenya* (Warsaw and Berlin: De Gruyter, 2014), p. 31; Paul Spencer, 'Becoming Maasai, Being in Time,' in *Being Maasai: Ethnicity and Identity in East Africa*, eds. Thomas Spear and Richard Waller (London: James Currey, 1993), pp. 140–141.

were not constituted of kinsfolk—members of the same family, in other words—but, instead, of men who were members of the same age-sets, who were not, then, necessarily related to one another. They brought to these villages their wives—polygyny was encouraged—and fathered children. The boys within each of these new villages who were members of age-sets would go on, then, to form new villages in the same fashion. New villages were established when the members of age-sets were still children: at around the age of ten or eleven years, boys would build huts for themselves at the edge of their fathers' village and, while they would still eat at their mothers' huts, socialised together as a group and lived together, apart from adults. As Wilson observed, this 'system' was 'regarded not only as being congenial to small boys ... but also as moral. For the Nyakyusa eating with age-mates is a corner stone of morality.'[11] It was within these small communities constituted of boys of the same age-set that children learned the norms governing Nyakyusa society. These bonds would then endure well into old age.

This example of Nyakyusa age villages is precisely this: an example. It should not be extrapolated across the continent, nor can it be projected into the past. Wilson observed Nyakyusa society during field trips undertaken in the 1930s to Southern Tanzania, which had been transferred from German to British rule after the First World War. These villages certainly changed over time, and particularly as a result of the imposition of colonial rule. However, it is likely that these age villages bore similarities to those which had been formed in the precolonial era. It is also important to emphasise that not only did age-sets and age grades vary across the continent and over time, but they were inflected by gender too. Wilson noted explicitly that Nyakyusa age villages were formed as a result of processes of male socialisation.

But this example does help us to understand some of the dynamics present in generational systems. Firstly, they were gendered. Age intersected with other categories of identity in apportioning social roles and power to particular kinds of people, and gender was one of the most significant of these categories. Because of the patriarchal structure of many precolonial African societies, boys' processes of initiation and entry into age-sets were entangled with the distribution of power and accessing of wealth. However, it is clear that membership of age-sets for girls and women—even if they might not have wielded the same forms of power as those allotted to boys and men—was extremely important for making meaning too. Observing young people in early twentieth-century Pedi society in contemporary South Africa, the anthropologist Godfrey Pitje noted that young women not only were responsible for providing others in their age-sets with information about puberty, sex, and contraception, but also actively patrolled the behaviour of girls with men.[12] The relationships which

---

[11] Monica Wilson, 'Nyakyusa Age-Villages,' *The Journal of the Royal Anthropological Institute of Great Britain and Ireland*, vol. 79, no. 1/2 (1949), pp. 21–22.

[12] G.M. Pitje, 'Traditional Systems of Male education among Pedi and Cognate Tribes,' Part I, *African Studies*, vol. 9, no. 2 (1950), pp. 58–59.

developed between girls in puberty carried through into adulthood. Recognising that gender shaped age systems helps with moving away from using men's and boys' experiences as the template for all African societies. Historically, anthropological scholarship which used boys' and men's experiences of initiation into age grades assumed the universality of the male experience. Yet it is clear that even if women in some societies did not enter into age grades—or did so differently—they, too, found ways of making meaning of particular stages in their lives.[13] Regardless, as Corrie Decker notes, 'maturation was not a biological fact or a particular chronological age but a status that was earned'.[14]

Secondly, age was not necessarily in itself a marker of who was a youth and who counted as an adult. While biological markers of the onset of puberty separated adolescents from children, entry into adulthood was far less sharply delineated, and not accessible for everyone. In Hausa society in what is now Nigeria and Niger, for example, there are two broad categories of people: the young (*yara*) and the elders (*dattijai*), with separate groups for the very young and the very old. Age was only one factor in ascribing membership to these categories: gender (men could achieve elder status through marriage, while women could remain *yara* even after wedlock), wealth (for a man, the ability to marry a second wife), behaviour (a younger person deemed to behave with the dignity of an elder), position within a family (the first wife of a man was more powerful than subsequent wives, regardless of their ages), and free and unfree status were as important. Murray Last explains:

> [*Y*]*ara* include all those of low status, whatever their biological ages. Slaves, for example, or free-born servants remain *yara*, especially in a large, powerful household: they are a 'son of the house'. But *yara* of a royal house may be of higher status than an ordinary free man; the latter's greater age, though, might protect him in a dispute. In a large family it is possible for an uncle to be younger than his nephew, in which case age can sometimes trump generation.[15]

To be a member of the *dattijai* is to have the capacity and influence to make decisions. Also, *dattijai* have dependents. The youth, on the other hand, are subject to decisions taken by the *dattijai*, whose chief concern is the maintenance of harmony within the household and the community more broadly. *Yara* can under some circumstances rebel against or disobey the *dattijai*, but potentially at some cost. As Last notes, though, '[a] key point is that "junior" status is temporary, except for slaves, and that there are always people junior to you (unless you are the last wife or the last child, and then you are a "favourite").'[16]

---

[13] Corrie Decker, 'A Feminist Methodology of Age-Grading and History in Africa,' *The American Historical Review*, vol. 125, no. 2 (Apr. 2020), pp. 422–423.

[14] Corrie Decker, 'A Feminist Methodology of Age-Grading and History in Africa,' p. 420.

[15] Murray Last, 'Toward a Political History of Youth in Muslim Northern Nigeria, 1750–2000,' in *Vanguard or Vandals: Youth, Politics, and Conflict in Africa*, eds. Jon Abbink and Ineke von Kessel (Leiden and Boston: Brill, 2005), p. 39.

[16] Last, 'Toward a Political History of Youth in Muslim Northern Nigeria,' p. 40.

This example demonstrates, firstly, that biological age could be relatively insignificant in determining what might be described as an individual's *social* age. Writing about the Atwot people—a Dinka-speaking group who live in contemporary South Sudan—John W. Burton notes that 'the factor of physiological maturity is self-evident', while more useful markers of age classification were 'evidenced in the course of daily life by divergent economic and symbolic attributes'.[17] Secondly, this example shows the degree to which generation was a system of ranking, dependent partially on age, but also on a range of other factors, ranging from free or unfree to status, to gender. It did not fix individuals forever in one specific category; rather, most people could move up (and occasionally down) according to circumstances. The system could also be challenged, and especially by younger men wanting access to senior status.

Thirdly, and perhaps unsurprisingly, systems of generation could be a powerful source of conflict within these societies. Precisely because age categories were also social ranks with responsibilities and privileges associated with them, maturation offered young people access to power. At the same time, older generations—particularly older men—controlled who could attain the markers of maturity, usually through processes of initiation and then the accumulation of wealth to allow for marriage. Maintaining a balance between the demands of junior men and women and the maintenance of social, political, and economic power by senior men and women was a complex act. For example, the societies clustered in the Great Lakes in what is now Tanzania and Uganda were gerontocratic, with hierarchical, centralised political systems. Gender and age ranking worked together to bolster the power of older men, but their authority could be challenged by junior men if they abused their position. To become an adult—to claim status as senior within these societies—men needed to reach biological maturity, as well as accumulate particular markers of prestige: an independent household on land and with livestock claimed by the male head of household, and marriage and parenthood. As Shane Doyle explains, 'there were degrees of adulthood, and the physically mature who were unmarried or childless would not be treated in the same way as children, although real autonomy was acquired through the successful negotiation of independence.'[18] Independence meant marriage, and the ability to marry was determined by wealth. For a marriage to occur, the groom's family was required to pay bridewealth. Men from wealthy families might be loaned this payment—in the form of livestock, for instance—by wealthier male relatives. Men whose families were less wealthy could enter into a client relationship with wealthier men, working in exchange for livestock, or borrow livestock to repay the debt over time.

Either way, notes Doyle, marriage 'involved the young in a network of debt, both moral and material' and which entrenched the power of older, wealthier

---

[17] John W. Burton, 'Atuot Age Categories and Marriage,' *Africa*, vol. 50, no. 2 (1980), p. 146.
[18] Shane Doyle, 'Premarital Sexuality in Great Lakes Africa,' in *Generations Past: Youth in East African History*, eds. Andrew Burton and Helene Charton-Bigot (Athens, OH: Ohio University Press, 2010), p. 240.

men who controlled when their juniors could marry and, thus, claim seniority themselves.[19] Generational conflict arose when younger men felt that their elders were abusing their power. These men could organise violently against their elders, meaning that chiefs and kings needed to govern with the interests of junior men in mind. Writing about the region which would become the British colony of Kenya in the early 1890s, Paul Ocobock points out that generations were in constant debate with one another over what constituted adulthood and authority, meaning that the criteria by which seniority or junior status was measured could and did change over time. Age-based systems were characterised by generational conflict, but they were also flexible and capable of adjusting to new challenges and circumstances.[20]

This flexibility helps to explain why generation as well as the family were so important for African societies. The family—or the lineage, more precisely—was, as Temilola Alanamu makes the point, all-encompassing: it 'was an economic, political, religious, judicial, and social unit' comprised of the blood members of the lineage as well as, depending on the particular norms of a society, spouses, and, for instance, 'slaves, pawns, followers, and hangers-on', who often lived together.[21] The precise composition of the village, compound, homestead, or household differed across time and space. The lineage linked children to their ancestors, who, in many societies, could intervene in the lives of the living; the lineage could provide access to land or trade. Its power, in other words, extended from the spiritual to the material. Lineages tended to be either patrilineal or matrilineal—tracing their origins through either their fathers or their mothers to an original ancestor. However, as Rhiannon Stephens notes, because 'lineage models are supposed to determine behaviour—e.g., who inherits what—it can be difficult to avoid deterministic arguments'.[22] Put another way, scholars must beware of using lineage as a template to account for all people's behaviour—it was not an absolutely totalising system in which people exercised no agency. Also, people negotiated lineage, and definitions of who or what constituted the lineage changed over time.[23]

Nevertheless, the point is that most children were born into lineages, and their socialisation, education, and futures were shaped substantially by that lineage. Noting the significance of the lineage or the family to African societies becomes one way of explaining why generation was such a powerful force on the continent. Large families were particularly valuable for accessing and working the land, mainly for agriculture but also hunting, for instance. Across the continent, people could gain the right to use land usually by joining a

---

[19] Doyle, 'Premarital Sexuality in Great Lakes Africa,' p. 241.

[20] Paul Ocobock, *An Uncertain Age: The Politics of Manhood in Kenya* (Athens, OH: Ohio University Press, 2017), p. 8.

[21] Temilola Alanamu, 'Yoruba Childhood,' *Transition*, no. 121, Childhood (2016), pp. 96.

[22] Rhiannon Stephens, 'Lineage and Society in Precolonial Uganda,' *The Journal of African History*, vol. 50, no. 2 (2009), p. 205.

[23] Peter Geschiere, '"The African Family is Large, Very Large": Mobility and the Flexibility of Kinship, Examples from Cameroon,' *Ethnography*, vol. 21, no. 3 (2020), pp. 335–354.

land-holding group, and this could be, for example, through marriage or entering into client relationships (agreeing to be under the authority of a wealthy patron), among other strategies. Becoming part of a lineage brought with it access to land. Labour to work the land could also be accumulated through marriage (multiple wives and their children would contribute their labour to the household), kinship relations (betrothed young men might work for their prospective in-laws), pawnship (an institution which allowed adults and children to be pawned, by themselves or their relatives, in exchange for capital), or buying enslaved people.[24] Although pawnship, slavery, and other forms of unfree labour will be the focus of the following chapter, suffice it to note here that both of these systems incorporated more people, and often children, into the family group. On a continent where land was frequently difficult to cultivate, a large workforce meant being able to work more land, grow and store more food, and keep and herd more livestock.[25]

It is perhaps no surprise, then, that one of the key terms developed by scholars to describe African systems of value is 'wealth in people'. The concept of 'wealth in people' captures how many societies on the continent understood wealth to reside in the size of individuals' kinship networks. The term was developed specifically to apply to Equatorial Africa, and partly to explain the existence of systems of enslavement in precolonial societies. Originated first by Suzanne Miers and Igor Kopytoff in their collection *Slavery in Africa: Historical and Anthropological Perspectives* (1977), 'wealth in people' applies particularly to societies where prosperity depended on the existence of sufficient numbers of people to work the land. Writing about the region which is now called Angola, Joseph Miller explains that in the 'minds of virtually all Western Central Africans loomed the assumption, visible in the ideology of kinship that they employed in structuring and discussing human relations of all sorts, that wealth was people and that its sources resided in the propagation of descendants owing proper respect to their elders'.[26] However, as Miller points out, subscribing to this view of the centrality of the family did not preclude the purchase of enslaved people to increase the numbers of a household. While polygyny could contribute more children to a family than monogamous marriage, enslavement and pawning were useful tools too. Regardless, the idea that wealth resided in people—or that people were vital for the production of wealth—meant that children possessed enormous value in African societies. A bigger kinship group or family signified greater wealth. Children represented future labour, future bridewealth, and future alliances.[27]

[24] Sara Berry, 'Social Institutions and Access to Resources,' *Africa*, vol. 59 (1989), pp. 41–42.
[25] John Iliffe, *Africans: The History of a Continent*, second ed. (Cambridge: Cambridge University Press, 2007), pp. 1–4.
[26] Joseph C. Miller, *Way of Death: Merchant Capitalism and the Angolan Slave Trade, 1730–1830* (Madison, WI: University of Wisconsin Press, 1988), p. 44.
[27] Jane I. Guyer and Samuel M. Eno Belinga, 'Wealth in People as Wealth in Knowledge: Accumulation and Composition in Equatorial Africa,' *The Journal of African History*, vol. 36, no. 1 (1995), pp. 91–120.

To study children and young people in precolonial Africa is, then, to understand the most fundamental structures of many societies, and, in fact, the origins of political organisation itself. Writing about the Bantu migrations in Central and West Africa before 1600, Jan Vansina shows how children were central to the expansion of these communities: the birth of more children grew families and helped to establish new lineages. As these broke off to establish new villages, so the frontier of human settlement was pushed forward, dispersing the population over a bigger region. The organisation of lineages—whether descent was matrilineal or patrilineal, for instance—shaped the emergence of political systems in these regions.[28]

However, it is also to centre the most intimate and emotionally vulnerable aspects of human life in an account of a continent's history. As Kathryn M. de Luna writes, accounts of precolonial Africa 'might seem dry and overly instrumental to colleagues (and students) studying more recent periods ... because they lack the narrative depth of human emotion', a conundrum produced largely by the sources available to historians.[29] Generation refers both to a system which structured many African societies politically and to the relationships between parents and children, grandparents and grandchildren; wealth in people brings to mind marriage and women's experiences of childbearing and childrearing. While we must be careful not to superimpose contemporary definitions of what it means to love, or to care for, or, even, to resent, it is nevertheless vital to recognise that these institutions were shaped by feeling and thinking people, both young and old.

Growing Up in Precolonial African Societies

To return to the *Sundiata*, after the joyous celebrations of the birth of the hero, Sundiata Keita, the epic goes on to describe how, contrary to all expectations, he was initially a disappointment to his parents, and particularly his father. Unlike his peers—including his half-brothers—Sundiata Keita failed to reach developmental and social milestones:

> Sogolon's son had a slow and difficult childhood. At the age of three he still crawled along on all-fours while children of the same age were already walking. ... He had a head so big that he seemed unable to support it; he also had large eyes which would open wide whenever anyone entered his mother's house. He was taciturn and used to spend the whole day just sitting in the middle of the house. Whenever his mother went out he would crawl on all fours to rummage about in the calabashes in search of food, for he was very greedy.[30]

---

[28] Jan Vansina, *How Societies are Born: Governance in West Central Africa before 1600* (Charlottesville, VA: The University of Virginia Press, 2004).

[29] Kathryn M. de Luna, 'Affect and Society in Precolonial Africa,' *The International Journal of African Historical Studies*, vol. 46, no. 1 (2013), p. 125.

[30] Niane, *Sundiata*, p. 15.

Sundiata Keita, with his large head, big eyes, and crawling instead of walking, remained both physically and developmentally akin to a baby:

> Malicious tongues began to blab. What three-year-old has not yet taken his first steps? What three-year-old is not the despair of his parents through his whims and shifts of mood? What three-year-old is not the joy of his circle through his backwardness of talking?[31]

The narrator defines in the negative all that was expected of a child who might in contemporary terms be described as a toddler: wilful, babbling, and alternatively a source of joy and exasperation to its parents. In contrast, Sundiata Keita's older half-brother was not only meeting but also exceeding the expectations held of an eleven-year-old boy, much to his mother's pride:

> He was a fine and lively boy, who spent the day running about the village with those of his own age. He had even begun his initiation in the bush. The king had had a bow made for him and he used to go behind the town to practise archery with his companions.[32]

What is so striking about this section of the *Sundiata* is the shame that Sundiata Keita's apparent backwardness brings to his parents, and especially his mother. His seeming inability to be 'normal' reflects ill on her, with Sogolon already occupying a relatively lowly status in his father's household as a junior wife. Powerful emotions—like shame—are as important for understanding people's behaviours in the past as the institutions which structured their societies.[33] In the case of the *Sundiata*, Sogolon's shame is produced by her son not participating in the rituals and practices associated with ageing. Unlike Dankaran Touman, his older half-brother, he does not leave his mother to join other young boys to play in and beyond the village, and to practise hunting; he may not be initiated. As a result, he remains a perpetual child, apparently unable to be set on the path to manhood: to marriage and his own family, to the founding of his own household, the accrual of wealth, and his ascension to political power. For his parents, Sundiata Keita's lack of progress represents profound crisis.

Most African societies gradually produced systems and rituals for bringing children and young people formally into their communities as full members and participants. As they grew out of childhood, young people learned what was expected of them as adults through socialisation carried out in play and in games, as well as via rituals at key moments in their development. These processes differed across the continent, changed over time, and were shaped by children's gender, free or unfree status, and religious belief, among other

---

[31] Niane, *Sundiata*, p. 15.
[32] Niane, *Sundiata*, p. 15.
[33] Barbara M. Cooper, *Countless Blessings: A History of Childbirth and Reproduction in the Sahel* (Bloomington, IN: Indiana University Press, 2019), pp. 27–29.

considerations. This section takes a closer look at what it was like to grow up in some precolonial African societies.

As the *Sundiata*'s joyous description of the birth of a young princeling suggests, while children were certainly valued for their future labour and capacity to marry and bring wealth to their families, it is also clear from the ceremonies and celebrations which accompanied the birth of babies that parents and families loved babies and children for the fact of their being babies and young children. Across the continent, societies found a range of ways of marking the arrival of a new child—although at different times in the child's development and in different ways. In what is now Burkina Faso, nineteenth-century Mossi babies were not regarded as full persons within the family until they were weaned, a strategy to cope with high rates of infant mortality.[34] Among the Hausa people in the nineteenth century, for example, children were named seven days after birth, a moment followed by celebration the day after. Slaughtering a ram, distributing kolanuts, gifting new bolts of cloth, and an evening of drumming and singing, all marked the entrance of a new person to the community.[35] These naming ceremonies also established the responsibilities of certain adults in relation to the new child. In nineteenth-century Akan society in contemporary Ghana, the 'father's right of access to his children was initiated with his completion of the rites of naming' during which 'the father accepted the responsibility for training' the child. In return, that child owed his or her father particular obligations in adulthood.[36]

For their parents, babies held a transformative power, although those changes depended on the context in which the baby was born. Writing about precolonial North Nyanza society between c. 800 and 1200, in what is now Uganda, Rhiannon Stephens explains that motherhood was both a biological and a social process. She writes: 'to be a mother a woman should do more than conceive and give birth: she should do these in a specified and socially recognised context', and for North Nyanzans, this context was marriage. Marriage was a long process, beginning with the young woman—the future bride—reaching physical maturity, at which point she would receive instruction about married life, and a suitable husband would be sought for her. He and his family would present a negotiated bridewealth to her and her family, to be distributed among her kin. After these ceremonies, the bride would leave to live with her husband and his family. She shifted from cultivating food with and for her mother and her mother's children to becoming a cultivator of food for herself, her husband, and her future children (who would also work for her). Wifehood offered an increase in status, but bearing children—and particularly sons—could

---

[34] Lisa McNee, 'The Languages of Childhood: The Discursive Construction of Childhood and Colonial Policy in French West Africa,' *African Studies Quarterly*, no. 4 (2004), p. 25.

[35] Mary Felice Smith, *Baba of Karo, a Woman of the Muslim Hausa* (New Haven and London: Yale University Press, 1981).

[36] Jean Allman, 'Fathering, Mothering and Making Sense of "Ntamoba": Reflections on the Economy of Child-Rearing in Colonial Asante,' *Africa*, vol. 67, no. 2 (1997), pp. 301–302.

increase her seniority further. North Nyanzan women who bore the most children or the first son in a household would take the position of senior wife, regardless of the order in which they had married the groom. A woman incapable of bearing children for whatever reason occupied low status, although a married childless woman could potentially foster or adopt a child from another household.[37]

Children born within marriage in North Nyanzan society were enmeshed in a complex, dense web of relations, first established with the payment of brideprice: the goods which constituted this payment would be distributed among the bride's kin, linking them, then, socially and materially to the kin of the groom. Children were, too, a powerful presence within this society, with their arrival raising or otherwise adjusting the social positions of their parents. After the birth, babies and their mothers remained in seclusion, in the house in which the birth had occurred, until the stump of the umbilical cord had dried and withered off. (The placenta—considered to be the twin of the infant—would have been ritually buried near the entrance to the house, partly to placate the spirit associated with it.) Upon emerging from their isolation, they participated in a ceremony to assert the legitimacy of the child, and to take its rightful place among its father's kin.[38]

What happened, though, when a child was born outside of social convention? Unmarried girls in nineteenth-century Xhosa society, in contemporary South Africa, who fell pregnant faced both immediate and lifelong consequences. While pregnant, she would be excluded from her age group and prevented from participating in their activities. As one young woman remarked to the anthropologists Philip and Iona Mayer in the early twentieth century, the '"fallen" girl "no longer belongs to us from the moment she is pregnant. She has become a grown-up person."' The young man who impregnated her might pay a fine, and there was some possibility of a hastily organised marriage. But if this did not occur, she faced an uncertain future in which she might not be able to marry, or would only be able to receive a reduced brideprice.[39] Most likely, she would have remained as part of her father's household, cultivating her own land, and her child raised among her nephews and nieces. As Peter Delius and Clive Glaser remark, extra-marital pregnancy was disapproved of 'not because sex was in any way "sinful" but because of the familial and custodial complications it created'. Here, the baby was not brought into the same kind of network of kin relations established by marriage and the payment of brideprice. However, it would not bear the stigma of illegitimacy—and, if born a girl, her

---

[37] Rhiannon Stephens, *A History of African Motherhood: The Case of Uganda, 700–1900* (Cambridge: Cambridge University Press, 2013), pp. 39–46.
[38] Stephens, *A History of African Motherhood*, pp. 53–55.
[39] Philip and Iona Mayer, 'Socialization by Peers: The Youth Organization of the Red Xhosa,' in *Socialization: The Approach from social Anthropology*, ed. Philip Mayer (London: Tavistock, 1967), pp. 176–177.

Photograph 2.1 A mother and baby in Pondoland, South Africa, 1931, Monica and Godfrey Wilson Collection, University of Cape Town Libraries

brideprice would be paid to her maternal grandfather, thus recouping what he might have lost when her mother became pregnant.[40]

Given the care with which babies were enmeshed in their social worlds on birth, the nurturing and rearing of infants and young children was a deliberate and careful process. In his research on the Pedi people, Pitje describes how a newborn baby is welcomed into its community: having been bathed by the chief midwife, '[i]t is cheered up and spoken to as if it understands. Honorific expressions are showered on it when it sneezes. If their actions are any guide, one may safely say that the Pedi believe that the education of a child begins right from birth.' This education might—too—be shaped by the possibility

---

[40] Peter Delius and Clive Glaser, 'Sex, Disease, and Stigma in South Africa: Historical Perspectives,' *African Journal of AIDS Research*, vol. 4, no. 1 (2005), p. 30.

that the baby might be a returned deceased relative.[41] Regardless, its socialisation was of vital importance, even a few hours after its arrival. What was, then, the education of the child in Pedi society?

In its earliest years, the baby was in the care of its female relatives—its mother, grandmother, and younger female relations—who fed, weaned, and cared for it as they went about their daily tasks. Pitje observes: 'From birth until the age of three or four, a child's education is very simple. Priority number one is speech-training and the stimulation of its senses—particularly the senses of sight and hearing.' Its first words were usually '*Ma-ma* and *Pa-pa*, also *Ta-ta*'. Learning to crawl, sit, and stand were considered to be 'great achievement[s] for which the child is usually rewarded by being praised'. As young children move around, they were taught how to stay out of harm's way—about the dangers of fire and sharp blades, the necessity of being careful around fragile objects—and, around the age of three, how to relieve themselves appropriately. These skills were complemented by an emotional and social education: children were taught 'cheerfulness' and to practise self-control; they were taught how to greet their elders and how to dress modestly.[42]

Between the ages of three and six years, children began to leave the constant care of their mothers and enter into the world of their peers, but this was a gendered process. Girls stayed within the orbit of their female relatives, cultivating crops, collecting water and firewood, and assisting in domestic tasks. Boys, on the other hand, moved further away and by the age of six or seven spent full days in the countryside, herding cattle with their peers. It was in this phase that their socialisation intensified, as they learned the structure of the kinship system, how to behave among adults, and the correct attitude towards the opposite sex. Adult behaviour adjusted too, with boys being treated with 'firmness'. Pitje explains that Pedi adults

> assume that a boy is naturally tough, aggressive and war-like; a useless good-for-nothing sort of individual who is full of mischief. Only rough handling can turn him into a good citizen. Besides, man is destined to live a tough life, and therefore the boy must be hardened for it. Hence when it is cold, and the girls sit by the fireside, boys must play outside, if they are not running errands.[43]

In this way, boys were taught how to perform manliness, as girls—playing at keeping house—were taught a womanliness linked closely to the care of the household.

Not all childhoods were uniformly harsh, in comparison to those in contemporary industrialised societies. The existence of a strand within oral tradition intended mainly for children suggests the presence of a distinct children's world: a sphere inhabited by children and their caregivers. Folktales, for

---

[41] Pitje, 'Traditional Systems of Male Education among Pedi and Cognate Tribes,' Part I, p. 63.
[42] Pitje, 'Traditional Systems of Male Education among Pedi and Cognate Tribes,' Part I, p. 64.
[43] Pitje, 'Traditional Systems of Male Education among Pedi and Cognate Tribes,' Part I, p. 66.

instance, are a rich source for understanding how the carers of babies and young children might have conceptualised early childhood, and thought about how children should learn about the world. For example, scholars engaged in the study of Yoruba traditional literatures have noted that these encode precolonial Yoruba childrearing practices. Stories, lullabies, 'game poetry' (rhymes associated with children's games), and riddles helped to socialise children into Yoruba society, teaching them appropriate behaviour, inculcating cultural norms and values (such as the importance of hard work and resilience in the face of adversity), and preparing them for future roles within the community.[44]

The task of educating Yoruba children about their position within their society intensified, though, at around the age of four years. Similar to Pedi people, the Yoruba in the nineteenth century recognised a period of infancy lasting three to four years (*omo agbo* or *omo owo*), in which the young child learned to speak and to walk. As Alanamu notes, among the Yoruba, 'the social category of child, known as *omode*, denoted the totality of the period that commenced at birth until an individual was considered mature enough to marry, generally between the ages of eighteen to twenty for girls and mid-twenties to early thirties for boys'. Because 'childhood was not seen as an end unto itself but a preamble to adulthood', in the years leading up to marriage, children and young people's purpose was to learn. Alanamu suggests that this work occurred in three key areas: socialisation into children's specific household and lineage, labour learned and done in childhood, and play.[45]

As in many societies across the continent, all children were born into a specific lineage, where, in the case of the Yoruba, all members of the lineage traced their origins through their paternal line to a single, male ancestor. Children were raised within the lineage, living 'in a polygamous spatial patrilocal dwelling, known as the compound, or *idile*'. Children were marked—literally, through processes of cutting marks into the skin—as members of this lineage. Regardless of the fact that children belonged to the male line—for girls, that was, until marriage, when they would leave to join another lineage—they spent most of their time with their mothers, and, like Pedi children, were required to learn the history of their lineage (after all, their ancestors could be called upon to intervene in the world of living), and their obligations to other members of the lineage.[46]

It was under the supervision of both parents—and other relatives—that children learned how to work. This was possibly the most important feature of their education, as Alanamu explains: because 'economic independence was crucial to adulthood, socialisation largely consisted of teaching children *ise*, or labour. All young children, without exception, were taught some means of livelihood.' While very young children performed housekeeping tasks around

---

[44] Akínyemí, Akíntúndé, 'Yoruba Oral Literature: A Source of Indigenous Education for Children, *Journal of African Cultural Studies*, vol. 16, no. 2 (Dec. 2003), pp.161–179.
[45] Alanamu, 'Yoruba Childhood,' pp. 95, 96, 98.
[46] Alanamu, 'Yoruba Childhood,' pp. 96–97.

the compound, and cared for visitors and elderly and ailing relatives (another form of socialisation), from about the age of six years, girls learned how to trade from their mothers, gradually acquiring knowledge about motherhood and wifehood as they aged. Older girls also became increasingly independent traders themselves, working as hawkers, for instance, near their mothers' market stalls. Boys spent more time with older men, in whose company they became familiar not only with Yoruba political traditions, but also with specific skills, apprenticing to become blacksmiths or farmers, for instance.[47]

Social and cultural norms were also communicated in the activities which constituted children's leisure time—something which boys tended to have in greater abundance than girls, who were employed both in trading and in housekeeping. Games, rhymes, and tales, told to and between children, taught listeners to distinguish between what was moral and what was not, and what was good behaviour and what was not. Stories featuring and intended for girls emphasised 'generosity, responsibility, respect, loyalty, and even financial acumen' while those for boys—who were destined to establish their own households and to become involved in Yoruba governance—'focussed on morality and emphasised good versus bad behaviour'.[48]

These descriptions of typical Yoruba and Pedi childhoods in the nineteenth century should not be taken to represent each individual's experience of growing up in these societies. It is worth noting broad similarities, though, which were shared by other societies: the primary unit for socialising the child was the lineage or the family, about whose history and structure the child was expected to learn; the purpose of childhood was a preparation for adulthood; childhood was gendered; and education was as practical as it was emotional. There were also children who were raised outside of lineages and households. The following chapter will pay attention to children who were pawned and enslaved, but children were cast out for other reasons. Because missions were frequently places of refuge for abandoned children, missionaries are a valuable source of information on children who were not welcome at home. Missionaries working among the Yoruba noted that children suffering from disease, or who were accused of being responsible for the deaths of their parents, were left to fend for themselves. They also took in foundlings: infants whose mothers may have been enslaved, and babies (like twins) who had been discarded.[49]

The reasons for children's exclusion from society changed over time, and according to context. Although frowned upon, illegitimacy—being born out of wedlock—might not necessarily permanently mark a child. Equally, attitudes towards multiple births varied. While members of precolonial Igbo society practised twin infanticide in the belief that twins and other multiple births were

---

[47] Alanamu, 'Yoruba Childhood,' pp. 98–100.
[48] Alanamu, 'Yoruba Childhood,' pp. 101–103.
[49] John Iliffe, 'Poverty in Nineteenth-Century Yorubaland,' *The Journal of African History*, vol. 25, no. 1 (1984), pp. 43–57.

an abomination to the earth deity,[50] attitudes differed elsewhere. The Akan—also in West Africa—regarded twins as a sign of good luck, and celebrated their parents.[51] Similarly, in North Nyanzan society, twins were 'feared and respected', and their parents were 'granted special respect and awarded honorific titles'.[52] These beliefs were not static either: while some precolonial Yoruba did kill or abandon twins, those who lived within the Oyo Empire between the seventeenth and nineteenth centuries abandoned the practice.[53]

A child who was not a full member of a lineage would not participate in the key rituals which marked that child's integration into new age categories and into society. Ceremonies at puberty and at marriage—the latter only possible if the former had been undergone—marked two decisive breaks in the life of a young person, shifting from childhood to youth, and from youth to adulthood. Those who were not included in these rituals might not join their age-set, their comrades who would accompany them into adulthood and seniority; they would not be marked out as ready for marriage and, thus, maturity. Fellow initiates formed bonds—encouraged in some cases by the taking of oaths or the sharing of secret knowledge or names—which the cohort maintained through marriage, parenthood, and the assumption of positions of seniority or leadership (particularly in the case of men), depending on the political formations of the regions in which they were located.

Puberty was the key moment which signalled a young person's readiness to leave behind childhood, and was frequently marked by ceremonies initiating young people into new age grades, in preparation for full adulthood. Depending on context, these rituals might be presided over by peers or much older adults of the same gender as the initiates (whose activities were segregated by gender), with much of the information provided focusing on sex and sexuality. Given the contemporary stereotypes about the prudishness of African societies, this emphasis might seem surprising. But as many scholars have noted, providing youth with information about sexual reproduction and allowing limited—usually non-penetrative—sexual contact provided, as Susan Kiragu writes of precolonial Gĩkũyũ society in contemporary Kenya, 'a restricted form of sexual release' where 'young people were given the free will to sexual desire, exploration and release' but 'within a restrictive moral code, with boundaries and

---

[50] Misty L. Bastian, '"The Demon Superstition": Abominable Twins and Mission Culture in Onitsha History,' *Ethnology*, vol. 40, no. 1, Special Issue: Reviewing Twinship in Africa (Winter, 2001), pp. 13–27.

[51] Wolf Bleek, 'Did the Akan Resort to Abortion in Pre-Colonial Ghana? Some Conjectures,' *Africa*, vol. 60, no. 1 (1990), p. 125.

[52] Stephens, *A History of African Motherhood*, p. 55.

[53] Elisha P. Renne and Misty L. Bastian, 'Reviewing Twinship in Africa,' *Ethnology*, vol. 40, no. 1, Special Issue: Reviewing Twinship in Africa (Winter, 2001), pp. 1–11.

public regulations'.⁵⁴ Early twentieth-century Xhosa society made similar allowances, classing what was defined as appropriate sexual activity between young people as 'play'. As the Mayers remark, this had two purposes: 'encouragement, and direction into harmless channels'. Directed entirely by slightly older peers, nearly pubescent girls learned 'about the permissibility of *metsha*, external sexual intercourse' or intercrural (thigh) sex. This sexual 'play' was encouraged in the period before marriage as a sanctioned outlet for sexual curiosity and desire between heterosexual couples. Those who broke the rules—those who had penetrative sex—faced consequences from members of their age-sets. While young people were taught not to speak of sex to their parents, this was not because sex was regarded as shameful, but, rather, as a component of *hlonipha*—the respectful attitude owed to parents and older people.⁵⁵

It is worth pausing for a moment to emphasise that although these examples describe heterosexual relationships, young people of the same gender were attracted to one another sexually too, and had same-sex sexual relationships. Historians, anthropologists, and activists in LGBTQ communities across Africa have all pointed to long histories of same-sex relationships on the continent, and especially between young people in the period between childhood and marriage.⁵⁶ Similar to how scholars are attentive to how contemporary definitions of 'childhood' cannot be imposed on precolonial African societies, so they need to be alert to how Africans defined gender. As Nwando Achebe explains, precolonial Africa provided

> a milieu that recognizes that biological sex and gender do not coincide; that gender is a social construct and is flexible and fluid, allowing biological women to become gendered men, and biological men, gendered women.⁵⁷

As a result, under certain circumstances, women with access to wealth could assume the status of husbands, taking younger women as wives—becoming thus 'female husbands'. Adult daughters could become sons in order to inherit wealth from their fathers, in the absence of other heirs. Women could govern as kings. Men could exist as priestesses.⁵⁸ For all this flexibility, these gendered

---

⁵⁴ Susan Kiragu, 'Conceptualising Children as Sexual Beings: Pre-Colonial Sexuality Education among the Gĩkũyũ of Kenya,' *Sex Education: Sexuality, Society and Learning*, vol. 13, no. 5 (2013), p. 585.

⁵⁵ Philip and Iona Mayer, 'Socialization by Peers,' p. 175.

⁵⁶ Stella Nyanzi, 'Dismantling Reified African Culture through Localised Homosexualities in Uganda,' *Culture, Health & Sexuality*, vol. 15, no. 8 (2013), pp. 961–962; Stephen O. Murray and Will Roscoe, 'Africa and African Homosexualities: An Introduction,' in *Boy-Wives and Female Husbands: Studies in African Homosexualities*, eds. Stephen O. Murray and Will Roscoe (Albany, NY: SUNY Press, 1998), p. 8.

⁵⁷ Nwando Achebe, *Female Monarchs and Merchant Queens in Africa* (Athens, OH: Ohio University Press, 2020), p. 24.

⁵⁸ Ifi Amadiume, *Male Daughters, Female Husbands: Gender and Sex in an African Society* (London: Zed Books, 1987).

identities existed within systems in which age and other factors—wealth, free or unfree status, for instance—determined how individuals fitted into the homestead, the lineage, and the society more broadly. Overwhelmingly, young people were taught that heterosexual marriage was their future, and that the attainment of adulthood and seniority (depending on context) depended on heterosexual marriage. Nevertheless, there was room within this framework for same-sex sexual attraction and sex to occur.

In many societies, one of the most significant markers of the attainment of adulthood was circumcision, for boys and, less frequently although not unusually, for girls too. The removal of the foreskin, a procedure frequently undertaken by a senior man, was a vital component of a series of events held in the seclusion of initiation. Nelson Mandela—leader of the anti-apartheid movement and the first President of democratic South Africa—described his circumcision during his youth in the early twentieth century in the countryside, where he lived as a ward of one of the Xhosa royal families:

> When I was sixteen, the regent decided that it was time that I become a man. In Xhosa tradition, this is achieved through one means only: circumcision. In my tradition, an uncircumcised male cannot be heir to his father's wealth, cannot marry or officiate in tribal rituals. An uncircumcised Xhosa man is a contradiction in terms, for he is not considered a man at all, but a boy. For the Xhosa people, circumcision represents the formal incorporation of males into society. It is not just a surgical procedure, but a lengthy and elaborate preparation for manhood. As a Xhosa, I count my years as a man from the date of my circumcision.[59]

Mandela goes on to describe his enjoyment of the camaraderie between him and the other twenty-five initiates, who occupied two specially built, secluded huts for the duration of their initiation. Having been circumcised, the young men were coated in white clay to symbolise their purity, and remained apart from society as they healed from their wounds. Once ready to re-enter the world, now as men, they were coated with red ochre, suggesting their readiness for marriage. At the end of their 'seclusion, the lodges and all their contents were burned, destroying [their] last links to childhood, and a great ceremony was held to welcome [them] as men to society'. A key marker of this new status was the awarding of each initiate with livestock—cattle and sheep—to signify their adult status.[60]

In the *Sundiata*, the hero—having lagged behind his peers developmentally—becomes a youth through the exercise of supernatural powers. Having been provoked by the machinations of his father's senior wife, Sundiata lifts an extremely heavy iron bar, standing and walking for the first time. In an instant, he is a child on the point of adolescence, who gathers around him a group of friends, who spend their days hunting. He learns the history of his society and

---

[59] Nelson Mandela, *Long Walk to Freedom: The Autobiography of Nelson Mandela* (London: Abacus, 1995), p. 30.

[60] Mandela, *Long Walk to Freedom*, p. 34.

Photograph 2.2 A group of boys in Gonja, Tanzania, described by the German missionary Wilhelm Guth as being 'newly circumcised', c. 1913–1938, the Leipzig Mission Picture Archive

lineage from his mother, and from an older companion he receives 'education and instruction according to Mandingo rules of conduct'.[61] He is, in other words, on his way to becoming a man—so that when he and his mother flee into exile to escape persecution, Sundiata achieves full maturity outside of his kingdom, before returning to conquer it. A key component of Sundiata's childhood and youth is learning how to fight, and there are echoes of this emphasis in the childhoods of many young men, especially, across the continent.

In Xhosa society, young boys in the years preceding initiation engaged in stick fighting among one another. This tremendously popular pastime had multiple purposes. Perhaps most obviously, it was a preparation to bear arms and to participate in warfare, in a society which, particularly in the nineteenth century, was engaged in a series of brutal wars with the colonial state. In addition to this, the rules governing stick fighting taught boys and young men what constituted manliness. As Anne Mager explains, this was a game, a practice, and a spectacle in which 'hierarchies of age, respect and physical prowess were established' and also 'constantly challenged, tested and re-established'. During a period when young men were forming their own identities, stick fighting

---

[61] Niane, *Sundiata*, p. 23.

offered 'a ritual language' in which identities were 'articulated', and allowed participants to '"fix" and stabilise a sense of self'.[62] Circumcised men abandoned stick fighting—its association was with preparation for adulthood.

Young women's initiation into their societies occurred differently. As described earlier, this could include being brought into the world of women's market trading in parts of West Africa, where girls began as assistants to their mothers, moved on to working as hawkers, and, eventually, operated their own stalls. In some societies—in what is now Kenya and Mali, for instance—girls underwent forms of circumcision too, in which the clitoris was excised or nicked, depending on context. This procedure was accompanied by the provision of knowledge about wifehood and motherhood, usually from older women, even if girls' subsequent behaviour might have been monitored by their peers. An excised girl was ready to be married, and, thus, to attain maturity.[63] But—again—excision or elaborate initiation rites for women were not characteristic of every society over time. Information about menstruation was conveyed to both girls and boys in many societies, and for girls and women, menstruation was associated, frequently, with a range of beliefs and practices, many of them linked to regulating the position of women in society. Writing about the nineteenth-century Akan—where elite women could wield significant political power— Emmanuel Akyeampong and Pashington Obeng note that it was the capacity to menstruate—to transmit blood to new generations, to make life—that rendered women potentially powerful and, thus, dangerous. Learning rituals around menstruation became, then, important for young women as they learned to negotiate gendered power dynamics within this society.[64]

All rituals and other practices instituted to mark people's navigation of age-based systems were subject to modification over time, and for a range of factors. The introduction of Islam to West Africa in the nineteenth century changed forms of initiation for young men and women, being less tolerant of the encouragement of premarital sexual play, among other things.[65] In the early nineteenth century, Shaka Zulu is said to have ended the practice of male circumcision in his kingdom, meaning that—unlike other Nguni-speaking groups in the region (like the Xhosa further south)—Zulu speakers do not mark entry into male adulthood with circumcision. However, in the twenty-first century—200 years later, in other words—health professionals campaigned to (re) introduce circumcision in KwaZulu-Natal province in an effort to stem rates of HIV infection. King Goodwill Zwelithini supported this campaign because, as

---

[62] Anne Mager, 'Youth Organisations and the Construction of Masculine Identities in the Ciskei and Transkei, 1945–1960,' *Journal of Southern African Studies*, vol. 24, no. 4 (1998), p. 658.

[63] Cooper, *Countless Blessings*, pp. 103–104.

[64] Emmanuel Akyeampong and Pashington Obeng, 'Spirituality, Gender, and Power in Asante History,' *The International Journal of African Historical Studies*, vol. 28, no. 3 (1995), pp. 481–508.

[65] Cooper, *Countless Blessings*, pp. 51–53.

Liz Timbs points out, it 'provided an opportunity to recentre himself as the heart of the Zulu nation'.[66] This reinvention of tradition served both medical and political ends.

Conclusion

Even if colonial conquest can be understood as a significant moment of rupture in Africa's long history, the processes described in this chapter did not cease suddenly with the imposition of European rule. Many institutions and ceremonies changed, often as a result of social and economic change, and particularly as young people left the countryside in search of waged labour. What is often described as 'tradition' was, thus, malleable. As Thomas Spear argues, under colonial rule 'older traditions were continually reinterpreted' and 'customs were endlessly debated …. All were dynamic historical processes that reconstituted the heritage of the past to meet the needs of the present.'[67] Occasionally, these rituals developed new, sharply politicised meanings. Lynn Thomas has described how efforts to end the circumcision of girls in Kenya during the mid-1950s—a practice condemned by British feminists, missionaries, and the colonial state—remade excision as an anti-colonial act, as girls declared—in opposition to colonial authorities and Kenyan elders who attempted to enforce the ban—that they would circumcise themselves. In so doing, they changed the practice and, to some degree, the meaning of circumcision.[68]

A history of childhood and youth in the precolonial era is, thus, a history of the more recent past too, and an account of social change which helps to illuminate the present. As this chapter has shown, it is impossible to generalise a distinctive precolonial 'African' childhood over such a long period of time, over such a varied and complex continent. But there are a number of key ideas which are widely applicable across Africa and for much of the precolonial period. The first is that children and young people existed in communities where generation was one of the most important institutions which structured societies. Intersecting with other factors—like gender and free or unfree status—age apportioned power to certain people at particular moments. Children and young people existed on the lower rungs of a ranking system which shaped the status, behaviours, relationships, and expectations of all the people—adults and children—within that system. Also, those children would ascend this system as they aged, although how they did so was also dependent on their gender, for example. Secondly, biological age and social age did not necessarily map onto one another precisely. In many societies, adulthood was achieved

---

[66] Liz Timbs, 'An In(ter)vention of Tradition: Medical Male Circumcision in KwaZulu-Natal, 2009–2016,' *Journal of Natal and Zulu History*, vol. 32 (2018), p. 8.

[67] Thomas Spear, 'Neo-Traditionalism and the Limits of Invention in Colonial Africa,' *Journal of African History*, vol. 44 (2003), p. 25.

[68] Lynn M. Thomas, '"*Ngaitana* (I will circumcise myself)": The Gender and Generational Politics of the 1956 Ban on Clitoridectomy in Meru, Kenya,' *Gender & History*, vol.8, no. 3 (Nov. 1996), pp. 338–339.

when an individual married, for instance, and not at a specific age. Signs of biological maturation were not insignificant—menstruation signalled in many societies that girls should be prepared for womanhood—but they were by no means the only signal that a young woman was leaving childhood.

Thirdly, childhood was a preparation for adulthood. The socialisation and education of children and young people encompassed their place within their lineage and society more broadly, their relationship with the spiritual (which was often linked to the lineage, as ancestors were believed to exercise influence over the lives of the living), social and cultural norms regarding the treatment of elders and peers, the behaviours associated with men and women, and, frequently, the kinds of work they would be required to do as adults. While the powerful ideology of the innocent child posits that sexual knowledge and labour are inimical to children's happiness, within many African societies, children were taught how to work alongside their parents, other adults, and their peers, and they were, particularly as they aged, provided with frank information about sexual reproduction and sexual mores. So while children were certainly loved and treasured in ways that might feel familiar in the twenty-first century, 'childhood' was certainly conceptualised very differently.

The multiple definitions of what constituted 'childhood' both confused and concerned European administrators and Christian missionaries in the nineteenth and twentieth centuries. As the following chapters will describe, African childhoods needed, in their view, to be reformed.

CHAPTER 3

Enslavement and Unfreedom

In about 1855, a married couple living around the border of contemporary Mozambique and Tanzania had a daughter and named her Swema. They were Yao speakers, the ethnic group which dominated this stretch of East Central Africa. Swema was one of several children in the family, and their father was a successful hunter, meaning that they had both abundant food to eat and could exchange the ivory and other animal products he collected with traders who worked between the coast and the interior. On the eastern littoral of the Indian Ocean world, Swema, her sisters, their little brother, and mother wore clothing from abroad, and had access to goods circulated by the trade caravans. Disaster struck, though, when a lion killed her father on a hunt, and the family fell into poverty and starvation: they could not maintain their livestock, and all of Swema's siblings died. Not yet ten years old, she and her mother left their village.

As Edward Alpers explains, it is difficult to understand why they left: in Yao society, both could have been taken in by Swema's maternal uncle, or by one of her father's brothers. Perhaps, Alpers speculates, her father was a recent arrival, with few social ties. Or her mother was enslaved, meaning that 'she would have had no social identity beyond that of her husband's wife.'[1] Regardless, conditions only worsened: their efforts to grow their own food failed and her mother became indebted, unable to repay the loan of two sacks of sorghum millet. One morning, with the arrival of an Arab caravan, the creditor appeared at Swema's mother's hut with two witnesses, and Swema was sold into slavery in payment for her mother's debt. Distraught, her mother begged to be taken along too—to not be separated from her daughter. Albers writes:

[1] Edward A. Alpers, 'The Story of Swema: Female Vulnerability in Nineteenth-Century East Africa,' in *Women and Slavery in Africa*, Claire C. Robertson and Martin A. Klein, eds. (Portsmouth, NH: Heinemann, 1997), p. 191.

Although she was not formally selling herself into slavery, this is what she was doing in effect. Indeed, had she remained in Yaoland, she probably would have suffered the same fate, since solitary survival was virtually impossible and her only option would have been to attach herself to a local lineage as a client with little security against being sold to the next caravan that came long. For the weak and defenceless, voluntary enslavement was the only sure form of protection in late nineteenth-century East Central Africa....[2]

Both mother and daughter began the long walk to the coast.

A number of factors shaped their predicament. Perhaps most obviously, their gender made them particularly vulnerable to impoverishment. The source of their woes was the death of Swema's father, the only person capable of supporting the family within Yao society (before his untimely death, Swema's younger brother would have been too young to contribute to the household). On their own, their options were limited to voluntary enslavement or entering into a client relationship, another form of unfreedom. Swema's status as a child also rendered her particularly appealing to slave traders. She had a lifetime of labour—reproductive and otherwise—ahead of her, while her mother represented only a potential burden to the caravan, another mouth to feed who might not fetch a good price at the slave market in Zanzibar. Undergirding these possibilities and obstacles was a system of enslavement which was regarded as legally legitimate in Yao society. The presence of the two witnesses at the formal enslavement of Swema confirmed that her mother's creditor had every right to sell her to cover the debt.

Enslavement existed across precolonial and colonial Africa. As G. Ugo Nwokeji points out, until comparatively recently slavery existed in most societies around the globe, and, thus, 'it would have been an anomaly if slavery did not exist on the continent.'[3] Slavery occurred in multiple forms across Africa over a long period of time, as a result of which there was no single African system or experience of slavery. Swema and her mother were drawn into the trade of enslaved people along the east coast of the continent in the Indian Ocean. Africans' participation in the Indian Ocean trade in the nineteenth century (or earlier) differed from those caught up in the trans-Atlantic trade in the seventeenth century, or in systems of enslavement which operated across the Sahara or in Muslim societies in West Africa, or precolonial Central Africa, for instance. But there were certainly continuities of experience: Swema was sold to pay a debt, like many other enslaved Africans across time and place. Children were enslaved and traded in all of these systems—and were also subject to other forms of unfree labour, such as pawning. Importantly, they were enslaved, bought and sold, or pawned, on the grounds of their status as children. Not only were children more easily seized and enslaved in some cases—and after the

---

[2] Alpers, 'The Story of Swema,' p. 192.
[3] G. Ugo Nwokeji, 'Slavery in Non-Islamic West Africa, 1420–1820,' in *The Cambridge World History of Slavery*, vol. 3: 1420–1804, David Eltis and Stanley L. Engerman, eds. (Cambridge: Cambridge University Press, 2011), p. 81.

abolition of the trans-Atlantic trade, children could be hidden more successfully than adults on illegal slave ships—but they were also attractive as slaves or as pawns. For example, they represented years of future labour, and could be potentially incorporated into new households, especially as wives in the case of girls. Children were born into enslavement, and systems of kinship were bound up with slavery in many contexts.

As the previous chapter demonstrates, the fact that children in precolonial African societies worked was not regarded as an anomaly. While in contemporary societies the idea that childhood innocence is compromised by wage labour has proven to be remarkably powerful, this was not the case in pre- and early colonial Africa (and around the world in most places until the twentieth century). In fact, work was one of the primary activities through which children were socialised into the communities into which they were born. The difference between enslaved (or pawned) children in Africa and those who were free was precisely their status as slaves or as pawns: all children worked—to lesser and greater degrees—but enslaved or pawned children occupied specific legal and social statuses which, for enslaved children, foreclosed the usual initiation into new age categories, and full integration into society. Pawned children occupied a more ambiguous position: their labour assisted in paying off a debt to the creditor, who was responsible for their care and welfare during the period of pawnship.

Thus, an understanding of the history of slavery in Africa—a history which is focused on the continent as well as Africa's position within larger systems, across the Atlantic or Indian Oceans, for instance, or as part of the Muslim world—requires an attentiveness to the enslavement and unfreedom of children. Their experiences of enslavement were both similar and different to adults on the grounds of their status as children. However, as historian Benjamin Lawrence observes, the lives of enslaved children ask historians to think more carefully about how they describe and define enslavement and emancipation. The lives of enslaved children defy a 'slavery/freedom dichotomy,' he writes, because even after having been freed 'children were never free and autonomous.' As the previous chapter demonstrates, in pre- and early colonial societies, for all that they were loved and valued, children and young people occupied social positions of relative powerlessness, and were subject to the authority of their parents and other adults. Even before enslavement, children were not necessarily 'free'. Upon being freed, children remained under adult supervision, in roles dependent on the context in which they settled: as apprentices or domestic servants, or school pupils. As Lawrence notes, children's 'paths toward liberty and autonomy erupted in fits and jerks, sometimes forward, sometimes backward.'[4] Of course, this is not to suggest a fundamental similarity between enslavement and the condition of childhood, but, rather, to ask what constituted freedom in the context of slavery.

[4] Benjamin N. Lawrance, *Amistad's Orphans: An Atlantic Story of Children, Slavery, and Smuggling* (New Haven and London: Yale University Press, 2014), p. 54.

This chapter examines children and young people's experiences of enslavement and other forms of unfree labour. It begins with a definition and overview of histories of enslavement in Africa, and then shifts to an account of children in precolonial systems of slavery and pawning across the continent. The chapter then expands its focus, pulling in the Atlantic and Indian Ocean trades in Africans, and concludes not with abolition, but with the persistence of enslavement and pawning well into the nineteenth and twentieth centuries under colonial rule. The study of the enslavement and freeing of children helps to illuminate the complex and unintended consequences of ending slavery in Africa.

Enslavement in Africa

During the partition of Africa in the final decades of the nineteenth century, in most parts of the continent under European domination, slavery was nearly ubiquitous, with enslaved people constituting half of the subjugated population in some areas.[5] The Treaty of the Berlin West Africa Conference (1884–1885) required that colonising powers eradicate all forms of enslavement in the territories they claimed, using the abolitionist logic that slavery was antithetical to free trade. While many colonies did make some effort—to varying degrees—to abolish enslavement, other forms of unfree labour either emerged (or re-emerged) or persisted clandestinely. Colonial rule was, then, another moment in the long, complex, and changing history of enslavement in Africa. The widespread nature of slavery shortly before the 'Scramble' for Africa was not produced by colonialism, although the continent had certainly changed as a result of contact with Europeans involved in the trans-Atlantic slave trade, especially. Rather, slavery had long existed in Africa. Although it was one of the forms of trade which linked the continent to other regions—across the Sahara, the Indian Ocean, and the Atlantic—it also pre-dated those forms of contact and existed in regions which were not necessarily drawn into intercontinental trade.

How, then, to define slavery in Africa? As Frederick Cooper emphasises, slavery in Africa neither existed in isolation from slavery in other regions of the world, nor was it necessarily different from slavery elsewhere.[6] Equally, though, other scholars suggest that the term 'slavery' is, at best, too broad to capture the variety of forms of enslavement and unfreedom on the continent and, at worst, potentially misleading for writing histories of unfree labour in Africa. On the one hand, as the historian Paul Lovejoy notes, the fact that it is possible to 'translate "slave" into any language in Africa, such as *nikla* (Tamasheq), *bawa* (Hausa), but also *bella* (Songhay), *maccuBe* and *rimaaybe* (Puular), *'abd*

---

[5] Paul E. Lovejoy, 'Slavery in the Colonial State and After,' in *The Palgrave Handbook of African Colonial and Postcolonial History*, Martin S. Shanguhyia and Toyin Falola, eds. (Basingstoke: Palgrave Macmillan, 2018), p. 104.

[6] Frederick Cooper, 'The Problem of Slavery in African Studies,' *The Journal of African History*, vol. 20, no. 1 (1979), p. 106.

(Arabic), *jam* (Wolof), among others,' suggests the ubiquity of its existence across the continent. But, on the other, economic historian Joseph Inikori counters that 'slavery' collapses a range of highly specific, local social relationships under one over-simplifying category.[7] African terminologies and practices might not map precisely onto what might be understood as 'slavery' by contemporary readers—and particularly when the plantation slavery which existed in the Americas tends today to dominate debates over the legacies of enslavement. One route out of this impasse is to identify some broad characteristics of slavery in Africa, to determine 'how extensive it was and when it assumed significance in … the political economies, as well as its extent, character, and dynamics.'[8] Writing about West Africa before or beyond the imposition of Islamic rule and the institution of the trans-Atlantic slave trade, Nwokeji offers a description of the nature of slavery which holds for most of the continent too:

> Slavery in most African societies was, in various configurations, a means of labour recruitment, a system of domination and exploitation, and an important means of expanding the lineage. Africans also acquired slaves as status symbols, bureaucrats, and soldiers.[9]

Slavery was not necessarily always a response to a specific crisis or difficulty—for instance, the necessity of access to labour to work the land, or as markers of status of their masters—but, rather, served a number of purposes.

As historian Sean Stilwell explains, slavery is usually defined by three major characteristics: enslaved people are regarded as social outsiders, with no familial or other links to the societies in which they work; enslaved people exist as property; and slavery is a form of violent domination in which enslaved people are powerless.[10] In the case of Africa, historians have tried to account for the existence of slavery on the continent, drawing precisely on these factors. One explanation—associated mainly with the scholars Suzanne Miers and Igor Kopytoff—places particular emphasis on the relationship between slavery and kinship. While enslaved people may exist as social outcasts—they have suffered 'social death' or are not regarded as social beings, as Orlando Patterson argues—over time they might be gradually incorporated into the kinship group. As the previous chapter demonstrated, the size of kinship groups in precolonial African societies was linked, often, to the wealth of the head of that family. Adding enslaved people to the kinship group was one strategy for expanding the group. This interpretation of slavery in Africa has at its heart the

---

[7] Paul E. Lovejoy, 'Slavery in Africa,' in *The Routledge History of Slavery*, Gad Heuman and Trevor Burnard, eds. (London: Routledge, 2011), p. 35.

[8] G. Ugo Nwokeji, 'Slavery in Non-Islamic West Africa, 1420–1820,' in *The Cambridge World History of Slavery*, vol. 3: 1420–1804, David Eltis and Stanley L. Engerman, eds. (Cambridge: Cambridge University Press, 2011), p. 81.

[9] Nwokeji, 'Slavery in Non-Islamic West Africa,' p. 85.

[10] Sean Stilwell, *Slavery and Slaving in African History* (Cambridge: Cambridge University Press, 2014), pp. 5–6.

question, in Stilwell's words, 'can slaves be placed along a continuum of statuses that included kin (those who belonged)?' Or, put another way, was enslavement 'not the opposite of freedom or kinship but similar to other institutions that emphasized dependency?'[11] Perhaps unsurprisingly, many scholars have critiqued this understanding of enslavement in Africa, pointing out its elision of the violence inherent to the system, and the suffering experienced by enslaved people. It also seems to imply, as Cooper writes, that slavery was 'indelibly written into particular cultures and not the ever-changing product of conflicting pressures from slave-owners, non-slave-owners, and the slaves themselves.'[12] His point is that Miers and Kopytoff's approach implies that slavery in Africa is ahistorical: that it exists within broader kinship systems, impervious to political, economic, or other forms of change.

An opposing view emphasises, then, enslavement as a system produced by the labour market. Buying or capturing enslaved people was a choice made when paying for or acquiring labour through other means was too difficult or expensive. Marxist scholars of slavery—most famously the anthropologist Claude Meillassoux—link an economic interpretation of slavery with one attentive to kinship.[13] Interested specifically in questions of reproduction—in other words, how societies maintain and pass on their structures, culture, and so on—these scholars suggest that enslaved people constituted a class which contributed to the reproduction of that society through their labour, without necessarily becoming part of that society. Enslaved people produced more food or other commodities than a free person and their family would have. As a result, the owners of the enslaved could accrue wealth and power more effectively. In this interpretation of slavery in Africa, scholars suggest that enslavement became vital to the maintenance of elite power.[14] However, neither of these interpretations accounts for how slavery changed over time.

A thread connecting these varying interpretations of enslavement is the tension between social insiders and outsiders. Instead of understanding slavery in Africa as existing in a binary with absolute freedom, it would be more accurate to think of enslavement as resting on a 'distinction between people defined as insiders—those who belonged to and in local and regional social, religious, and political systems—and slaves, who were outsiders.'[15] As social outsiders, the enslaved were without the kinship connections which embedded them within social, political, and economic structures, allowing them access to resources, political relationships, and other kinds of meaningful and useful connection. It was precisely because enslaved people existed without these connections that they were rendered useful to their owners: they could be put to whatever kind of work needed by insiders, without recourse to the protective relationships

[11] Stilwell, *Slavery and Slaving in African History*, p. 7.
[12] Cooper, 'The Problem of Slavery in African Studies,' p. 104.
[13] Cooper, 'The Problem of Slavery in African Studies,' p. 108–110.
[14] Joseph C. Miller, 'The World according to Meillassoux: A Challenging but Limited Vision,' *The International Journal of African Historical Studies*, vol. 22, no. 3 (1989), p. 476.
[15] Stilwell, *Slavery and Slaving in African History*, p. 9.

available to insiders. Over time, enslaved people could become or take on some of the characteristics of insiders—through manumission, through high-ranking work—but the key feature of enslavement was maintaining the kinlessness of slaves. Stilwell writes:

> slaves in Africa were usually produced through violence, were often the objects of a property-like relationship, and initially had the status of kinless outsiders within their host societies. … slavery in Africa provided the most efficient and complete means for some human beings to exploit other human beings. …slaves were valuable … because they were outsiders and thus were open to more profound exploitation than those who belonged—or the free.[16]

Perhaps most importantly, 'slavery in Africa—as in the rest of the world—was fundamentally about economic, sexual, social, or political exploitation.' Most enslaved people were women. They contributed labour to the household—they produced food or other commodities for sale—as well as their reproductive capacity. Children born to enslaved women belonged to the household, and were also enslaved, inheriting their mothers' status. The sexual exploitation of enslaved women was one of the key features of slavery, both in Africa and elsewhere (although women could and did own slaves, both male and female, too).[17]

Another way of defining enslavement in Africa would be to compare it to other kinds of unfree labour. Pawnship—dubbed debt bondage in other contexts—existed across many African societies, well into the twentieth century. Most of these societies appear to have stretched from contemporary Sierra Leone and Liberia in the west, across Central Africa, to Kenya and Mozambique in the east. (Like slavery, pawning existed in other parts of the world too. It was not a uniquely African form of labour.) Historians Toyin Falola and Lovejoy explain that a 'pawn was a person held as collateral for a loan'. Not only was the pawned individual security for the loan (the pawn would remain with the creditor until the loan was paid back), but the pawn's labour was also interest on the debt.[18] Clearly, there were powerful similarities between pawnship and enslavement, and they existed alongside each other within many societies, with the practice of pawning often increasing after the abolition of slavery in the late nineteenth and early twentieth centuries. Enslaved people could be pawned in cases where their owners were in debt or needed to raise capital. However, there were also important differences. Falola and Lovejoy write:

> the pawning contract, not the pawn, was the property of the creditor, while under slavery, the slave was the direct property of the master. Pawns, or more often their

---

[16] Stilwell, *Slavery and Slaving in African History*, p. 12.
[17] Stilwell, *Slavery and Slaving in African History*, p. 12, 24.
[18] Toyin Falola and Paul E. Lovejoy, 'Pawnship in Historical Perspective,' in *Pawnship, Slavery, and Colonialism in Africa*, Paul E. Lovejoy and Toyin Falola, eds. (Trenton, NJ: Africa World Press, 2003), p. 3.

relatives who had placed them in pawn, had legal recourse in the case of abuse or dispute on the basis of the contract, and the contract could be terminated on the repayment of the original debt. Slaves had no such legal recourse....[19]

Pawns were not regarded as social outsiders, even if they occupied socially marginalised positions. They might even be treated as 'quasi-kin' of the creditor. Being a pawn was intended only as a temporary condition, and the children of pawned people were free. Individuals could—and did—pawn themselves in particularly desperate situations of indebtedness.[20] While most of the people who pawned themselves were men, as in the case of slavery, the overwhelming majority of people pawned by others across most societies over time were women, and usually girls or young women.

Unlike enslaved people, pawning involved negotiations between creditor and debtor and, possibly, a ceremony which placed the pawn formally in the care of the debtor. Enslaved people did not experience any such formalised or ritualised institution of their new status. Beyond those who were born into enslavement, most slaves were captured during wartime, on raiding missions, or via kidnapping. Enslavement was always a violent experience. As Swema's example demonstrates, people could be sold into slavery to pay a debt, and to professional slave traders. Enslaved people could be bought at markets in many societies.[21] As noted above, slavery was a status that children born to enslaved people inherited—except in the case of Muslim societies if the father of the child was free—and could only be ended if the slave was able to run away and escape their master, as well as through buying their own freedom, 'death-bed acts of charity, or actions derived from legal proceedings'.[22]

It is imperative to emphasise, though, that systems of slavery varied extensively across time and place, and that well before debates over abolition emerged in Europe during the Enlightenment, enslavement was contested across the continent. It did not persist because it was somehow indelibly part of how African societies or economies functioned.[23] Slavery appears to have emerged in Africa between 3000 BCE and 500 CE, as settled, agrarian societies with a constant need for more labour began to put war captives to work as enslaved people.[24] While some slaves continued to be sacrificed at funerals, religious ceremonies, or at festivals, the majority became labourers.[25] Only in larger states—particularly in what are now Ethiopia and Egypt—did slavery become crucial to the functioning of those societies and polities. Elsewhere, it was between 500 and 1600 that slavery expanded far more significantly. This change was driven by a series of significant transformations. The East African

---

[19] Falola and Lovejoy, 'Pawnship in Historical Perspective,' p. 4.
[20] Falola and Lovejoy, 'Pawnship in Historical Perspective,' pp. 4–6.
[21] Lovejoy, 'Slavery in Africa,' pp. 38–39.
[22] Lovejoy, 'Slavery in the Colonial State and After,' p. 104.
[23] Lovejoy, 'Slavery in Africa,' p. 43.
[24] Stilwell, *Slavery and Slaving in African History*, p. 36.
[25] Lovejoy, 'Slavery in Africa,' p. 40.

coast was drawn increasingly into the monsoon-driven trade across the Indian Ocean, meaning that enslaved Africans were traded alongside other goods across the Indian Ocean world. In West Africa, large, increasingly Muslim states used enslaved people to administer, defend, and expand their borders. Enslaved people were also traded across the Sahara, into the Mediterranean world. Indeed, one similarity between the East and West African trades was the use of Islamic law to regulate—and occasionally contest—enslavement. During this same period, enslavement grew with the founding of states and the emergence of powerful local Big Men in Central Africa, the Great Lakes region, and Central East Africa. More political and economic inequality fuelled the acquisition of more slaves whose labour contributed to and defended courts and large households.[26]

But by far the most significant force which changed Central and West African societies—including both free and enslaved people—was the trans-Atlantic slave trade from the early seventeenth century. This trade removed Africans from the continent on a scale never before experienced, causing a decline in the overall population (particularly of young people, who were the most sought-after by traders on the coast), and major social, political, and economic transformations. New states were founded (like Oyo and Dahomey), which drew on the trans-Atlantic trade for their power, while others—like the Kongo Kingdom in Central Africa—collapsed. While some states and kingdoms resisted involvement in the trade periodically, other societies became profoundly entangled in the capture and sale of ever-increasing numbers of people, exchanging them for commodities brought from Europe and elsewhere.[27]

Britain's abolition of the slave trade in 1807 altered slavery significantly, although not necessarily always predictably. An illicit trade persisted well into the nineteenth century, focusing more and more on children. British rule brought the emancipation of slaves to the Cape Colony in contemporary South Africa (and elsewhere in the British Empire) in 1833. The Cape—which had been colonised initially by the Dutch East India Company in the seventeenth century—was drawn particularly into the Indian Ocean trade in enslaved people. This trade lasted well into the late nineteenth century, with the slave market in Zanzibar only closed—partly as a result of British pressure—in 1873. The imposition of colonial rule by European powers across the continent may gradually have eradicated slavery, but in particular places pawning and forced labour emerged as replacements for enslavement—both within African communities and, for instance, in the Congo Free State where forced labour was conscripted on rubber plantations by European businesses.

Slavery existed, then, across Africa over a very long period of time, altering in response to changes occurring within African societies, and as a result of contact with people from abroad. Not every society kept enslaved people, nor was every society which did enslave people absolutely reliant on them, although

[26] Stilwell, *Slavery and Slaving in African History*, p. 38–47.
[27] Stilwell, *Slavery and Slaving in African History*, p. 48–50.

there were some states which were. Slavery involved all Africans, to lesser or greater degrees, including children and, even more specifically, girls and young women. Enslavement's link to kinship—the fact that kinship groups could be made larger and wealthier through the incorporation of enslaved and pawned people, and the fact that the condition of enslavement was defined as being without kin—positions the history of slavery firmly within histories of age and of children and young people.

CHILDREN, SLAVERY, AND UNFREEDOM BEFORE 1600

Swema's account of her enslavement was published in France in 1870, but this was not an unmediated telling of her story. While her experiences of the forced march to the coast and her time in Zanzibar are described later in this chapter, it is important to note here that after her rescue, Swema narrated what had happened to her to the other little girls at the Catholic mission at Zanzibar. This was done not in Swema's mother tongue—Yao—but, rather, in the lingua franca of the east coast of the continent, Swahili, which she may have learned while enslaved. There is no date for her address to the other children of the mission, but her account was translated into French in Zanzibar on 26 July 1866 by Père Anton Horner, Superior of the Congrégation du Saint-Esprit mission in East Africa. Père Horner's aim in transcribing and translating Swema's enslavement and rescue was to communicate to Christian children and young people how grateful they should be that God had saved or protected them from undergoing similar terrors. As historian Edward Alpers remarks, Père Horner does not explain why he chose Swema's story in particular, and, even more than this, if what Swema described is what he wrote down. To what degree did he embellish or alter her account to suit his own aims? Alpers speculates that her tale was chosen because she had likely converted to Christianity, and she offered, thus, 'an opportunity to publicise the work of the mission.' Moreover, her account had in it 'all the elements of the Christian metaphor' of an innocent who undergoes appalling suffering, but who is redeemed through baptism. Partly as a result of this, as Alpers admits, the translation of her story was 'shaped to conform to mid-nineteenth-century French literary conventions. Her story simply does not read like that of a ten-year-old'.[28] In addition to this, the publisher of the piece, Monsignor J. Gaume, Apostolic Pronotary to Paris, hoped to use the text—which he addressed to middle-class young women in France—to raise funds for the mission in Zanzibar, as well as other charitable organisations working to rescue or protect girls in other parts of the world. Alpers explained:

> As part of his appeal for funds, Monsignor Gaume took considerable liberties with Père Horner's original French text, frequently changing words and adding or deleting passages in Swema's testimony, while also adding a considerable

[28] Alpers, 'The Story of Swema,' pp. 186, 188.

amount of linking text between chapters that did not exist the original manuscript in order to give the book added dramatic effect.[29]

However, Alpers maintains that due to Père Horner's longer track record of accurate descriptions of life in Zanzibar, as well as the fact that most of Swema's story does remain intact in the Gaume edition, this text is a useful source for historians, despite being so heavily mediated.

The publication history of Swema's story is by no means unusual. Memoirs by enslaved and formerly enslaved people were of enormous value to missionaries, churches, and abolitionist societies, and especially those focused on the Atlantic world. Because of children's association with innocence and moral purity in the eighteenth and nineteenth centuries, their stories were particularly valued by missionaries. And many memoirs written in adulthood included accounts of childhood, and, often, enslavement while in childhood. Perhaps the best known of these is by Olaudah Equiano who, as Gustavus Vassa, published *The Interesting Narrative of the Life of Olaudah Equiano* in 1789. In it, he describes Igbo society, his family, and his childhood in the Bight of Biafra, in what is now Southern Nigeria. Equiano devotes a chapter to his and his sister's kidnapping by traders while his parents were away. They were sold, separately, to a series of owners, before being taken to the coast, from which he was transported across the Atlantic. There is some debate over the veracity of Equiano's memoir: among other issues, the degree to which he crafted it for use by fellow British abolitionists (he settled in London having attained his freedom), and how much of his childhood and early years he could remember with accuracy.[30] Nevertheless, Equiano's writing echoes other accounts from the region (and will be discussed in greater depth further in the chapter).

The narrative of Swema's enslavement and liberation and Equiano's memoir are similar to many of the sources that historians of childhood rely on, which, even if purportedly authored by children, are usually mediated by adults in some way. Put another way, the flawed nature of these two texts is not unique to them and, despite these weaknesses, these documents do still open up the worlds and experiences of enslaved children in ways that other sources—accounts of the slave trade by travellers or missionaries, for instance—do not. This is particularly evident when writing about enslaved children and young people in Africa before 1600, when enslavement and the trade in enslaved people remained largely within the continent (although with some notable exceptions—like the trade across the Sahara). Here, children's perspectives are notably absent—as are those of other enslaved people.

But it is possible to reconstruct children's experiences of enslavement and other forms of unfreedom—partly in recognition of the fact that the lives of enslaved children were different from those of adults. Perhaps most obviously,

---

[29] Alpers, 'The Story of Swema,' p. 189.

[30] Paul E. Lovejoy, 'Autobiography and Memory: Gustavus Vassa, alias Olaudah Equiano, the African,' *Slavery and Abolition*, vol. 27, no. 3 (2006), pp. 317–347.

children could be born into enslavement, but the majority of enslaved children were—like Swema—caught and sold in childhood. During wartime and raids conducted by slavers, children were easy targets for capture, and tended to be less inclined to attempt escape. A captured man of status—a king, or Big Man—might be punished through the enslavement of his household, including his children. In times of famine or other severe deprivation, children might be sold to ease the burden on a household, or to raise capital, and particularly if those children were orphans or on the margins of a lineage. But this seems to have been a relatively infrequent occurrence.[31] Equiano and his sister were victims of kidnapping and although their enslavement within the Bight of Biafra was certainly shaped by that region's significant place within the Atlantic trade, some of what he experienced would have been similar to enslavement before 1600. Equiano's first significant period of enslavement was in the household of 'a chieftain, in a very pleasant country.'[32]

Life there was both familiar and strange. While 'these people spoke exactly the same language' as his family, and his master's family 'used me extremely well, and did all they could to comfort me; particularly the first wife, who was something like my mother,' he remained 'oppressed and weighted down by grief' at the loss of his mother, and so took every opportunity to plot his escape. A telling observation describes how he did not dare 'to eat with the free-born children' despite being 'mostly their companion'. He was reminded at every turn that he had no position or connections in this household to protect him. His master was a goldsmith, and Equiano's 'principal employment was working his bellows', but he also assisted an elderly enslaved woman, particularly in taking care of poultry. One morning he accidentally killed one of the chickens and, terrified of what punishment awaited him potentially, he hid from the family, its servants, and the slaves who looked for him. Convinced he was to be beaten or killed, he eventually gave himself up. But even though his master only 'slightly reprimanded' him and 'ordered' that he 'be taken care of and not be ill-treated', Equiano was sold on again soon after, after the death of the household's eldest daughter.[33] Historian Robyn P. Chapdelaine speculates that his sale may have been to fund the daughter's funeral, demonstrating again that Equiano was always regarded as an asset to be bought and sold, despite being treated—to some extent—like the other children in the household.[34]

As historian Trevor R. Getz remarks, 'slavery and youth were ... to some degree, linked statuses' in many precolonial societies, in that both enslaved people and children and youth occupied subordinate positions within these societies, subject to the dictates of those of higher rank. But as Equiano's

---

[31] Nwokeji, 'Slavery in Non-Islamic West Africa,' pp. 98, 101.

[32] Olaudah Equiano, *The Interesting Narrative of the Life of Olaudah Equiano, of Gustavus Vassa, the African, Written by Himself*, ed. Werner Sollors (New York and London: W.W. Norton, 2001), p. 33.

[33] Equiano, *The Interesting Narrative*, pp. 34–35.

[34] Robyn P. Chapdelaine, *The Persistence of Slavery: An Economic History of Child Trafficking in Nigeria* (Amherst and Boston: University of Massachusetts Press, 2021), p. 27.

experience suggests, enslaved children negotiated precisely the ambiguity of these positions: while life among his master's kin may have felt similar to that in his own household, Equiano was also always unambiguously without any of the protections afforded to full members of the lineage. While the children he played with would have entered into the processes of initiation which marked their entry into youth and adulthood, Equiano and other enslaved people would not necessarily have undergone the same ceremonies. As Nwokeji points out, while in some societies slave masters' children may have addressed enslaved people as 'uncle' or 'aunt', slaves 'were effectively perpetual minors' in most cases.[35] Had Equiano remained with the goldsmith's household, he might have eventually been regarded as a member of the lineage over a long period of time. Getz explains that the 'position and the condition' of enslaved people's 'captivity could change over time as they were drawn into kinship webs.' But, as Equiano's case demonstrates, they were always at risk of being sold on.[36]

Like the majority of enslaved children, Equiano was captured and enslaved. A minority of enslaved children were the offspring of enslaved women. As was the case among enslaved people around the globe, rates of fertility among enslaved women in Africa were low. Those women who did bear children could, though, enhance their status, depending on circumstance. Generally speaking, women and children had the greatest potential to be gradually incorporated into the societies in which they had been sold. Proximity to the enslaver and their kinship network produced an opportunity to become part of that group eventually—and for those people whose relatively lowly social position posed little threat to the already existing lineage. While they entered as kinless strangers—this status allowing for their exploitation—over time they might be treated as kin, and their descendants fully incorporated into the lineage. Lovejoy explains:

> Women and slaves born in the family were easily assimilated, and the sale of such individuals was rare. Those taken as slaves when they were children also were seldom sold. These slaves were treated very much as members of the household. Their tasks may have been more menial, but they were often granted responsibilities in trade, craft production, or other occupations. Second-generation slaves could fare as well or better.[37]

This process of assimilation was not without violence. All enslaved women were subject to sexual exploitation. Those who achieved the status of concubines or even junior wives did so on the grounds that they had contributed children as well as their labour to the household. Even so, their position likely

---

[35] Nwokeji, 'Slavery in Non-Islamic West Africa,' p. 102.
[36] Trevor R. Getz, 'British Magistrates and Unfree Children in Early Colonial Gold Coast, 1874–1899,' in *Child Slaves in the Modern World*, Gwyn Campbell, Suzanne Miers, and Joseph C. Miller, eds. (Athens, OH: Ohio University Press, 2011), p. 158.
[37] Paul E. Lovejoy, *Transformations in Slavery: A History of Slavery in Africa* (Cambridge: Cambridge University Press, 2012), p. 14.

remained lowly. As Nwokeji makes the point, usually enslaved parents 'had no substantive parental rights over their children.' The key figures in the lives of enslaved children were not their parents, but, rather, whoever owned their parents, and hence the desirability of marrying an enslaved woman, or taking her as a concubine: 'Marrying a slave woman gave a man unhindered ability to appropriate his wife's labour and reproductive power.'[38]

However, in Muslim societies, where enslavement was considered to be a tool for converting unbelievers (Christians and Jews, as people of the book, were exempted from this rule), children were nearly always assimilated, and the birth of children secured important protections for enslaved women. Historian Rudolph T. Ware notes that in Islamic Africa, female slaves could be

> granted the status of *umm walad* (mother of children) upon bearing a child… An *umm walad* could not legally be sold, nor could her children, whether or not they were explicitly recognized by their owner. She was granted freedom upon her master's death, as were her children. In the case that the owner formally recognized the children as his own, they were immediately free.[39]

As Ware warns, there is little way of knowing if the owners of enslaved people did indeed follow the law, but it is significant that this provision existed in the first place.

What these examples attest to is that for enslaved children, in particular, freedom and enslavement did not necessarily exist in a binary. While it is certainly true that being enslaved placed children in positions of exceptional vulnerability, liable to be abused as their enslavers so wished, it is also true that those children often occupied ambiguous positions within households and could become members of lineages. In addition to this, they were also occasionally the means by which enslaved women could gain status—if not necessarily freedom—within households. Pawnage—frequently confused with slavery by outsiders, particularly during the Atlantic slave trade—further complicated this binary. With a significant proportion of pawns being young, this was a status linked especially (although not necessarily) to childhood. While adult men could also pawn themselves, most pawns were nevertheless women and children. Pawning was usually governed by rules which were intended to ensure the good treatment of the pawn and, perhaps even more importantly, the return of the pawn.

As noted above, pawning was debt bondage, where a person was held as collateral for credit. It is vital to understand that pawns and slaves existed as 'separate social and legal categories'. Significantly, while some pawns were sold into slavery (in other words, while the boundaries between the two states could be porous under particular conditions), pawnship was never a position of

---

[38] Nwokeji, 'Slavery in Non-Islamic West Africa,' p. 96.

[39] Rudolph T. Ware, 'Slavery in Islamic Africa, 1400–1800,' in *The Cambridge World History of Slavery*, vol. 3: 1420–1804, David Eltis and Stanley L. Engerman, eds. (Cambridge: Cambridge University Press, 2011), p. 57.

kinlessness—in fact, it 'relied on social relationships, often kinship, to protect those being held in pawn'.[40] As Chapdelaine observes, the 'fundamental contradiction' of pawnship was that the pawn was 'both a dependent within a kinship network and part of an economic transaction.'[41] The fact of pawns' embeddedness within kinship groups meant that they operated under protections unavailable to enslaved people and could reasonably expect not to remain a pawn forever. Unlike slavery, pawnship was always intended to be a temporary status. This is all to demonstrate that there were rules governing the pawning of a child, although these did differ between societies, ensuring that pawning a relative was not an easily or quickly made decision. Writing about precolonial Asante society, Jean Allman notes that fathers were not allowed to pawn their children, although they could accept pawns into their households. There, pawning was the preserve of the mother's family.[42] Contracts established between the debtor and the creditor determined what kind of labour the pawn would undertake, and at what point that contract would be concluded. In the case of girls, pawnship might end with marriage. As Falola and Lovejoy note, the 'possibility that a pawn might become a wife is probably the most important reason that many, probably most, pawns were female.'[43] With marriage, the debt would be cleared, and the creditor would gain another—probably junior—member of his household, expanding his kinship group. The overlaps in status between pawns, junior wives, and children show the continuities of experience between those who were free and those who were not. Becoming a pawn for an adult man was a demotion of status—not necessarily to that of a child or a youth, but it was a similar shift in power within a household.

That the majority of pawned children were from poorer families or those under difficult circumstances—as a result of poor harvests or conflict, for instance—suggests that pawning was among the solutions of last resort. Creditors might also take pawns for social reasons. As Falola and Lovejoy make the point, children 'were less likely to contribute substantially to the income of the creditor' and may well have been a drain, financially, on the household if they fell sick or were injured. They might not, in fact, be able to work off the debt owed to the creditor. In addition to this, 'a creditor might well spend considerable money on education and clothing without expecting to recover those costs.'[44] Bearing in mind the harshness of the experience of pawning—especially when pawned individuals were enslaved—it is also worth emphasising that pawnship was, then, a means of caring for children when their closest kin were not capable of doing so. Writing about pawning in early colonial Yoruba

---

[40] Paul E. Lovejoy and David Richardson, 'The Business of Slaving: Pawnship in Western Africa, c. 1600–1810,' *Journal of African History*, vol. 42 (2001), pp. 71–72.

[41] Chapdelaine, *The Persistence of Slavery*, p. 29.

[42] Jean Allman, 'Fathering, Mothering and Making Sense of "Ntamoba": Reflections on the Economy of Child-Rearing in Colonial Asante,' *Africa*, vol. 67, no. 2 (1997), pp. 301–302.

[43] Falola and Lovejoy, 'Pawnship in Historical Perspective,' p. 12.

[44] Falola and Lovejoy, 'Pawnship in Historical Perspective,' pp. 7–8.

society, E. Adeniyi Oroge argues that 'putting a child in pawn in times of wars and famine represented an attempt by parents to reduce to the minimum the risk to the child's life and freedom and to secure his future.' As a result, 'the decision of Yoruba parents to put their children in pawn in times of famine stemmed more from parental love than from depravity and selfishness.'[45] While other historians may disagree with this generous appraisal, Oroge's point is valuable: parents and senior relatives chose to pawn children usually under difficult conditions, attentive not only to the necessity of paying off debts but also to the care and wellbeing of the child. Pawning might have involved a formalised contract, but in many cases children were not returned to their immediate families, having either married while pawned or been sold into slavery, for instance. This was an intensely precarious position.

In fact, the increasing involvement of West and Central Africa in the trans-Atlantic trade made the lines between pawning and enslavement even fainter. As Chapdelaine notes, the pressure of this trade exerted enormous change on enslavement and pawnship in these regions, rendering children even more vulnerable to capture.[46]

Children in the Atlantic Trade

On 11 July 1761, a ship weighed anchor in Boston harbour, concluding a journey which had begun on the shore of the same city slightly less than a year previously. The *Phillis* was owned by the wealthy Massachusetts merchant Thomas Finch, who traded both human beings and commodities between the northeastern coast of the United States and the west coast of Africa. In November 1760, he had commanded the crew of the *Phillis* to set sail for what is contemporary Senegal and Gambia, and buy about 100 enslaved people, exchanging them for rum and other goods. This expedition did not, however, go as planned: not only did the journey take far longer than usual, but the ship's commander appears also to have struggled to collect the number of enslaved people which Finch demanded. Also, they bought girls and women, where the preference was usually for men.[47]

Ironically, for contemporary readers, the name of this slave vessel—the *Phillis*—is probably familiar because of one of its younger (if not youngest), most vulnerable, and—for slave traders—least valuable passengers: the poet who was named Phillis Wheatley by the people who bought her in Boston in 1761. Historian Vincent Carretta speculates that Wheatley was loaded on to the *Phillis* towards the end of the ship's period along the African coastline, near either Sierra Leone or Ghana. She was likely a 'refuse' slave, meaning that she

---

[45] E. Adeniyi Oroge, 'Iwofe: An Historical Survey of the Yoruba Institution of Indenture,' *African Economic History*, no. 14 (1985), pp. 78–79.

[46] Chapdelaine, *The Persistence of Slavery*, p. 29.

[47] Vincent Carretta, *Phillis Wheatley: Biography of a Genius in Bondage* (Athens, GA: University of Georgia Press, 2011), pp. 11–17.

had not been bought immediately on arrival at the coast, from having been kidnapped in the interior. Her youth—she was seven years old or younger—and gender made her less attractive to buyers of enslaved people in the Americas, who overwhelmingly sought men for the hard labour on plantations. This little girl was one of 75 out of 96 Africans who survived the Middle Passage. She was bought soon after by Susanna and John Wheatley, prosperous members of Boston's middle class. Susanna was in search of an enslaved woman to work as a companion and servant, and to care for her in old age. Phillis—young and probably in ill health—was by no means the obvious choice for this position, but Carretta suggests that she may have resembled the Wheatleys' youngest daughter, Sarah, who had died at the age of seven, nearly exactly nine years previously.[48]

In a 'memoir' of Wheatley published in 1834—well after Wheatley's death in 1784—Margaretta Matilda Odell, a relative of Susanna Wheatley's, observed that Phillis had not 'preserved any remembrance of the place of her nativity, or of her parents, excepting the simple circumstance that her mother poured out water before the sun at his rising—in reference, no doubt, to an ancient African custom.'[49] The reason for Phillis's lack of memory was, Odell surmised, connected to her kidnapping, sale, and transport:

> We cannot know at how early a period she was beguiled from the hut of her mother; or how long a time elapsed between her abduction from her first home and her being transferred to the abode of her benevolent mistress.... This interval was, no doubt, a long one; and filled, as it must have been, with various degrees and kinds of suffering, might naturally enough obliterate the recollection of earlier and happier days.[50]

Odell describes Phillis as 'bereaved'—in a 'long season of affliction'—as she mourned the loss of both kin and home. She recognised, in other words, the profoundly traumatising effects of the brutalities of enslavement.

Phillis received an education at the Wheatleys, and developed an international reputation for her poetry, which was allied to the cause of abolition in both the United States and Britain. Hers was in many ways a profoundly unusual life: an enslaved African woman who received an education, existed on the edges of white, middle-class Bostonian society, and was celebrated in her lifetime for her writing. In addition to this, she had survived capture and enslavement in Africa, as well as the Middle Passage. But—at the same time—she was also part of a large group of children who had been sold into enslavement into the Atlantic world. Children had always been part of this trade. In fact, during the early centuries of the Atlantic trade in enslaved people—from the fourteenth to the sixteenth centuries—the majority of people taken from

---

[48] Carretta, *Phillis Wheatley*, pp. 16, 20.
[49] *Memoir and Poems of Phillis Wheatley, A Native African and a Slave* (Boston: Geo. W. Light, 1834), p. 10.
[50] *Memoir and Poems of Phillis Wheatley*, pp. 10–11.

Africa, often to Europe, were women and children.[51] Writing about enslaved Africans in Portugal, historian António de Almeida Mendes explains that more than seventy per cent of the enslaved Africans who arrived there between 1499 and 1522 were women and children, most of them from West Africa, and often from Muslim societies in the region.[52] Women and children were easier to capture, even if they might be sold for less than young men, who were in greatest demand. Having made the arduous journey up the coast to Europe, once in Lisbon the captives were sold and children went to work as domestic servants or as labourers, intensely vulnerable to whatever forms of violence and exploitation might await them in the households of their owners.[53] The quality of the lives of enslaved African children and youth in Portugal was dependent entirely on the people who owned them. Unlikely to be freed until the deaths of their enslavers, child slaves might attempt to earn enough to buy their freedom and establish their own families as they grew up. They occupied an invidious position: 'If most slaves were treated roughly and cruelly, some became parts of extended families' and 'even after they were freed, ties remained between former owners and their former slaves.' Children, in particular, were more likely to assimilate (as far as was possible) into Portuguese society, learning the language quickly, converting to Christianity, and potentially having access to some form of education.[54]

Echoing De Almeida Mendes, historian Audra Diptee argues that children were certainly involved in the later Atlantic trade, and in greater numbers than historians have tended to acknowledge. But, as she notes, one of the primary obstacles for identifying precisely how many children were taken to the Americas is determining who actually were children.[55] Enslaved Africans arriving at the island of Arguin, off the coast of contemporary Mauritania, in the fifteenth and early sixteenth centuries, came under the scrutiny of Portuguese traders and were divided according to sex and age. But 'since precise ages were not known, they were divided according to "life stages": children, (pubescent) youths, adults, and old people.' These age categories were meaningful to the Portuguese sailors and merchants who plied the West African coast, but did not necessarily overlap with the systems of age categorisation which existed in the societies of the enslaved. De Almeida Mendes explains that these ages 'corresponded to the Christian schema of growth, maturity, and decline' but that judging the age of the enslaved used relatively arbitrary criteria, like the presence or extent of body hair in young men.[56] By the eighteenth century, British

---

[51] António de Almeida Mendes, 'Child Slaves in the Early North Atlantic Trade in the Fifteenth and Sixteenth Centuries,' in *Children in Slavery through the Ages*, Gwyn Campbell, Suzanne Miers, and Joseph C. Miller, eds. (Athens, OH: Ohio University Press, 2009), p. 59.

[52] De Almeida Mendes, 'Child Slaves in the Early North Atlantic Trade,' p. 42.

[53] De Almeida Mendes, 'Child Slaves in the Early North Atlantic Trade,' pp. 56–57.

[54] De Almeida Mendes, 'Child Slaves in the Early North Atlantic Trade,' p. 59.

[55] Audra A. Diptee, 'African Children in the British Slave Trade during the Late Eighteenth Century,' *Slavery and Abolition*, vol. 27, no, 2 (2006), pp. 184–185.

[56] De Almeida Mendes, 'Child Slaves in the Early North Atlantic Trade,' pp. 56–57.

sailors and traders in coastal West and Central Africa were using as imprecise metrics. Diptee adds that slave traders used captives' height as a gauge: 'enslaved individuals were considered children if they were under four feet, four inches tall', a measure used elsewhere around the Atlantic where British planters, sailors, and merchants operated.[57] This definition of the category of children was not introduced to better monitor the welfare of those onboard slave ships, but, rather, was linked to the fact that slave ships did not pay a tax on enslaved people listed as children. This new provision was designed to force ships to pay their full taxes (and Britain was not unique in introducing this measure—the Portuguese had similar rules).[58]

Around a quarter of the enslaved people on French ships in the eighteenth century were children.[59] The numbers were—overall—lower on British ships, although slightly more than a third of the enslaved who left the Gold Coast on British ships between 1751 and 1775 were children, a figure which dropped to nineteen per cent during the last quarter of the eighteenth century. During this period, the same proportion of children was shipped by British ships from the Bight of Biafra, and sixteen per cent of the total of Africans exported from West Central Africa on British ships were children. Obviously, as these estimates demonstrate, numbers as well as the gender ratio of children captured and sold varied between the sixteenth and nineteenth centuries, in response to events within Africa itself, as well as to shifting demand in the Americas and alterations in the trans-Atlantic trade. A range of factors increased the likelihood of children being sold into slavery: drought and famine caused more children to be exported. For instance, during a major drought in West Central Africa in the final two decades of the eighteenth century, 'the proportion of enslaved children ... increased and accounted for approximately 27 per cent of the captives leaving' the region. The majority of those children were boys.[60]

Equiano and his sister had been captured and sold into the domestic trade in enslaved people in the middle of the eighteenth century. This trade was woven into the Atlantic trade and some of the children who were shipped to the Americas were probably pawns, sold to traders by unscrupulous masters. Equiano was eventually taken to the coast and placed on a vessel bound for Barbados, the most important sugar-producing island in the British Empire. Equiano's sister disappears from his memoir during their enslavement after capture, and it is possible that she remained in West Africa and was not transported. As Diptee explains, girls 'were highly valued in West Central Africa not only for their labour but also because ... they could more easily be socially

---

[57] Diptee, 'African Children in the British Slave Trade during the Late Eighteenth Century,' p. 185.
[58] Gwyn Campbell, Suzanne Miers, and Joseph C. Miller, 'Children in European Systems of Slavery: Introduction,' *Slavery and Abolition*, vol. 27, no. 2 (Aug. 2006), p. 165.
[59] Paul Lovejoy, 'The Children of Slavery—the Transatlantic Phase,' *Slavery and Abolition*, vol. 27, no. 2 (Aug. 2006), p. 203.
[60] Diptee, 'African Children in the British Slave Trade during the Late Eighteenth Century,' pp. 186–187, 189.

incorporated into African societies.'[61] The siblings' experiences of enslavement were, then, fairly representative of many children's capture and sale. Like other enslaved children, they 'passed through many hands before reaching the coast', meaning that the trip from inland to the shore could last many months, even years. In regions where this journey was overland and on foot, its arduousness probably increased mortality rates among women and children, although in places where the trip could be made by canoe—especially in what is now Southern Nigeria—enslaved people arrived sooner and healthier to be sold. On the coast, children were inspected by either local merchants or ships' captains for sale, and, in the Gold Coast, they might be held for many months at the 'factories' or forts built by the British, Dutch, and Portuguese, before setting sail. There are some accounts of children on the journey to the coast or before being removed to the Americas being rescued by their parents or relatives, but these were rare events. Most children crossed the Atlantic without their relatives, although infants—those who had survived the journey to the coast, and who were not killed by traders unwilling to sell women caring for babies—tended to remain with their mothers.[62]

Equiano describes his terror of his arrival at the coast, and of being carried on board a waiting slave ship. His account of the Middle Passage captures the depth of the suffering of the enslaved onboard, and the viciousness and cruelty meted out to them by the ship's crew. Once onboard and slowly aware of his fate:

> I even wished for my former slavery in preference to my present situation, which was filled with horrors of every kind... I was not long suffered to indulge my grief; I was soon put down under the decks, and there I received such a salutation in my nostrils as I had never experienced in my life: so that, with the loathsomeness of the stench, and crying together, I became so sick and low that I was not able to eat, nor had I the least desire to taste anything. I now wished for the last friend, death, to relieve me; but soon, to my grief, two of the white men offered me eatables; and, on my refusing to eat, one of them held me fast by the hands, and laid me across I think the windlass, and tied my feet, while the other flogged me severely. I had never experienced anything of this kind before; and although, not being used to the water, I naturally feared that element the first time I saw it, yet nevertheless, could I have got over the nettings, I would have jumped over the side, but I could not....[63]

Contemplating suicide as a result of the conditions onboard before the ship had even weighed anchor, Equiano's circumstances only worsened as the ship set sail across the ocean, as he was confined to the hold, which was packed with enslaved people:

---

[61] Diptee, 'African Children in the British Slave Trade during the Late Eighteenth Century,' p. 187.

[62] Diptee, 'African Children in the British Slave Trade during the Late Eighteenth Century,' pp. 188–190.

[63] Equiano, *The Interesting Narrative*, p. 39.

The closeness of the place, and the heat of the climate, added to the number in the ship, which was so crowded that each had scarcely room to turn himself, almost suffocated us. This produced copious perspirations, so that the air soon became unfit for respiration, from a variety of loathsome smells, and brought on a sickness among the slaves, of which many died, thus falling victims to the improvident avarice, as I may call it, of their purchasers. This wretched situation was again aggravated by the galling of the chains, now become insupportable; and the filth of the necessary tubs, into which the children often fell, and were almost suffocated. The shrieks of the women, and the groans of the dying, rendered the whole a scene of horror almost inconceivable. Happily perhaps for myself I was soon reduced so low here that it was thought necessary to keep me almost always on deck; and from my extreme youth I was not put in fetters. In this situation I expected every hour to share the fate of my companions, some of whom were almost daily brought upon the deck at the point of death, which I began to hope would soon put an end to my miseries.[64]

If this account describes Phillis Wheatley's crossing—only a few years later—then it is little wonder that she suppressed her memory of the Middle Passage. Equiano's writing is so evocative that he is worth quoting at length. He makes clear that his experience of the Middle Passage was shaped significantly by his status as a child. Although subject to the same inhumane treatment as the adults around him, the fact of his youth meant that he was allowed outside and above board for longer periods of time, and without being shackled. This freedom may well have saved his life. As Diptee notes, children's rates of mortality in the Middle Passage appear to have been lower than those of adults, and possibly as a result of their treatment onboard. While adult men were kept fully shackled, women and girls existed in appalling conditions (as Equiano describes) but were not restrained. Boys might be allowed to move about the ship. Regardless, even if—like Equiano—they were allowed more freedom to roam than adults, the journey across the Atlantic was fraught with danger: from disease, malnutrition, and accident, to the ever-present threat of sexual exploitation and other violence from the crew.[65]

Ironically, the movement to abolish slavery—a movement which invoked the figure of the suffering child, among other strategies, to appeal to the public for support—had the effect of increasing the numbers of children and young people captured and transported across the Atlantic. As Colleen A. Vasconcellos explains, by the end of the eighteenth century, planters in Jamaica were so alarmed by the debates over ending the slave trade in Britain that they began to buy more and younger enslaved Africans (and especially young women, whose reproductive labour was increasingly valuable) in the fear that they could no longer rely on a steady supply of African labour from across the ocean. As a

---

[64] Equiano, *The Interesting Narrative*, p. 41.
[65] Diptee, 'African Children in the British Slave Trade during the Late Eighteenth Century,' pp. 191–192.

result, ships began to respond to this demand.⁶⁶ In addition to this, the nature of plantation agriculture was also changing. For instance, in Brazil—and the vast majority of enslaved Africans were taken to South America—the introduction of coffee plantations meant that planters were willing to buy children, who would be able successfully to harvest this crop.⁶⁷ Britain abolished the slave trade in 1807, and the trans-Atlantic trade came to an end in the 1860s, even if slavery was still legal in most of the Americas until well after that date. During this period of slightly more than half a century, children shifted from constituting twenty-two to more than fifty per cent of those transported across the ocean. This produced a vicious trade in children, as Lawrence describes:

> As prohibitions on the slave trade expanded, slave traders turned to children in increasing numbers. These traders designed their ships with specifications "intended for children only," such as the "hellish nurseries" of the *Tragos Millas* and *Pharafoal*, with slave decks of fourteen and eighteen inches in height. ...The peak period for child slave shipment, circa 1825–55, made it possible to specialise entirely in child transportation. In 1840, the *Jesús María* sailed from Sherbro near Sierra Leone for Havana with a cargo that was ninety-eight per cent children. Later in the decade, the *Triumfo* sailed with a cargo exclusively of children; all but one of its 105 Africans were between the ages of four and nine years. To be clear, these ships were not outliers.⁶⁸

Clearly, this trade emerged partly in response to the fact that people in the Americas—especially in Cuba and Brazil—were willing to buy them. But children were also useful to slave traders as the trade became illegal. Children were easier to capture, and to control onboard. They were less likely to escape. They were smaller and took up less space. On arrival in the Caribbean or elsewhere in the Americas, they could be quickly offloaded, concealed if necessary, and then sold. In fact, children were not necessarily guaranteed to be believed if they protested that they were enslaved.⁶⁹

The world these children encountered on the other side of the Atlantic was brutal in many ways—and one which they would navigate without the protections afforded by kinship. As they crossed the Atlantic, African children not only acquired new names (Phillis Wheatley gained the name of the ship which transported her, for instance), new roles, and new languages, but also forged new forms of kinship. As Vasconcellos writes, those enslaved people in Jamaica who had survived the Middle Passage identified 'with those who shared similar experiences' and recreated kinship groups via connections forged onboard slave ships: shipmates become siblings, cared for one another's children, and prohibited sexual relations between those who had travelled together on the

---

[66] Colleen A. Vasconcellos, *Slavery, Childhood, and Abolition in Jamaica, 1788–1838* (Athens, GA: University of Georgia Press, 2015), p. 4.
[67] Lovejoy, 'The Children of Slavery,' p. 207.
[68] Lawrance, *Amistad's Orphans*, pp. 35–36.
[69] Lawrance, *Amistad's Orphans*, pp. 36–37.

same ship, thus reinforcing the transformation of shipmates to family members.[70] The integrity of these new kinship groups was under constant threat from enslavers: from the possibility of sale, from being moved to another property, and from rape. But they provided their members—young and old—with support and care in the face of extreme cruelty.

The lives of those children who remained in Africa changed, too, as the transatlantic trade altered, and colonial conquest intensified. This chapter will return to West and Central Africa, but moves for the moment to the experiences of children in the Indian Ocean.

CHILDREN IN THE INDIAN OCEAN TRADE

One of the ways Equiano manifested extreme distress while on the ship which transported him to the Caribbean was his refusal to eat. He lost his appetite, and, in response, he was beaten by two members of the vessel's crew, seeking to make him eat. Similarly, when Swema and her mother began their long walk to the coast in a caravan of other enslaved people and slave traders, she, too, ceased eating. Initially, the journey had begun well: neither of the women found the walk too difficult, and Swema's mother—as an adult—was given a burden which she carried with relative ease. They were also provided with enough food, something they had not had during the hard months preceding their enslavement. However, approaching the Kilwa coast they entered drier country, and Swema's mother struggled both with thirst and the heavier load she had been tasked with bearing. She weakened and fell several times.[71]

> [W]hen it came time to receive their rations ... the Arab [leading the caravan] ordered, "The mother of Swema is worthless; she will no longer have a ration!" When Swema tried to share her food with her mother, she was taken to eat her meal in front of the Arab. The following day, Swema's mother sought nourishment by eating some grasshoppers, some millet leaves, and a little red earth. Unable to eat in the knowledge of her mother's need, Swema had to be force-fed by her master's servants.[72]

Equiano, Swema, and other enslaved children—especially those who were smaller and younger—had few tools available to them to resist the adults who enslaved them. Although it is unlikely that Equiano and Swema conceptualised their unwillingness to eat in these terms, in refusing to eat they were both striking at precisely what made them valuable: their relatively good health. The crew and caravan traders who force-fed Equiano and Swema did not do so out of compassion or care, but, rather, because malnutrition or starvation undermined the chances of them earning from the sale of these children. Not eating was, under these circumstances, an act of rebellion, and one which was taken

---

[70] Vasconcellos, *Slavery, Childhood, and Abolition in Jamaica*, pp. 25–26.
[71] Alpers, 'The Story of Swema,' pp. 194–195.
[72] Alpers, 'The Story of Swema,' p. 195.

exceptionally seriously. However, because Equiano and Swema were small, there were limits to what protest they could mount. While Equiano was allowed slightly more freedom on board, he still lived under the threat of more violence, and, in Swema's case, her refusal to eat could not save her mother. Under the same brutal logic which caused Swema to be force-fed, so her mother was beaten and abandoned by the caravan, left to die on her own.[73]

Swema survived the journey, albeit in enormous distress. In Kilwa—a major trade centre on the East African coast, and in the Indian Ocean world more broadly—she and her caravan were kept in a house for a few days, before being loaded on to a dhow—a light sailed ship which traders had long used to traverse the Indian Ocean—to the slave market in Zanzibar. Grieving and probably malnourished and dehydrated as a result of the packed, badly provisioned almost week-long sail to the island, Swema could not be sold by the trader who had brought her from Yao country. He was ordered, instead, to wrap her in a straw mat and to bury her—which he did, leaving her in a shallow grave.[74]

As Alpers remarks, it is difficult to know if this was a 'typical decision or if it only reflected the market situation at the time of Swema's arrival in Zanzibar.'[75] Because although Swema's experiences were in some ways unusual—the fact of her finding refuge at a Christian mission, the transcription of her story—she was also one of many children caught up in the trade in enslaved people in the Indian Ocean. As historian Gwyn Campbell explains, it is misleading to understand the history of enslavement in the Indian Ocean world in the same terms as that in the Atlantic. While an excruciating experience regardless of circumstance, the lives of Africans caught up in the trade of enslaved people in the Indian Ocean were different to those in the Atlantic. Slavery and other forms of unfree labour were present throughout the Indian Ocean world for nearly two millennia. People were enslaved for a range of reasons: through conquest, debt, and in times of hardship as a result of war, famine, or natural disasters. There were other forms of unfree labour too: pawning existed in many East African societies, particularly in relation to children; serfdom linked groups of people to specific tracts of land and the owners of that land; and debt bondage involved people voluntarily entering servitude in order to pay off a loan. These forms of enslavement and bondage occasionally overlapped and changed according to time and place. The point is that slavery and unfree labour were important features of economies and societies throughout the Indian Ocean world—slaves constituted between twenty and thirty per cent (and occasionally more than this) of many societies around this ocean.[76] Most unfree people in this vast region were traded overland, and relatively near to where they had been captured. Enslaved people were also moved over much greater distances,

---

[73] Alpers, 'The Story of Swema,' pp. 195–197.
[74] Alpers, 'The Story of Swema,' pp. 197–198.
[75] Alpers, 'The Story of Swema,' p. 198.
[76] Gwyn Campbell, 'Slavery in the Indian Ocean World,' in *The Routledge History of Slavery*, Gad Heuman and Trevor Burnard, eds. (London: Routledge, 2011), pp. 54–57.

either on land or by sea: during the medieval period, for instance, Turks and Slavs were transported to South Asia, while Africans and Central Asians were taken to the Middle East. Africans were, then, one group of enslaved people among many. Most slaves and unfree labourers worked in households as servants, as labourers on farms, miners, and fishermen, and in skilled trades in businesses, as soldiers, and occasionally as bureaucrats. Enslaved women could become wives, but more usually were concubines and were prostituted. There were plantations on some Indian Ocean islands—such as sugar cane on the French colonies of Mauritius and Réunion—but generally enslaved people were not used for plantation labour.[77] While French, British, Dutch, and other Europeans were involved in the trade in enslaved people in the Indian Ocean, merchants from India, the Persian Gulf, Southeast Asia, and elsewhere traded in human beings too.

Swema's rescue was at the hands of a man originally from Réunion, who heard her cries from the shallow grave, dug her out, and carried her to the Catholic mission in Zanzibar. There she received medical treatment, rested, and recovered. Unsurprisingly, she was encouraged to learn about Christianity, and to consider conversion. But her inability to forgive her enslaver and the man who had, in effect, caused the almost certain death of her mother hindered her full embrace of Christianity. In a section of her story which feels almost too apt to be true, Swema re-encountered that man—described simply as the Arab—when he was brought to the mission for treatment, having been wounded in an attack on his dhow carrying enslaved people, led by a British anti-slave patrol:

> Overcoming her deepest feelings, Swema dressed his wounds, as ordered by the Sister in charge, and through that act, she tells us, she found salvation. She was shortly thereafter baptised as Madeleine. By 1875, when she was about twenty years old, she was preparing to become a Sister of Mercy, and in April 1876 she had received her novice's habit at Réunion, having taken the name of Sister Marie Antoinette. In July 1876 she took her first vows.[78]

Swema—or Madeleine, or Sister Marie Antoinette—was part of a much longer history of enslavement in the Indian Ocean world, but her experiences were also shaped by a confluence of forces specific to the nineteenth century: the presence of the French Catholic mission, Swema's movement within the French Empire, and the anti-slaving work of the British navy. As Campbell explains, an increasingly industrialised global economy, European imperialism, pressure on states to modernise, and European demand for commodities in the Indian Ocean world all enormously increased commercial activity in the regions around the Indian Ocean. Alongside millions of Indian and Chinese indentured workers, among other unfree labourers, greater numbers of enslaved

---

[77] Campbell, 'Slavery in the Indian Ocean World,' pp. 56–61.
[78] Alpers, 'The Story of Swema,' p. 199.

Africans left the continent, although in numbers far lower than in the Atlantic world, with some estimates suggesting about a million were transported elsewhere.[79] At the same time, anti-slavery patrols by the British navy—supported by Christian missionaries and other philanthropic organisations present or linked to the Indian Ocean through imperial connections—sought to end the slave trade. Eventually, the slave market in Zanzibar was closed in 1873 and the Sultanate of Oman, under whose authority Zanzibar fell, declared the ending of the trading of slaves over the ocean, and slavery was gradually eradicated in the region.

African children had certainly long been traded across the Indian Ocean, and mainly to the Middle East, Persian Gulf, and South Asia, but records pertaining to children specifically are scanty—both for African children and those from elsewhere. Unlike the Atlantic trade, in the Indian Ocean African children were traded alongside children from South Asia, Southeast Asia, and elsewhere in the region. Separating African children out from a larger history of enslaving children is difficult in this context. And, once again, records are vague as to who counted as a child in this trade. European traders in the seventeenth and eighteenth centuries did not rely on height but rather on perceived age to classify enslaved people. In the French Mascarenes children were considered to be those fourteen years old or younger, while the British in the Moluccas in present-day Indonesia pegged this age at ten years in the early nineteenth century. Children were usually sold—sometimes by their families—or kidnapped into the trade, and their numbers increased during times of famine or economic collapse, despite the fact that, as in the Atlantic, they were usually sold for the lowest sums of money. They worked as domestic labourers, or were occasionally trained into skilled trades or as labourers.[80]

Considering the increase in the numbers of enslaved Africans removed from the east coast in the nineteenth century—some of them on illegal slave vessels, particularly from Mozambique to South America—it is possible that more children were sold into the trade during this period. However, as historian Fred Morton argues, enslaved children became important for domestic trade in the region, before they were taken by dhow to Zanzibar and sold on to other nodes along the Swahili coast, the Middle East, the Persian Gulf, and South Asia. Morton explains:

> In a system of collecting and supplying slaves to long-distance caravan routes, children commonly changed hands at least once or twice in the catchment areas, again along long-distance trade routes, and again at the coast, before embarking for their ultimate destination. To the slave traders, children served as small capital suited for negotiating deals, settling debts, or establishing credit. Most young-

---

[79] Campbell, 'Slavery in the Indian Ocean World,' pp. 57–58.

[80] Richard B. Allen, 'Children and European Slave Trading in the Indian Ocean during the Eighteenth and Early Nineteenth Centuries,' in *Children in Slavery through the Ages*, Gwyn Campbell, Suzanne Miers, and Joseph C. Miller, eds. (Athens, OH: Ohio University Press, 2009), pp. 69–85.

sters were easily controlled, impressionable, and teachable. As slave traders waited to sell or trade them, child slaves could be put readily to a variety of temporary, productive uses and usually appreciated in value.[81]

As in Swema's account, most children appear to have been enslaved as a result of being sold to pay off debts, were war captives, or were kidnapped. Traders were both Arab and African, and—unlike Swema—children often passed through multiple hands before reaching the coast, a process which might take months or years, and which might increase children's value as they aged. Also unlike Swema, most children were not enslaved alongside their parents or kin, and were reliant on their enslavers for care. Before reaching the coast, children performed domestic tasks, similar to what they might have done at home (e.g. caring for younger children, herding animals, and fetching wood and water). As Morton observes, these enslaved children seem to have been integrated fairly quickly into the communities of the people who bought them, learning the language, for example. For those whose journeys—like Swema— to the coast were immediate and direct, the walk was arduous, even if children tended not to be shackled. As in the Atlantic trade, infants might be killed by traders unwilling to be slowed down by nursing mothers.[82]

Once they reached the coast, those children who were not sent on to Zanzibar might work again as servants. Those who reached Zanzibar would be sold on, either to places beyond Africa or further down the Swahili coast. Some children might be freed by the patrolling British navy, and some attempted escape. An account of the capture of a dhow by *HMS Daphne* in the 1880s provides some sense of the miserable conditions experienced by enslaved children on their voyage to Zanzibar:

> In a space two feet high, in heat unimaginable, were literally packed like herrings 300 human beings, fifty of whom were children. The dhow, after sheltering at Zanzibar, started off for Arabia, when the wretched slaves heard shots fired, one of which came among them and wounded a little girl. For about ten minutes a desperate battle was fought, and then the Arabs left the ship and swam to land; the fresh air was let in, and the miserable slaves, who had only uncooked rice to eat, and who were wasted to skeletons, were put on board a British man-of-war, and liberated.[83]

Freed or runaway enslaved children might find refuge at missions, but many integrated into the society on the coast, often converting to Islam, speaking Swahili, and learning local trades. (Enslaved children sold into Muslim

---

[81] Fred Morton, 'Small Change: Children in the Nineteenth-Century East African Slave Trade,' in *Children in Slavery through the Ages*, Gwyn Campbell, Suzanne Miers, and Joseph C. Miller, eds (Athens, OH: Ohio University Press, 2009), p. 97.

[82] Morton, 'Small Change,' pp. 100–110.

[83] Morton, 'Small Change,' pp. 113–114.

Photograph 3.1 Two girls (named Mumbi on the left, Mwabura on the right), described as 'freed slaves' and employed at a mission station in Rungwe, Tanzania, c. 1894, the Moravian Archives Herrnhut

households along the same coast would, ironically, have undergone a similar assimilation.)[84]

Enslaved children from elsewhere in the Indian Ocean world were brought to Africa too. In the Cape Colony, established by the Dutch East India Company (DEIC) in 1652, enslaved people from Southeast and South Asia, as well as from West and East Africa, were bought and sold from 1658. While some of them worked for the DEIC, the remainder were purchased and used

---

[84] Morton, 'Small Change,' pp. 114–116.

mainly as domestic and agricultural labour by the settler population. Children were certainly brought to the Cape from elsewhere, but most were born into slavery—frequently the result of the rape of enslaved women—and worked in settler households. It was the mistreatment of children and the denial of parental authority over children which was partly at the root of one of the very few slave rebellions in the colony: Galant's 1825 slave uprising, which demanded the better treatment of enslaved people on an isolated farm in the colony.[85]

The abolition of slavery in the Cape and elsewhere in the British Empire in 1833 did not end children's enslavement or involvement in forms of unfree labour. In fact, in some contexts, children were sold into slavery or were pawned in even greater numbers than before. The final section of this chapter pays closer attention to the unintended consequences of abolition.

Abolition, Children, and Unfreedom

The literary scholar Patrick Brantlinger argues that 'abolitionism contained the seeds of empire'.[86] In other words, the arguments advanced by abolitionists for the righteous task of civilising Africa through ending slavery were also mobilised by European powers. Documents like the General Act of the Berlin Conference—referred to earlier—demanded that European rule be founded on a commitment to ending slavery in Africa. While the following chapter will explore the making of the idea of the 'African child' and the childlike African in, particularly, abolitionist and colonial rhetoric, it is vital to note here that as abolition was entangled with European imperialism, so the ending of enslavement did not mean freedom, for either children or adults. European empires ended slavery over the course of the nineteenth century. Britain announced the abolition of slavery in that empire in 1833, with the ending of a period of involuntary apprenticeship of former slaves in 1838. France followed suit in 1848. However, despite these laws, slavery—and especially the enslavement of children—persisted. Stilwell makes an important distinction: while '*individual* slaves continued to work in some places ... slavery as an *institution*, for the most part, ceased to exist.'[87] This occurred for a number of reasons, one of which was colonial states' tolerance of its clandestine continuance or emergence in new forms after the formal abolition of slavery. This emergence was shaped by the social, political, and economic transformations wrought in African societies by the introduction, especially, of wage labour and taxation.[88]

---

[85] Helen Bradford, 'Women, Gender and Colonialism: Rethinking the History of the British Cape Colony and Its Frontier Zones, c. 1806–70,' *The Journal of African History*, vol. 37, no. 3 (1996), pp. 358–360.

[86] Patrick Brantlinger, 'Victorians and Africans: The Genealogy of the Myth of the Dark Continent,' *Critical Inquiry*, vol. 12, no. 1, *"Race," Writing, and Difference* (Autumn, 1985), p. 167.

[87] Stilwell, *Slavery and Slaving in African History*, p. 178. Italics in the original.

[88] Stilwell, *Slavery and Slaving in African History*, p. 179.

Children bore the brunt of the remaking of unfree labour. For instance, with the abolition of slavery in the French Empire in 1848, all formerly enslaved children—all people who were under the age of eighteen—became wards of the state. In Senegal, where a majority of these children were girls, the colonial state created a guardianship system—*tutelle*—which allowed both individuals and institutions (like missions and schools) in Saint-Louis, the capital, and other towns to take on responsibility for these children, who would continue to work, largely as domestic servants while some were apprenticed.[89] The numbers of children pulled into this system were significant: in Saint-Louis between 1868 and 1888, thirty-nine per cent of freed slaves were part of the *tutelle* system.[90] As historian Martin Klein writes, this was undoubtedly a form of unfreedom.[91] *Tutelle* ensured the continuity of children's labour, while, at the same time, allowing the French state to claim that it had abolished slavery as part of its commitment to furthering humanitarian goals.

But neither guardianship nor the capture of enslaved children by French administrators or African leaders affiliated to the colonial state, nor, indeed, the implementation of more legislation intended to end slavery in French Sudan (1900) and new territories in French West Africa (1905), ended slavery, and especially the enslavement of children. For instance, in Sokolo in Mali, children were found on sale on the eve of the outbreak of the First World War. The continued enslavement of children was due to familiar reasons: they were small and easily moved and concealed. They could also be frightened into docility.[92] The demand for enslaved children also reflected the unwillingness of the owners of the enslaved to give them up as the French state passed ever more stringent anti-slavery legislation, particularly in the first decade of the twentieth century. As a result of this legislation, more than a million enslaved people left their owners in French West Africa. Those owners often retaliated by seizing the children of the enslaved, partly because—as Klein suggests—they 'undoubtedly believed that the children were theirs.' This was not as a result of those children being related to them biologically (although this was probably true in some cases), but mainly a consequence of believing that the offspring of enslaved people were the property of their owners. French officials did intervene in some places to allow enslaved children to be claimed by their freed parents, but this was a fraught process.[93] *Tutelle* did allow for a relative lack of disruption because it largely preserved the relationships between former slaves

---

[89] Kelly M. Duke Bryant, 'A "Sentiment of Humanity"? Child Protection, Surveillance, and State Guardianship in Senegal, 1895–1910,' in *Diverse Unfreedoms: The Afterlives and Transformations of Post-Transatlantic Bondages*, Sarada Balagopalan, Cati Coe, and Keith Michael Green, eds. (New York and London: Routledge, 2020), p. 35.

[90] Klein, 'Children and Slavery in the Western Sudan,' p. 128.

[91] Martin Klein, 'Children and Slavery in the Western Sudan,' in *Child Slaves in the Modern World*, Gwyn Campbell, Suzanne Miers, and Joseph C. Miller, eds. (Athens, OH: Ohio University Press, 2011), p. 128.

[92] Klein, 'Children and Slavery in the Western Sudan,' pp. 124, 127.

[93] Klein, 'Children and Slavery in the Western Sudan,' p. 131.

and former masters. Despite a series of scandals which revealed the degree to which *tutelle* was slavery by another name, the French colonial state moved slowly to address them, demonstrating, in Bernard Moitt's words, the 'duplicitous' position of the French state as regards the enslavement of children in all but name.[94]

In the case of French colonies in West Africa, a combination of the colonial state's complicity and the consequences of colonial conquest allowed for a continuance of enslavement or, perhaps more accurately, a remaking or modification of the institution. Similarly, pawning changed in reaction to both the abolition of slavery and the shifting economic circumstances in which colonised people found themselves. Writing about Akan-speaking Akuapem society in contemporary Ghana—the Gold Coast under British rule—anthropologist Cati Coe traces how pawning persisted in the colony after its abolition (along with slavery) in 1874. The Emancipation Ordinance did not necessarily free all enslaved people: it banned the sale of enslaved people, allowed enslaved people to buy their freedom, and made the children born to enslaved people free. At the same time, pawning increased not necessarily to replace enslaved people, but, rather, in response to the emergence of a new economy based on the cultivation of cocoa. Children were pawned often to raise capital to buy land to grow cocoa trees. In some cases, pawning established a relationship in which those children would stand to inherit the land from their parents. The pawning of the child could, thus, potentially establish that child's future economic status.[95] But pawning was illegal. As a result, pawned children were passed off to officials as fosterage: 'a common practice in West Africa' mostly 'practised between women, in which women gave their children to other women, whether kin or non-kin, to raise and take care of for a variety of reasons.'[96] Coe asks, then, to what degree the practice of pawning changed as it was argued to be the same as fosterage. She suggests that—in the context of Akuampem society—'what pawning became was, most broadly, debt relations with children, in which care and maintenance of children gave adults rights to children's residence, labour, and marriage payments, but increasingly in a diffuse and long-term way, as entrustment rather than direct exchange.'[97] In other words, the resources that parents invested in their children—medical care, food, and, increasingly, formal education—were used to create relationships in which children owed their parents their labour and other obligations. However, these relations were not formalised in the way that pawning had been in the precolonial period.

---

[94] Bernard Moitt, 'Slavery and Guardianship in Postemancipation Senegal: Colonial Legislation and Minors in *Tutelle*, 1848–1905,' in *Child Slaves in the Modern World*, Gwyn Campbell, Suzanne Miers, and Joseph C. Miller, eds. (Athens, OH: Ohio University Press, 2011), p. 141.
[95] Cati Coe, 'How Debt became Care: Child Pawning and its Transformations in Akuapem, the Gold Coast, 1874–1929,' Africa, vol. 82, no. 2 (2012), pp. 295–299.
[96] Coe, 'How Debt became Care,' p. 299.
[97] Coe, 'How Debt became Care,' p. 305.

Coe's research demonstrates the degree to which the introduction of the capitalist mode of production and colonial efforts to eradicate slavery and pawning shaped relationships within families and between parents and children. But writing about Southern Nigeria in the 1910s and 1920s, Chapdelaine shows that precisely the same forces—the effects of cash economies, new colonial administrations, and prohibitions on slavery—pulled families apart. She demonstrates that even as both pawning and slavery were abolished by the Nigerian colonial state, both practices persisted, with the pawning of children used to 'gain access to currency or other goods for the purpose of paying colonial taxes and other expenses'.[98] In the chaos of new forms of governance—in which already existing precolonial systems were replaced by African warrant chiefs and other colonial officials—the distinction between pawning and enslavement wore away, with increasing numbers of pawned children sold into slavery by the people in whose care those children were placed. In need of more labour, the colonial state was willing to ignore the continuance of bondage and exploitation, even as it faced increasing pressure from Britain to end slavery and pawning.[99] Similarly during the Great Depression, the government of French West Africa ignored or even encouraged the growing incidence of pawned children, most of whom were girls. The drop in commodity prices around the world during the 1930s had a dramatic impact on Africans across the continent, many of whom produced for international markets. In French West Africa, those producers struggled to pay their taxes to the state and so turned to pawning to raise those funds. Under these circumstances, colonial officials were willing to tolerate the practice as long as taxes continued to be paid.[100]

While the French government contemplated various interventions to end pawning, as incomes began to rise again during and after the Second World War, the issue was slowly resolved. Klein and Richard Roberts add:

> When disaster struck again in the years after 1968, pawning seems not to have been a serious option to those in need. By this time, fathers no longer had the same control over their families, relief supplies were available, and for most, other sources of money were available.[101]

Pawning was in most cases a last resort, a choice made with great reluctance. It was also facilitated by existing social and economic structures, and familial relations—and by the willingness of the state to allow it to function. It was not, thus, inevitable, and, as this chapter has shown, it changed significantly over time, to the extent that it began to disappear over the course of the twentieth century.

---

[98] Chapdelaine, *The Persistence of Slavery*, p. 76.

[99] Chapdelaine, *The Persistence of Slavery*, pp. 76–77.

[100] Martin A. Klein and Richard Roberts, 'The Resurgence of Pawning in French West Africa during the Depression of the 1930s,' *African Economic History*, no. 16 (1987), p. 23.

[101] Klein and Roberts, 'The Resurgence of Pawning in French West Africa,' p. 34.

Conclusion

Swema, Equiano, and Phillis Wheatley were among the lucky few children who managed to escape enslavement, finding freedom as adults. However, they were shaped, indelibly, by the experience of having been torn from their homes, forced to endure the horrors of the Indian and Atlantic Ocean slave trades, and the constitution of new identities in new societies. Even these three—who attained various forms of success as adults—always bore with them the appalling consequences of enslavement. Freedom was not necessarily freedom from all forms of distress. As this chapter has shown, the inclusion of children in histories of slavery and other forms of unfree labour in pre- and colonial Africa upsets the binaries which are often invoked in considerations of slavery and abolition. Firstly, enslavement in precolonial Africa was not the opposite of freedom. Rather, it was the status of being kinless—of no longer being embedded within a lineage, a network of kin, which granted the individual protection and support. As a kinless person within another society, an enslaved person occupied the same position as a child: always a minor, on the lowest rung of power. While it would be an exaggeration to suggest a parallel between the lives of children and those of enslaved people, there were certainly similarities in how they were both subject to the power wielded by higher-status adults. Secondly, enslavement was not necessarily the opposite of pawning, and the opposite of pawning was not freedom either. Although pawning and slavery could blur into each other, pawned children were never kinless, but, rather, derived their status as temporary unfree labourers from the fact of their connection to their kinship group.

Thirdly, abolition was not the opposite of enslavement. The ending of the Atlantic slave trade, efforts to eradicate the Indian Ocean trade, and the abolition of slave trading and enslavement in African colonies often increased the likelihood of the enslavement and the pawning of children. The fact of their being children—of being small and vulnerable—made them the ideal targets for the illicit slave trade. The introduction of capitalist agriculture, taxation which had to be paid in cash, the need for more labour to produce commodities for the international market, and the imposition of new forms of rule all produced circumstances where parents were often forced to pawn their children to raise funds (although occasionally pawning could assist in ensuring the economic stability of a family over generations). In these contexts, the meanings and nature of unfree labour changed, and could alter family relationships too. In the early twentieth century, pawning appears slowly to have disappeared by changing into different kinds of unequal relationships between adults and children, begging the question, then: What is the difference between free and unfree labour?

This history of children's involvement in slavery and pawning also helps to address narratives spun by abolitionists in the nineteenth and twentieth centuries, who invented the figure of the innocent African child, and of the childlike African adult, to gather support for their demands to end the slave trade and slavery. As children were vital to the maintenance of slavery within Africa and in the trades which took Africans from the continent, so they were of exceptional importance to the abolitionist cause—and thus, ultimately, to the project of European imperialism itself.

CHAPTER 4

Race and Childhood

In 1855, a Zulu boy in his early teens went to live at Ekukhanyeni ('place of light'), a mission school newly founded by Bishop John W. Colenso in the Natal Colony to educate the children of the Zulu elite. Manawami's father had agreed that his son should receive a Western education with the Bishop, and, later, consented that Manawami be baptised as a Christian in about 1859, after which the young man was renamed Magema. Today, Magema Magwaza Fuze (c.1840–1922) is known to South Africans as the author of *Abantu Abamnyama Lapa Bavela Ngakona* ('The Black People and Whence They Came'), the first account of the history of the Zulu people written by a Zulu speaker. Fuze was also a journalist and owned a printing press, having learned how to print at Ekukhanyeni, under Colenso's guidance. But Fuze began his career as a writer long before his magnum opus was published in 1922. In his early teens, he described life at the mission school, and in 1860, along with two other young converts, wrote an account of Colenso's then-recent tour of Zululand, on which they accompanied the Bishop and facilitated an introduction to the Zulu king, Mpande.

These accounts written by the young Fuze, as well as his descriptions of his childhood as an adult, are valuable and unusual sources for historians interested in precolonial childhoods, and in children's experiences of the entrenchment of colonial rule. Even more significantly, the grown-up Fuze understood that it was his status as a child which rendered him interesting and useful to Colenso. While the British had annexed the Natal Colony in 1843, Zulu chiefs had retained some independence under the system of indirect rule established by Theophilus Shepstone, the powerful director of native policy. The Zulu kingdom north of the colony remained largely self-governing until the Anglo-Zulu War in 1879, and its final remnants were conquered and incorporated into the colony in 1898. On his arrival in Natal in 1853, Colenso went to work among the Zulu, and particularly elite families, attempting to persuade parents willingly to send their children to the school as a way of introducing Christianity to Zulu society. With children at the school, parents would visit the mission station frequently and 'by degrees', he wrote, they might come into contact with Christianity, and agree for them and their children to be baptised.[1] Colenso met with a great deal of resistance, and for a variety of reasons, ranging from parents' belief that children sent to the school might be conscripted into the British imperial army, to concerns that children would no longer respect their parents.[2] In fact, Fuze's father, Magwaza, initially objected to his son's baptism on those grounds, saying to Colenso:

> Sir, I am afraid of my child becoming a Christian. There is a son of So-and-So at the Edendale Mission School over yonder who went there to study, and when his mother went to see him she found he was no longer there, and it was said he had simply left and no longer lived there. I am afraid, Sir, and I do not wish my child to become a Christian, because he will defy me and his mother.[3]

Colenso reassured him, noting that the Bible commands Christians to honour their parents. On hearing this, Magwaza agreed to his son's conversion. Fuze left his father's homestead where, he remembered as an adult, he 'was always happy when he was not at home but out herding calves with other young boys who were his age'[4] and enrolled at school at Ekukhanyeni. In an essay written in Zulu shortly after he commenced his education and later sent to Bishop Grey in the Cape Colony, Fuze described a different kind of childhood to the one he had led at home—with Colenso, life was regulated by the ringing of a bell, and divided between the school and the church:

> we cypher [sic], we read, we sing hymns of God. It is, on Sunday, that we enter into the house of prayer early, we pray… Daily, the Lady [Mrs Colenso] teaches us to draw pictures. Now we learn to cypher and to add, and to subtract on the slates which we cypher on. Now we read a book of the English: but we do not know that perfectly.[5]

On the mission, Fuze was introduced, too, to the race politics of settler society. In that same essay, he observed that whites and African converts prayed and worshipped separately, and was aware of his lowly position within the racial hierarchy of both the colony and Ekukhanyeni, as both an African and as a child. This was different to the age-based hierarchy he had slotted into at home, where he had spent his time with his peers, who taught him how to herd

---

[1] Hlonipha Mokoena, 'Christian Converts and the Production of Kholwa Histories in Nineteenth-Century Colonial Natal: The Case of Magema Magwaza Fuze and his Writings,' *Journal of Natal and Zulu History*, vol. 23, no. 1 (2005), p. 18.

[2] Hlonipha Mokoena, 'The Queen's Bishop: A Convert's Memoir of John W. Colenso,' *Journal of Religion in Africa*, vol. 38, no. 3 (2008), p. 324.

[3] Quoted in Mokoena, 'Christian Converts,' p. 19.

[4] Quoted in Mokoena, 'The Queen's Bishop,' p. 322.

[5] Quoted in Mokoena, 'The Queen's Bishop,' p. 319.

cattle and who would have, later, accompanied him in the initiation ceremonies which marked his transition from childhood to youth, and from youth to adulthood.

Although Fuze had little say over whether he would go to school at Ekukhanyeni—the decision was entirely his father's—and occupied a relatively subordinate position there, despite an increasingly close relationship with Colenso whom he regarded as a father figure, his writing as a child and, later, as an adult about his childhood emphasises the degree to which he was an active participant in this move. Strikingly, in adulthood Fuze insisted that as a very young child he had known that he would be raised in the household of a white settler. He explains in the introduction to *Abantu Abamnyama Lapa Bavela Ngakona*, writing in the third person:

> When Manawami attained the age of six or seven (I am not certain about that), he began to talk in a manner unintelligible to his parents, but they paid no heed to it, regarding it merely as child's talk… In his conversation with the other children he used to say, 'I am not going to grow up here at home. A white man of high rank will be coming here from across the sea; he is the one for whom I will work, and who will call me by the name of Skelemu.' As he was always speaking in this way to the other children, his parents eventually discarded the name of Manawami and Skelemu became his permanent name.[6]

'Skelemu' means 'rascal' and probably refers to Fuze's habit of telling, what his parents and contemporaries believed to be, tall tales. The nickname stuck, as did Fuze's desire to narrate his own experiences. His insistence that he had known from early childhood his destiny in the white bishop's court positions him—as a child—in an unusually powerful position: both as a seer aware of his own destiny, but also as the narrator of his own life, as he navigated the worlds of an African homestead whose laws, norms, and daily rhythms had not yet been significantly disrupted by colonial conquest, and that of the English-speaking, white-dominated Christian mission, where he was expected to live like a 'civilised' (or 'Westernised') convert.

Fuze is a remarkable and unusual figure not only in the context of the Colony of Natal and the Zulu kingdom, but also in African history more broadly. Very few African children recorded their impressions of colonial conquest, and described one of the most profound changes caused by colonial rule over the continent: conversion to Christianity. Considering that Fuze knew that his writing would be read by his teachers, Colenso, and other powerful figures within settler society, it would be unreasonable to suggest that they describe his own, fully truthful feelings about life at Ekukhanyeni. Moreover—as in the case of Oluadah Equiano's memoir, for instance—his descriptions of his childhood as an adult must be read with an awareness of the failures of memory and Fuze's own attempts at self-fashioning in his writing.

[6] Quoted in Mokoena, 'The Queen's Bishop,' p. 321.

Nevertheless, his writing remains an important source for historians. Fuze demonstrates the degree to which children and young people were at the frontier of the colonial encounter, and precisely because they were children. Many African parents, particularly those who were members of elites, like Fuze's father, understood that allowing one or more of their children to attend mission schools would provide them with connections to, and insight into, colonial politics and, in the case of the Natal Colony, settler society. Colenso and other missionaries believed that children were the key to converting whole societies, as potentially malleable subjects and as conduits to their parents. At mission schools—either the relatively well-resourced institutions close to power like Ekukhanyeni, or the smaller, isolated, and badly funded school rooms and Sunday schools at many mission stations dotted across the continent—African children were envisaged as the future subjects of a Christian Africa under European control. Regardless of whether children themselves bought into these arguments, they experienced first-hand the material consequences of colonialism, negotiating the shift between different definitions of what should constitute childhood.

Western notions of childhood did not simply overlay or replace pre-existing definitions of childhood and youth. Rather, they existed alongside each other, with both African and European conceptualisations of the category of childhood subject to change and debate during this period. Beginning with a brief overview of the European conquest of Africa in the nineteenth century, this chapter pays closer attention to the making of 'childhood' in the colonial encounter and in the colonial state—or, more specifically, to how categories of race and childhood were co-constituted. Regardless of Colenso's increasingly sympathetic stance towards the Zulu, the world which Fuze and his peers inhabited at Ekukhanyeni was intensely racialised: he was not a child, he was an *African* child, a category which bore with it a range of associations, and which was mobilised by missionaries, humanitarians, and colonial states, among other entities, to pursue a range of aims. Moreover, 'African-ness' itself was constructed by colonial administrators and others in relation to childishness and childlike behaviour—one of the legacies of the abolitionist movement. The final section of this chapter focuses on multiracial children, whose existence both challenged the race thinking which underpinned colonial conquest, but was also used—in other contexts—precisely to bolster this rule.

From Abolition to Partition

The previous chapter invoked Patrick Brantlinger's observation that 'abolitionism contained the seeds of empire'.[7] We can interpret this point in a number of ways. On the level of discourse and ideas, the abolitionist movement imagined

---

[7] Patrick Brantlinger, 'Victorians and Africans: The Genealogy of the Myth of the Dark Continent,' *Critical Inquiry*, vol. 12, no. 1, 'Race,' Writing, and Difference (Autumn, 1985), p. 167.

Europeans as the saviours of Africa and of Africans: most pressingly from enslavement and its appalling consequences, but also from what Europeans believed to be Africans' ignorance and backwardness. This unequal relationship which—in the language of the nineteenth century—placed the burden of rescuing Africa from savagery on Europeans, began to justify the conquest and colonisation of the continent in the minds of some Europeans. But materially, European and other foreigners' trading with Africans did not end with the abolition of the trans-Atlantic trade. On the contrary, what was described as legitimate trade occurred alongside and in the place of the enslavement of people in many places, producing a shift in the relationship between Africans and European merchants (and states), and transformations within African societies too. As the previous chapter showed, the British abolition of the slave trade in 1807 did not end the enslavement and transportation of people across the Atlantic. Trade in other commodities complemented and sometimes depended on enslavement. In Southern Nigeria, for example, Yoruba-speaking people's trade in palm oil with the British grew significantly at the end of the eighteenth century, as demand for soap and industrial lubricants increased with industrialisation. Enslaved people certainly worked in the production of palm oil well after 1807, despite the British presence in the region. A steady trickle of missionaries into Southern Nigeria alongside traders, significant political change within Yoruba society (specifically the collapse of the Oyo empire, a major node in the trans-Atlantic trade), and French and German interest in the region caused the British to annex most of Southern Nigeria between the 1860s and the 1880s.[8]

This example touches on some of the most important factors which caused and shaped the European conquest of Africa: a combination of industrialising European states (especially Britain initially) pursuing trade in commodities in demand at home; the role of traders, missionaries, and also explorers in establishing a European presence in parts of the continent, often producing knowledge (of languages and terrain, for example) useful for colonial conquest; rivalry between European nations—some of them, like Germany, relatively new—seeking to accrue their own empires; and political, social, and economic change within African societies that determined the nature of conquest. Undergirding all of this, technological advances in weaponry and medicine made the conquest of the continent more possible than ever before. In addition to these circumstances, ideological and religious transformations in Europe helped to justify colonial conquest. Firstly, Christian evangelical revival in Europe and North America from the eighteenth century sought to convert all people across the globe to Christianity, in preparation for Christ's second coming. Colonial conquest was, in the minds of many missionaries, a tool for this process. As a result, the European imperial project in Africa was cast as a civilising mission even if the primary motives of European politicians in seeking

---

[8] Toyin Falola and Matthew M. Heaton, *A History of Nigeria* (Cambridge: Cambridge University Press, 2008), pp. 77–82, 93.

African colonies were usually firmly material. This noted, missionaries were proponents of commerce as part of the process of civilising colonial subjects. Secondly, scientific racism—which drew on the ideas propounded by a range of scholars, including Georges Cuvier, Herbert Spencer, and Francis Galton—attempted to explain differences between societies through an understanding of race rooted in biology. The various theories which constituted this race science usually posited that increasing European political and economic global hegemony was due either to the racial decline of Africans or Asians, for example, or the innate differences between race groups. Regardless, this profoundly racist pseudo-science was mobilised in the justification of both the partition of Africa and colonial rule there.

The Berlin West Africa Conference convened in the winter of 1884–1885 agreed, firstly, to recognise the right of Leopold II of Belgium to what was then the Congo Free State, a free trade zone whose revenues enriched Leopold II and the European traders and businesses which operated there, at brutal cost to the societies which inhabited this vast area. Secondly, the conference established that for European powers to claim a region of Africa, they needed to occupy it—a move which Germany used to bolster its efforts to establish its colony of Tanganyika (present-day Tanzania), which Britain argued was part of its 'sphere of influence' being on the border with Kenya. This was, then, no orderly division of Africa between European states. The 'scramble' for Africa was precisely that: 'a largely uncoordinated, often headlong rush from the coast into the hinterland and beyond, a multitude of military advances and engagements interspersed by diplomatic interactions', in historian Richard Reid's words.[9] Put another way, there was no coordinated military assault on Africa's multitude of societies from the late 1870s. Rather, European empires seized regions for themselves, and often where they had pre-existing economic interests—as in the case of Southern Nigeria, but also much of West Africa, for example—or strategic concerns (Britain's two colonies in South Africa were founded partly to guarantee the route to India for British ships). Much of this conquest was done via treaties signed by proxies for empires, usually chartered companies like Cecil John Rhodes's British South Africa Company in what became Northern and Southern Rhodesia (or Zambia and Zimbabwe) and the Imperial British East Africa Company in Kenya. African responses to the imposition of rule varied according to context. The British crushed the Zulu kingdom in 1879 after a revolt earlier that year; the Chimurenga uprising in Southern Rhodesia tried to cast out British rule in 1896–1897; Britain fought a series of wars against the Asante, before declaring control of the Gold Coast (now Ghana) in 1901; and the Maji Maji rebellion in 1905–1907 attempted to throw off German rule in Tanganyika. But in other cases, African elites could use the presence of Europeans to their own advantage: for example, in the Buganda Kingdom, a Protestant faction within the court formed an alliance

---

[9] Richard J. Reid, *A History of Modern Africa, 1800 to the Present*, second ed. (Chichester: John Wiley & Sons Limited, 2012), p. 117.

with the British in 1890 which, although resulting in the declaration of a protectorate in 1894, largely bolstered the power of Protestants over Catholics and other groups in the new colony.

Given that it is difficult to generalise a single account of colonial conquest, it is unsurprising, then, that colonial rule also changed over time and place. Settler colonies—Algeria under French rule, as well as South Africa, Rhodesia, and Kenya under British rule—were governed in the interests of white minorities, and, from the early twentieth century, by those whites themselves. The French Empire tended to be fairly centralised with governors implementing policy formulated in Paris, and informed by a view that assimilation could be possible for African subjects. To these ends, in 1848, the inhabitants of Saint-Louis, Dakar, Gorée, and Rufisque in Senegal were granted French citizenship, although in reality this only applied to a handful of people: those Africans (dubbed *évolués*) who spoke French fluently and were judged to be patriotic to France and to live like Europeans could attain full citizenship via a formal process, a system emulated in the Belgian Congo (after the appalling abuses of Congolese people were revealed, Belgium took over the governance of Leopold's Free State in 1907) and in the Portuguese colonies of Mozambique and Angola. In reality, very few people attained this status. The British developed a system of indirect rule, most comprehensively described in Frederick Lugard's *The Dual Mandate in British Tropical Africa* (1923). Drawing on his experience as governor of Northern Nigeria after the conquest of the Sokoto Caliphate in 1903, Lugard proposed that colonial administrations govern through already existing African political structures. In reality, few African societies resembled this Muslim Caliphate, resulting in British administrators creating African political structures through which to govern, usually 'chiefs' imbued with authority they would not have possessed before colonial conquest. In theory at least, indirect rule placed the burden of tax collecting and organising labour for mining, agriculture, and other industries required to make colonies profitable on African leaders. This social and political engineering produced a range of consequences. In Igbo society in Southern Nigeria, for instance, the Aba Women's War in 1929 was—among many other causes, including an increase in the pawning of children—a reaction against the African warrant chiefs whose role it was to collect taxes.

As the justification for indirect rule implies, European powers were often loath to invest heavily in their colonies, even in contexts where administrators expressed a desire to institute social or other kinds of reform. Education and healthcare provision were usually in the hands of missionaries. As historian Barbara Cooper explains, for all the French state's expressed anxiety about demographic decline within its empire, 'the real demographic decline concerned not the indigenous population but the inadequate numbers of appropriately trained colonial administrators.' In other words, 'France never invested sufficient human or financial resources to have an appreciative positive impact on reproductive health in the

Sahel.'[10] But colonial administrators did devote significant funds to infrastructure work or other projects which contributed to the economic exploitation of those colonies—such as the construction of the Uganda railway between 1896 and 1901, which joined Mombasa on the coast to Lake Victoria. European powers did not hesitate to draw on their colonies during difficult times: during the First World War (1914–1919), Africans fought for European rulers both in Africa and beyond, but by far the vast majority of those caught up in the conflict (often unwillingly) were porters who helped to provision armies, especially in East and West Africa. Altogether, between one and two per cent of the continent's total population was involved in the First World War in some way. Both during this conflict and the Great Depression, African colonies were squeezed for both their resources and tax revenues, creating circumstances under which impoverishment, hunger, and unemployment flourished. While anti-colonial politics and decolonisation will be discussed in later chapters, it is enough to note here that criticism of colonialism—in Africa and beyond—post-1919 and during and after the Second World War (1939–1945) did contribute to the emergence of policies designed to develop the economies, particularly, of many colonies, in preparation for potential independence.

In debates on colonies' preparation for independence, colonial administrators (and, occasionally, African politicians too) reached for the metaphors of youth and age to describe processes of decolonisation. The following section pays attention to how childhood and youth were mobilised by Europeans involved in the imperial project to understand Africa and Africans, and to justify colonial rule.

Abolition, Colonial Conquest, and the Childlike African

In her abolitionist novel *Uncle Tom's Cabin* (1852), the author Harriet Beecher Stowe set out explicitly to narrate a story which would persuade her white readers of the evils of enslavement, especially in the United States. One of her strategies for demonstrating slavery's inhumanity was to describe the childlike nature of Africans. This is particularly marked in the titular character of Uncle Tom who possesses 'the soft, impressionable nature of his kindly race' and, thus, is 'ever yearning toward the simple and childlike'.[11] Stowe makes clear that Tom's piety, refusal to engage in violence, and moral goodness stem from the fact of his African-ness, an identity she associates with being childlike. Towards the end of the novel, Stowe sends her surviving African-American characters to Liberia, a colony established in 1822 for freed enslaved people. She reflects on Africa and Africans:

---

[10] Barbara Cooper, *Countless Blessings: A History of Childbirth and Reproduction in the Sahel* (Bloomington, IA: Indiana University Press, 2019), pp. 117–118.

[11] Harriet Beecher Stowe, *Uncle Tom's Cabin, or, Life among the Lowly* (Cambridge, MA: Belknap Press of Harvard University Press, 2009), p. 192.

> If ever Africa shall show an elevated and cultivated race ... life will awake there with a gorgeousness and splendour of which our cold Western tribes faintly have conceived. ... the negro race, no longer despised and trodden down, will, perhaps, show forth some of the latest and most magnificent revelations of human life. Certainly they will, in their gentleness, their lowly docility of heart, their aptitude to repose on a superior mind and rest on a higher power, their childlike simplicity of affection, and facility of forgiveness.[12]

Stowe's point here is that if Africa were provided with adequate assistance to overcome the appalling consequences of the trans-Atlantic slave trade, then the continent would become a kind of heaven on earth, populated by childlike, morally perfect, innately Christian people. Instead of a place of darkness and backwardness—as Africa was frequently characterised as being—it would be a shining beacon for the whole of humanity.

Stowe was not alone in this imagining of Africa and of Africans, and although her intentions were to improve the lives of the enslaved and to counter the racism of those who described Africans as brutish heathens, the childish African is yet another racist stereotype—one which still shapes perceptions of the continent in the twenty-first century. Brantlinger argues that the trans-Atlantic slave trade was fundamental to shaping European—and, indeed, Western—perceptions of Africa and of Africans, partly because, '[i]ronically, the expansion of the slave trade ... from the 1600s on meant that Europeans had to develop more accurate knowledge of Africans',[13] but also as a result of shifting opinion of slavery itself. Describing Africans in a positive light was, crudely, intended to encourage Europeans to sympathise with the victims of enslavement. To these ends, discourses already circulating in eighteenth-century Europe—when popular opinion against slavery was first mobilised on a significant scale—were put to use: the stereotype of the 'noble savage', a term usually associated with the Enlightenment philosopher Jean Jacques Rousseau, posited that indigenous peoples beyond Europe lived lives which were perfect in their simplicity and freedom from modernity and industrialisation. The concept proved to be attractive to both scholars—including Marx and Freud—as well as explorers and missionaries. But however racist the conceptualisation of the noble savage is, in most iterations it still emphasises the full maturity of Africans or other indigenous people. Circulating at about the same time as this myth, another view of Africans as childlike also gained widespread popularity.

The myth of the childlike African relied on the emergence of new ideas about childhood in eighteenth- and early nineteenth-century Europe. Enlightenment philosophers—notably John Locke and Rousseau—described the child not as inherently sinful, but, rather, as a 'blank slate' (in Locke's words) to be raised and educated by parents and teachers into rational adults. At the same time, Romantic poets and writers went a step further, arguing that

---

[12] Stowe, *Uncle Tom's Cabin*, p. 235.
[13] Patrick Brantlinger, 'Victorians and Africans: The Genealogy of the Myth of the Dark Continent,' *Critical Inquiry*, vol. 12, no. 1, 'Race,' Writing, and Difference (Autumn, 1985), p. 173.

childhood was, in fact, an ideal state: the child, as the Romantic poet William Wordsworth wrote, could best understand the beauty and profundity of the world before the onset of the self-consciousness and disillusion of adulthood. Evangelical Christians drew on both sets of ideas when they conceptualised childhood as a period of moral innocence. For evangelicals, unselfconscious children possessed the purity of heart fully to devote themselves to Jesus Christ—whose own childhood was not only a model for Christian children, but also for Christian adults. Evangelical ministers urged their adult congregants to become 'childlike' in their faith.

These ideas were not formulated and circulated in a vacuum. They occurred at the same time as the industrialisation of European economies and the growth of the bureaucratic state. In the households of the growing and politically ascendant middle class, the changing nature of work altered the roles of men and women, and of adults and children. As men left households to work in offices—as the household was no longer a productive unit, in other words—so women presided over the domestic space (as 'angels of the house'), now imagined as a sacred, secluded world beyond the chaos and strife of the public sphere. Middle-class childhood was, over the course of the nineteenth century, made into an extended period of care, play, and education. The role of the child in this household was simply to be an innocent, and not to work. The material and ideological were intertwined. Not all middle-class childhoods changed in these ways, but this idealised description of white, bourgeois life—the subject of so many books published during this Golden Age (as scholars have dubbed it) of children's literature, like Louisa May Alcott's *Little Women* (1869) and *The Railway Children* by Edith Nesbit (1906)—proved to be immensely powerful. It was at the root of the child saving movement around the world in the nineteenth and twentieth centuries, which extended compulsory education, made the abuse and neglect of children illegal, and moved to eradicate child labour, among other measures.

This ideology of modern childhood was constituted during campaigns to abolish slavery and the expansion of industrialised European empires. Thus, from its inception, the idea of the innocent child was racialised and, unsurprisingly, in most cases the innocent child was imagined as white and middle class. This association was put to use in a number of ways. Writing about the United States, historian Robin Bernstein writes that as white children were 'constructed as tender angels' in popular discourse, their black counterparts 'were libelled as unfeeling, noninnocent nonchildren' in the second half of the nineteenth century, and, in so doing, justifying the exclusion of black children from school and their continued presence in wage labour, and contributing to their criminalisation.[14] While the application of ideas about innocence to African children on the continent will be discussed in the following section, it is worth emphasising here that, firstly, discourses and ideologies of childhood did not

---

[14] Robin Bernstein, *Racial Innocence: Performing American Childhood from Slavery to Civil Rights* (New York and London: New York University Press, 2011), p. 33.

necessarily map precisely on to the experiences of children and young people, even if those ideas were exceptionally important for shaping the institutions and norms in and under which children and their parents operated; and, secondly, these categories of age and identity were under constant debate and existed alongside other definitions of childhood. They existed alongside a variety of definitions of adulthood too.

A crucial factor in European thinking about Africans—both adults and children—from the late eighteenth century onwards was scientific racism. Although constituted of a range of theories, in sum it argued for the inferiority of Africans on the grounds that their racial constitution rendered them lesser than Europeans and some other racial categories. But it was mobilised in different ways as Europeans' relationship with Africa and Africans changed over time. For instance, historian William B. Cohen notes that French literary representations altered according to the popularity of the abolitionist movement: sympathetic portrayals of enslaved Africans in the eighteenth century came to an end with the commencement of the Haitian Revolution in 1792, but then re-emerged in the early nineteenth century, as French abolitionists lobbied the state to end enslavement in the French Empire. In the sentimental literature of the first decades of the nineteenth century, Africans were simple, good, and childlike. Even, as Cohen writes, 'most of the literature which glorified' Africans 'had as basic to it the understanding' that the average African person 'was a "child", a lesser being'. As a result, even as this literature protested the crime that was enslavement, informed as it was by scientific racism, it 'rarely denied the contemporary conviction that the white race had abilities and a destiny superior to that of Africans'.[15]

Insisting on the childlike nature of Africans may have assisted Stowe and some French abolitionist novelists in proving to their readers the necessity of abolishing slavery, but it served other purposes too. Being childlike implied a range of behaviours and characteristics. In Stowe's view, childlike Africans were the moral superiors to Europeans; but 'childlike'—although not the same as 'childish'—implies, also, the irresponsible, impulsive, and irrational actions of children in need of supervision (for their own benefit) and discipline. As Brantlinger makes the point, after the abolition of the slave trade, 'the British began to see themselves less and less as perpetrators of the slave trade and more and more as the potential saviours of the African'.[16] In this paradigm, Europeans take on the role of the adult parent to childlike Africans in need of careful rearing to full maturity. This infantilisation of Africans was a useful tool not only for justifying colonial conquest—Africans needed to be placed under the care of Europeans—but also for explaining the nature of colonial rule itself.

---

[15] William B. Cohen, 'Literature and Race: Nineteenth Century French Fiction, Blacks, and Africa 1800–1880,' *Race and Class*, vol. 16, no. 2 (1974), p. 184.

[16] Brantlinger, 'Victorians and Africans,' p. 173.

Cohen writes:

> The European imperial powers of the nineteenth and twentieth centuries viewed their African and Asian subjects as children, as men not fully grown, whose destiny had to be guided by the presumably more advanced states of Europe.[17]

In this scheme, the colonial state was both the 'generous mother' caring for childlike Africans and the stern father, serving to discipline wilful, immature subjects.[18] As philosopher and historian Achille Mbembe writes, imagining the relationship between coloniser and colonised as being analogous to that of a parent and child was a strategy for legitimising the violence of colonial rule.[19] He explains that the metaphor of the coloniser/colonised as parent/child elides the violence inherent in colonial rule by making 'familiarity and domestication ... the dominant tropes of servitude'.[20]

Yet as historian Carol Summers shows as regards colonial Buganda—contemporary Uganda, then under British rule—the metaphors of youth could work to the advantage of activists demanding reforms too. In the 1930s and 1940s, British officials and missionaries described the colony of Buganda and the Baganda as existing in an 'adolescent' state as protests against colonial rule increased: 'the Anglican bishop of Uganda complained "[T]he Baganda are in a very difficult adolescent period ... [e]merging from childhood where they were willing to be controlled but not yet having reaches sensible thinking manhood."' As Summers explains, 'the metaphor of adolescence suggested hope that such turbulence was finite and would end with the adolescent achieving maturity and the ability to stand alone, independent and self-supporting.'[21] It was also a way of belittling activists' work, dismissing it as a kind of rebellion for rebellion's sake. However, activists found this metaphor useful:

> ideas of an adolescent Buganda offered a way to legitimize rebellion and opposition to British guidance. An adolescent, after all, is more than a child. Her or she knows more, understands more, and is on the verge of adulthood and maturity. Adolescents achieve maturity, moreover, not through the dutiful obedience and acceptance of subordination of a client, but by rebelling, pointing out injustice, sometimes by 'making mistakes.' Adolescence was a stage on the path to self-determination, self-sufficiency, and independence.[22]

Adopting the language of youth became a means of demanding no longer to be treated as children. The term 'adolescence' was a relatively new one in the

---

[17] William B. Cohen, 'The Colonized as Child: British and French Colonial Rule,' *African Historical Studies*, vol. 3, no. 2 (1970), p. 427.

[18] Cohen, 'The Colonized as Child,' p. 427.

[19] Achille Mbembe, *On the Postcolony* (Berkeley, CA: University of California Press, 2001), p. 25.

[20] Mbembe, *On the Postcolony*, p. 27.

[21] Carol Summers, 'Youth, Elders, and Metaphors of Political Change in Late Colonial Buganda,' in *Generations Past: Youth in East African History*, eds. Andrew Burton and Hélène Charton-Bigot (Athens, OH: Ohio University Press, 2010), p. 176.

[22] Summers, 'Youth, Elders, and Metaphors of Political Change in Late Colonial Buganda,' pp. 176–177.

1930s, having been coined in 1904 by the American psychologist G. Stanley Hall. While the term was developed within the context of the American child study movement and referred to shifts in the experience of childhood and youth in the United States, it was taken up and used around the world. Clearly, colonial administrators and missionaries found the idea useful for justifying their responses to anti-colonial politics. But, as the case of Buganda demonstrates, Africans, too, adopted the term, mobilising it to justify struggle. As Summers notes, the concept as it was deployed in Buganda 'had little to do with real young people on the verge of adulthood'. Rather, it helped to reframe anti-colonial politics—which often took on the character of intergenerational strife, as younger African politicians accused their elders of benefitting from aspects of colonial rule (this will be discussed further in Chap. 7).[23]

How, then, were African children themselves understood by colonial rulers? The following section pays closer attention to the creation of the stereotype of the 'African child' under colonialism.

THE AFRICAN CHILD AND THE PROJECT OF EMPIRE

The figure of the emaciated, suffering child has become one of the most powerful symbols of African crises: on the cover of *Life* magazine in 1968 during the Biafran War in Nigeria; in the arms of the BBC journalist Michael Buerk, covering the Ethiopian famine in 1984; in the foreground of photographer Kevin Carter's photograph 'The Struggling Girl' taken in Sudan in 1993, as a vulture waits behind her. Unsurprisingly, African children have been used extensively in fundraising campaigns for international charities and aid agencies doing work on the continent, alluding not only to these exceptionally well-known depictions of suffering, but also linking to a much older, colonial discourse about African childhood.

Colonial administrators and missionaries were especially concerned about African childhood. In some ways, this is not surprising. As literary scholar Lisa McNee observes as regards French colonies in Africa where children were at the 'centre' of many policies designed to civilise African subjects, this was because 'they were to be the repositories of French culture, the agents of change who would anchor the French Empire'.[24] As young and potentially malleable, in the minds of missionaries and administrators, children could be educated into being civilised French subjects. But a more pointed question would be to ask how colonial administrators, missionaries, and others constructed the idea—or the category—of the 'African child'. The example of Magema Fuze is useful here: he moved between two definitions of what it meant to be a child. With his family and away from the mission station, as a young boy yet to be initiated whose chief activity was herding, and whose main

---

[23] Summers, 'Youth, Elders, and Metaphors of Political Change in Late Colonial Buganda,' p. 178.
[24] Lisa McNee, 'The Languages of Childhood: The Discursive Construction of Childhood and Colonial Policy in French West Africa,' *African Studies Quarterly*, vol. 7, no. 4 (Spring 2004), p. 22.

Map 4.1 Africa in 1914. Alison D. Ollivierre, Tombolo Maps & Design

companions were boys his own age, the next significant step in his life course would be the ceremonies which ushered him into adulthood and manhood, which he would undergo having reached puberty. Then he might be expected to fight in the Zulu army and, eventually, to marry and establish a homestead of his own, for which he would need access to cattle. But at the same time, at the mission school Magema Fuze was a 'child' in the European sense, meaning that his only occupation was learning, and not labour (which might, if it were wage earning, be considered to be a form of exploitation). Having converted to Christianity and learned a trade, he would enter young adulthood with the completion of his schooling. There were some similarities between these childhoods: obedience to adults, perhaps most obviously. But a key difference was that the latter was racialised. As mentioned earlier, Magema Fuze was on the mission station an African child, not simply a child. He would have been understood and treated differently to the white children of missionaries.

As historian Abosede George has described, the notion of the 'African child' as both a racial and an age category emerged in the early twentieth century and encapsulated the contradictions of European attitudes towards colonial rule and, in the interwar and post-war eras, of African development. The nineteenth-century ideology of the innocent child was capacious enough to include a range of ideas—some of them ostensibly contradictory—about childhood, particularly when this age category came up against stereotypes relating to race and class. As a result, while social reformers in the nineteenth and twentieth centuries argued that all children—regardless of identity—were innocent, they did also believe that white urban working-class children, for instance, were more inclined to behave badly, largely as a result of poor parenting and the impoverished circumstances of their upbringings. In this way, children were always innocent but could also be wild and dangerous, and this was especially the case for African children. The 'African child' was in perpetual need of rescue from backward parents and African institutions. This child represented a potentially developed and civilised future if only the child could be raised and educated by European, Christian schools and carers. But at the same time, the 'African child' was always dangerous, tempted by idleness and excess, emotionally uncontainable, and intellectually weak. The 'African child' could always be and not be saved. As George writes: 'the African child became articulated as a sign of vulnerability, African pathology, and the paradoxical (im)possibility of African development.'[25] The 'African child' captured colonial powers' thinking about the future potential and inherent backwardness of the continent.

Clearly, the idea of the African child was useful for colonial rule in the early twentieth century. As George explains, this was a figure through whom 'imperial liberalism became imaginable as an enterprise of proliferating vulnerabilities that (re)instated colony, empire, and imperial nation-states as guarantors of humanity and rights'.[26] Put another way, concerted efforts to rescue African children served to justify the intertwined colonial and humanitarian projects. Humanitarianism—the promotion of human welfare—emerged in the eighteenth century, and over the course of the following 200 years, became part of an international project to improve the lives of others abroad, and entangled in the promotion of human rights. Among the earliest and most powerful of the

---

[25] Abosede A. George, *Making Modern Girls: A History of Girlhood, Labor, and Social Development in Colonial Lagos* (Athens, OH: Ohio University Press, 2015), p. 63.
[26] George, *Making Modern Girls*, p. 72.

international humanitarian organisations which were founded in the early twentieth century were related to children. As historian Emily Baughan has argued as regards the Save the Children Fund (SCF)—which was founded in 1919 in Britain to aid children in Austria and Germany—the humanitarian movement could be mobilised in support of European imperialism. She writes that in its appeals for funding to the public, the SCF 'sought to show that humanitarian action was, in fact, integral to the imperial tradition'—in fact, 'it was partly through the performance of humanitarian works that imperial greatness was constituted.'[27]

The idea of the African child was formulated in this broader context, meaning that this category of identity, which drew on ideas of idealised childhood and racist notions of African-ness, would appeal to humanitarians and other social reformers in Europe and elsewhere. For instance, in her research on efforts to ban clitoridectomy in colonial Kenya during the first half of the twentieth century, Lynn Thomas demonstrates that while this campaign was driven locally by missionaries and colonial and African officials, it was vocally supported by humanitarians and feminists in the United Kingdom, where women 'parliamentarians and women's rights organisations argued before the House of Commons that clitoridectomy should be banned'. This on the grounds of dangers posed to mothers and also to infants.[28] But humanitarian ideas took root on the continent too. Writing about early twentieth-century Lagos, George describes the work of the Lagos Women's League in the 1920s, particularly as regards girls who worked as hawkers in that city. They were not the only group concerned about child hawkers: in 1922 Sylvia Leith-Ross, a British ethnographer, wrote a report for the British Association for Moral and Social Hygiene about the state of hawking and interracial sex in Lagos. She, the League, and colonial officials were especially concerned that girl hawkers doubled as sex workers—an anxiety they did not express about boy hawkers who, they all acknowledged, worked in order to attend school, for instance. They did not ask if girls did the same. At issue was the question of what constituted 'girlhood':

> Reformers were wedded to a particular idea of what girlhood was like, and it was an idea that involved notions of innocence, modesty, and chastity. Preserving the idea of girlhood in that way required designating girl hawkers to bear the burden of notions that fell outside their idea of girlhood. By the 1920s girl hawkers were viewed as immodest, unchaste, and definitely not innocent. In this way, girl hawkers remained in question, while girls could continue to be girls.[29]

---

[27] Emily Baughan, '"Every Citizen of Empire Implored to Save the Children!" Empire, Internationalism and the Save the Children Fund in Inter-War Britain,' *Historical Research*, vol. 86, no. 231 (Feb. 2013), pp. 128–129.

[28] Lynn M. Thomas, 'Imperial Concerns and "Women's Affairs": State Efforts to Regulate Clitoridectomy and Eradicate Abortion in Meru, Kenya, c.1910–1950,' *Journal of African History*, vol. 39 (1998), p. 130.

[29] George, *Making Modern Girls*, p. 57.

Ideas about gendered, racialised childhood could certainly, then, shape interventions in the lives of children—in the case of Lagos, the League demanded that the colonial state put an end to the employment of girls as hawkers.

As these examples attest, missionaries and women's and other kinds of social reform organisations tended to drive efforts to rescue African children (a rescue about which those children and their parents were frequently not consulted). But there were also some state interventions, even, as noted above, when colonial states were usually reluctant to pour money into social welfare programmes, especially before the Second World War. Writing about the Belgian Congo in the 1920s, historian and anthropologist Nancy Rose Hunt explores how the colonial state and mining companies embraced the pro-natalist interventions of the Ligue pour la Protection de l'Enfance Noir (the League for the Protection of Black Childhood). The Ligue opened the first of its clinics—called *gouttes de lait*, or drops of milk—in the Congo in 1914, aiming to reduce infant mortality 'by teaching African women the "art" of child rearing, cleanliness and hygiene' among other topics.[30] Despite the support of the Commission pour la Protection des Indigènes (Commission for the Protection of Aborigines) in Belgium, the Ligue's activities met with scepticism and resistance by doctors, missionaries, and the colonial state. This changed, though, as anxieties increased about low population growth and its implications for the colony's labour needs (one of the many appalling consequences of Leopold II's brutal regime in the Congo Free State). Efforts to extend hospitalised childbirth, provide propaganda promoting new forms of breast feeding and birth spacing, and schooling were all intended to grow and to civilise Congolese families. Similarly, some French colonies experimented with pro-natalist policies too. From the 1890s, the colonial state in Madagascar sponsored a public health system, efforts to disseminate modern (or Western) modes of childrearing to replace precolonial systems, and even festivals of children and the family to encourage the growth of the Malagasy population.[31] This pro-natalism was integral to labour policies, but it was also reflective of anxieties within France about a demographic decline and French power.

The image of the suffering African child has been useful to various institutions from the late nineteenth century onwards: from colonial states to international humanitarian organisations. This child embodied the contradictions of the racialised stereotyping of Africans—vulnerable and innocent, representing all the possibilities for a civilised African future, but also, at the same time, dangerous and in need of firm supervision—to help to justify colonial rule, and

[30] Nancy Rose Hunt, '"Le Bebe en Brousse": European Women, African Birth Spacing and Colonial Intervention in Breast Feeding in the Belgian Congo,' *The International Journal of African Historical Studies*, vol. 21, no. 3. (1988), p. 403.

[31] Margaret Cook Anderson, 'Creating a Labor Reservoir: Pronatalism, Medicine, and Motherhood in Madagascar,' in *Regeneration Through Empire: French Pronatalists and Colonial Settlement in the Third Republic* (Lincoln, NE, and London: University of Nebraska Press, 2015), pp. 110–158.

also interventions designed to reform African societies. As the examples cited above attest, the idea of the African child was a powerful one, producing significant efforts to alter childbirth and childrearing practices, and introduce forms of education and welfare improvement which would change the lives of children and young people.

But not all children on the continent fall into the narrow category of 'African'. The final section considers colonial states' responses to multiracial children, as childhood was progressively racialised.

Multiracial Children and the Racialisation of Childhood

Writing about the Lebanese population in West Africa, historian Andrew Arsan argues that historians and other scholars 'must find ways of making sense of the presence in colonial society of figures like the Eastern Mediterranean migrants of West Africa in terms which transcend the binary schemes of late colonial thought, and its anti-colonial obverse'.[32] His point is that while colonial states and anti-colonial activists on the continent may have believed that the societies in question were constituted solely of African subjects and European colonisers, the populations of these colonies were always more diverse than this binary would suggest. Not only Lebanese, but also Indian, Jewish, and other groups, found their way to Africa, and especially along the routes of trade and migration facilitated by empire in the nineteenth and twentieth centuries (although people from other parts of the world had settled in Africa before the partition of the continent too). They settled in African colonies alongside African and growing multiracial populations (the terminology for whom differed across time and place, including métis in French colonies and coloured or Anglo-African in British Southern African colonies). The children within these groups were understood by colonial states in a variety of ways: as contributing positively to the constitution of empires or, on the other hand, as representing a threat to the social order.

As historian TJ Tallie notes, 'The reproductive futurity established in settler states ... constitutes a privileging of the figure of the white colonial child as the hope for securing the occupation and legitimacy of the next generation of settlers.'[33] For white settlers in settler colonies, white children represented not only the future stability and prosperity of settler societies, but were also the means by which that stability and prosperity would be attained. As a result of this, settler states became increasingly interested in the welfare and education of white children, and especially from the end of the nineteenth century. One of the questions which concerned settler politicians, clergy, social reformers, and others was the difficulty of defining who precisely was a 'white' child. In

---

[32] Andrew Arsan, *Interlopers of Empire: The Lebanese Diaspora in Colonial French West Africa* (Oxford: Oxford University Press, 2014), p. 8.

[33] TJ Tallie, *Queering Colonial Natal: Indigeneity and the Violence of Belonging in Southern Africa* (Minneapolis and London: University of Minnesota Press, 2019), p. 8.

the nineteenth- and early twentieth-century Cape Colony, for instance, poor rural and urban communities were composed of people who, some commentators worried, were no longer 'white' or were in danger of becoming like the African or multiracial population. White poverty, in particular, appeared to undermine white people's claims to evolutionary, moral, and other forms of superiority. For this reason, white children—and particularly the children of the white poor—needed to be brought within the ambit of white respectability, usually through school, apprenticeship, or skilled employment (unlike black or multiracial children who were destined to be unskilled labourers). Like the girl hawkers of 1920s Lagos who did not conform to ideal notions of girlhood during the period, these white children in the Cape—and elsewhere in Southern Africa—did not conform to the ideal of innocent childhood.[34]

Writing about Southern Rhodesia—now Zimbabwe—between the 1930s and the 1950s, historian Ivo Mhike explains how anxieties about white children and families were heightened during the Great Depression:

> State officials were worried about the collapse of the white family because of the history and nature of Rhodesian settler white society. Rhodesia was built through white immigration, settlement and the exploitation of natural resources of the territory. … The family unit became an essential tool in driving natural population increase and fostering a specific set of values upon which Rhodesian settler society was based. … Natural population increase and the reproduction of 'white' values in children were key to the survival of white settler society.[35]

As a result—mirroring the South African state—the Southern Rhodesian government sponsored or supported measures aimed specifically at reducing the potential social upheaval caused by white girls described as delinquent. In these contexts, the ideology of the innocent child was progressively racialised: 'childhood' implied *white* childhood. In these societies, African children were not to have long periods of play and education under the supervision of parents, teachers, and other adults, but, rather, were sent out to work as soon as they were able. While the following chapter will consider the education provided to African children by missionaries, it is important to note here that making academically rigorous schooling available to African children was believed by many colonial officials in the nineteenth and twentieth centuries to undermine the project of colonial rule itself.

How, then, were multiracial children understood? The offspring of relationships between whites—in many contexts, colonial officials—and African (or Indian, or other not-white) women, these children and communities often occupied ambiguous positions within colonial societies, frequently as a result of

---

[34] SE Duff, 'Saving the Child to Save the Nation: Poverty, Whiteness and Childhood in the Cape Colony, c.1870–1895,' *Journal of Southern African Studies*, vol. 37, no. 2 (2011), pp. 229–245.

[35] Ivo Mhike, 'Intersections of Sexual Delinquency and Sub-Normality: White Female Juvenile Delinquency in Southern Rhodesia, 1930s–c.1950,' *Settler Colonial Studies*, vol. 8, no. 4 (2018), p. 577.

colonial and European disapproval of 'miscegenation' (or interracial sex). Historian Owen White explains:

> The lives of people of mixed race in French West Africa were shaped by a paradox. On the one hand, most métis could tell a story of individual rejection. The majority were left behind by their French father while they were still infants, if indeed they ever knew their father's identity, while a smaller number also found themselves abandoned by their mothers. At the same time, however, the French administration expressed great interest in their collective potential.[36]

This 'potential' lay in the fact that métis children were seen as mediators between French and indigenous societies, and, so, could act as interpreters of culture and language, for instance. As White concedes, this understanding of multiracial children in French West Africa did not necessarily produce better circumstances in which they would be raised and educated, but, rather, points to a different way of interpreting racialised childhood.

In British colonies, by contrast, interracial relationships were discouraged by colonial governments, which saw them as a threat to the colonial social order. In 1900, the Secretary of State for the Colonies, Lord Crewe, issued a circular prohibiting concubinage—unmarried sexual relationships—between indigenous women and British officers. The issue, argued colonial officials (who for the most part did not implement Crewe's rules), was not only that interracial sex was believed to undermine British claims to moral purity, but that it also drew colonial officials into webs of social relations and obligation with local families, undermining officers' capacity to act dispassionately in carrying out their official duties.[37] As a result, British administrators regarded multiracial people in their colonies as a conundrum: they could not fit neatly into any particular racial category and they potentially undermined the very project of colonial rule. Multiracial people were often regarded with suspicion by Africans too—and during the decolonial era were accused of having potentially pro-imperial political sympathies.

But as Christopher J. Lee argues in a study of multiracial people in Nyasaland—now Malawi—understanding interracial relationships within a longer history of inter-group relationships across Africa shows that marriage or sexual relationships across lines of identity were by no means specific to the colonial era. Multiracial children—or children belonging to more than one community, society, or culture—had long existed before the imposition of colonial rule.[38] The point is that colonial conquest, a modern ideology of childhood, and anxieties about race (specifically the maintenance of white suprem-

---

[36] Owen White, 'Abandonment and Intervention,' in *Children of the French Empire: Miscegenation and Colonial Society in French West Africa, 1895–1960* (Oxford: Clarendon Press, 1999), p. 33.

[37] Christopher J. Lee, 'Do Colonial People Exist? Rethinking Ethno-Genesis and Peoplehood through the *Longue Durée* in South-East Central Africa,' *Social History*, vol. 36, no. 2 (May 2011), p. 177.

[38] Lee, 'Do Colonial People Exist?' pp. 190–191.

acy) all combined to designate innocent childhood as white, produce the category of the African child, and position multiracial children as a problem. It is also important to remember that families understood themselves and their origins in their own ways too—their own accounts of their histories might not map precisely on to official thinking about appropriate or inappropriate relationships or childbearing.[39] As Arsan notes as regards children in the West African Lebanese community in the 1930s, they became vehicles for their parents' own ambitions for social mobility, attempts to maintain links with family and culture at home, and efforts to assimilate into Francophone society. Wanting to send their children back to Lebanon to receive a French education

> was driven not only by a diasporic longing for home, but also by … a desire for their children to acquire at once a sense of life in Lebanon and an acquaintance with French culture. And if they called their children Albert, Antoine, Michel, Hélène and Latifa … or Alfred, Adèle, Emilia and Joseph … it was only to keep up with the fashions of the Eastern Mediterranean, and to mark their accession to its Francophone middle classes while—at the same time—passing down the names of their fathers and mothers.[40]

Children carried with them, then, multiple meanings.

Conclusion

Four years after his arrival at Ekukhanyeni, Magema Fuze and two other young converts, William Ngidi and Ndiyane, accompanied Bishop Colenso on a visit to Mpande, the Zulu king, and his court. All three young men—then in their teens—wrote accounts of the journey and their time at court, and Colenso published these in 1860 as *Three Native Accounts of the Visit of the Bishop of Natal in September and October, 1859 to Umpande, King of the Zulus*. As the historian Hlonipha Mokoena points out, when Colenso asked the three to note down their experiences, this 'was not an open-ended invitation to write just anything'. Rather, 'he introduced his converts to those mainstays of Enlightenment letters—travel writing and the journal'.[41] As Mokoena observes, travel writing 'is a decidedly colonial genre'. And while Fuze, Ngidi, and Ndiyane did as they were told, they all recorded and emphasised different aspects of what they had experienced, producing, thus (and perhaps inadvertently), specific and personalised travelogues. Mokoena pays particular attention to an event recorded uniquely in Fuze's section: an encounter with two armed adult white men. One of them commanded Fuze to hold his gun while he jumped over a muddy stream, and, attempting to return the gun, Fuze 'sank into the mud'. Both men 'laughed' at him and one

---

[39] Lee, 'Do Colonial People Exist?' p. 186.
[40] Arsan, *Interlopers of Empire*, p. 187.
[41] Hlonipha Mokoena, *Magema Fuze: The Making of a* Kholwa *Intellectual* (Scottsville: University of KwaZulu-Natal Press, 2011), p. 98.

asked and said, 'Are you a boy of the Bishop, eh?' I assented, and said, 'Yes.' He said, 'Do you know it, to draw a bullock, and a horse, and a bird' I said, 'I know a little.'[42]

In this mocking exchange, the white men make clear that they understand—and probably disapprove of—the education Fuze has received with Bishop Colenso. They have marked him out as an educated convert and, thus, someone they might not regard in the same way as an unconverted Zulu boy of the same age, still living in the Zulu kingdom. Fuze's conversation with these men underscored how his education and time on the mission station had transformed him into a colonial mediator: in both the worlds of the settler colony and Zulu society, a translator between Bishop Colenso and Mpande, a Zulu young person writing in a colonial genre. He was both an insider and an outsider in a range of spaces, always acutely aware of how both his racial identity and age pushed him into positions of profound vulnerability. Although in many ways an unusual figure, Fuze is useful for exploring how children experienced the sharp edge of the imposition of colonial rule, because of their status as children: as embodiments of potential, as representatives of the future, children carried with them the plans and ambitions of their parents, missionaries, colonial administrators, and others. These burdens differed according to the race and gender of the child.

A melding of the relatively new ideology of the innocent child with scientific racism, and informed by shifting relationships between Europe and Africa, produced a stereotype of childlike Africans which served to justify colonial conquest. Or, put another way, the slave trade helped to produce a discourse which infantilised all Africans in the service of rescuing them from enslavement—and justified their colonisation. As a step further, African colonies were imagined as children, with their maturation resulting in the adulthood represented by decolonisation and independence. And yet, as the example of Buganda shows, Africans, too, could co-opt this language to anti-colonial ends. Children themselves became important for the making of colonial societies: while some became representatives of the future and were educated, others were regarded as undesirable and as signs of social collapse. In all of these debates, children's own views and perceptions of their experiences are often hard to grasp. But in accounts of their education, especially during and after colonial rule, it becomes easier to detect children and young people's motives, reactions, and interests. The following chapter turns, then, to schooling and education.

---

[42] Quoted in Mokoena, *Magema Fuze*, p. 100.

CHAPTER 5

Schooling and Education

In 1993, Chinua Achebe, the legendary author of the classic novel *Things Fall Apart* (1958), among other works, presented a lecture at Cambridge University, thinking through his experience of being educated at mission and colonial schools before, during, and after the Second World War in colonial Nigeria. Titled 'The Education of a British-Protected Child', Achebe addresses his audience from what he describes as the 'middle ground'. Invoking an Igbo children's rhyme which celebrates the good fortune of being in the middle, rather than first or last, Achebe explains that he chooses 'the home of doubt and indecision, of suspension of disbelief, of make-believe, of playfulness, of the unpredictable, of irony'.[1] He does this not to justify colonial rule—which he labels 'a gross crime'—but, rather, to make sense of what he gained and did not gain from his education as a 'British-protected child' or, in other words, as a subject of the British Empire in an African colony. It is interesting that this memoir of childhood is informed by attitudes and behaviours—playfulness, a desire for make-believe—which might be considered to be childlike.

Achebe was educated first at the Church Missionary Society's St Philips's School in Ogidi, Government College in Umuahia, and, finally, at what would become the University of Ibadan, the first institution of higher learning in Nigeria. Achebe's parents were Christian converts—his father was an evangelist—who had been educated at mission schools too, and he describes the bookish household he grew up in, complete with posters in English on the walls:

> My father filled our walls with a variety of educational material. There were Church Missionary Society yearly almanacs, with pictures of bishops and other dignitaries. But the most interesting hangings were the large paste-ups which my father created himself. He had one of the village carpenters make him large but

---

[1] Chinua Achebe, 'The Education of a British-Protected Child,' in *The Education of a British-Protected Child: Essays* (New York: Anchor Books, 2010), p. 6.

light frames of soft white wood onto which he then gummed brown or black paper backing. On this paper he pasted coloured and glossy pictures and illustrations of kinds from old magazines.[2]

These pictures ranged from 'a most impressive picture of King George V in red and gold' to advertisements for Johnnie Walker whisky and the Nigerian Railways. Achebe writes that his 'education went from the walls' of his family's home, 'through the village' to the mission school, 'and back again'.[3] Although the education that he received—from a good mission school and an excellent high school and university, from the first standard in primary school to a BA degree—marked him out as a member of a small, middle-class elite, Achebe captures something of the nature of education more broadly under colonial rule in the late nineteenth and early twentieth centuries. What schooling was made available to African children was provided most frequently by missionaries, whose chief interest was the conversion of children and their parents. From the interwar period and, especially, after 1945, colonial states became more willing to spend money on building secondary and tertiary institutions, many of which (like some mission schools) provided very high-quality teaching. But these institutions were beyond the reach of the vast majority of African children, most of whom only attended school in their numbers in the postcolonial period.

Achebe's emphasis on his ambivalent feelings about his education points to another feature of schooling under colonial rule. The emphasis of the syllabi at his high school, especially, was on introducing him and his peers to the literature and history of the United Kingdom. This was an overwhelmingly Eurocentric curriculum and one which he and his fellow students challenged while at university. At the same time, though, his parents were committed to ensuring that he and his siblings went to missionary and state schools, fully knowing the content of the education their children would receive. This education could serve many ends. As Christians, the mission school was an important site for the transmission of faith to the next generation. But high school and university also provided potential access to employment in the colony, and especially in the colonial administration. Being of the generation which was young during decolonisation, this education, perhaps ironically, positioned Achebe to take on significant roles in newly independent Nigeria, where new institutions needed skilled graduates to staff them (for instance, he worked initially for the colonial Nigerian Broadcasting Corporation and was later involved in founding the postcolonial Voice of Nigeria).

Achebe's reflections and trajectory help to explain why debates over education in colonial and postcolonial Africa were often fraught: they raised some of the key questions introduced by both colonial rule and decolonisation. Because education was often a tool for realising (or avoiding) different visions for the

---

[2] Chinua Achebe, 'The Education of a British-Protected Child,' pp. 10–11.
[3] Chinua Achebe, 'The Education of a British-Protected Child,' p. 11.

future, when educators, administrators, anti-colonial politicians, parents, missionaries, and young people debated education, they were concerned with more than simply what occurred in school. Understanding that interest in education extended beyond the colonial state and churches, and into African society, helps to illuminate how schooling was not simply a top-down imposition on parents and children but was also the terrain on which a range of ideas—about colonisation, African society, anticolonialism, nationhood, subjecthood, and citizenship, for instance—were worked out. To be sure—and as this chapter explores—forms of education existed well before the partition of the continent in the nineteenth century. As Chap. 2 showed, the socialisation of children in precolonial societies entailed their apprenticeship in a range of activities, from cooking and childcare to blacksmithing and herding. Madrasas and other educational institutions existed in Muslim societies. This chapter does not draw a sharp distinction between what might appear to be conventional schooling to contemporary readers—children gathered in a classroom overseen by an older or adult teacher—and those forms of education that occurred in households, workshops, or other venues. Rather, it uses an expansive definition of what constitutes education and schooling, surveying how children received intellectual and vocational training to prepare them for the lives they were to lead as adults. In addition to this, when missionaries and, later, colonial states founded schools in Africa, the model on which they drew in Europe was also in a state of significant change. The massification of education, the linking of schooling to the needs of the nation, the extension of schooling throughout childhood and adolescence, and the broadening of the curriculum, among other things, were debated and implemented to lesser and greater degrees in the nineteenth and early twentieth centuries in the industrialised regions of the globe.

Histories of education on the continent are, then, multiple and varied. Beginning with a section on precolonial forms of education, this chapter then moves on to the range of efforts to implement forms of education by Christian missionaries and also colonial officials in the nineteenth and twentieth centuries—uneven, complex, and fraught processes. As the third section demonstrates, African parents demanded or rejected education for their children for a range of reasons. And children and young people, too, responded to their experiences in schools and universities in a range of ways, to which the final section pays closer attention.

Precolonial Systems of Schooling and Education

When missionaries opened schools across sub-Saharan Africa in the nineteenth and twentieth centuries, they needed to persuade African parents that their children's best interests were served by sending them for hours every day to learn reading, writing, a little arithmetic, and about Christianity. Often, entry to the school was framed as being a step into colonial modernity—a process promoted by colonial authorities as well as by some African elites. While the curriculum and quality of teaching varied enormously across time and place and according to denomination, missionary society, and the resources of each school, the question they posed was the same: Why send children to these schools in the first place? In Achebe's novel *Arrow of God* (1964), Ezeulu, the chief priest of an Igbo village in the early twentieth century, decides to enrol one of his children in the local mission school:

> At first he had thought that since the white man had come with great power and conquest it was necessary that some people should learn the ways of his own deity. That was why he had agreed to send his son, Oduche, to learn the new ritual. He also wanted him to learn the white man's wisdom.

But this choice had left him with mixed feelings, as 'Ezeulu was becoming afraid that the new religion was like a leper', spreading quickly among the Igbo. Also, he had to speak 'strongly' to Oduche, 'who was becoming more strange every day' as a result of his exposure to both Christianity and Western schooling.[4] While *Arrow of God* is fiction and by no means an ethnography, this description of Ezeulu's reasoning for devoting one child to the mission school echoes the conversations Magema Fuze's father had with Bishop Colenso in nineteenth-century Natal. This was a strategic move, using a child to gain knowledge about and curry favour with a potential new power in the region. For both Magema Fuze and the fictional Oduche, though, this schooling did result in a complicated renegotiation of relationships with their families and their societies more broadly, and especially with unconverted Africans.

These two examples are also of elite families who could afford to lose a child to a mission school. For poorer parents, children were an important part of a homestead's labour force, contributing in multiple ways—varying according to the child's age, gender, and status—to its upkeep, from caring for livestock to collecting water. As Chap. 2 showed, all African societies inculcated in children and young people the skills they needed in adulthood. Writing about precolonial societies in what is now Ghana, historian Michael A. Kwamena-Poh identifies different forms of education occurring within households and villages. Through interactions with adults—their parents, close relatives, and, especially, those much older than them—children would learn cultural and social norms, as well as gain 'knowledge of their history, beliefs, and culture, thus enabling them to participate fully in social life'. But those destined to take on the 'office of priest, chief, hunter, state drummer, and musician' would need to acquire training from those individuals already occupying those roles, as would 'craftsmen, such as the weaver, the goldsmith, and the potter'. While these roles 'were, in general, hereditary and the acquisition of knowledge was through observation and practice, the training required for perfection might be long and specialised'.[5]

---

[4] Chinua Achebe, *Arrow of God* (New York: The John Day Company, [1964] 1967), p. 51.

[5] Michael A. Kwamena-Poh, 'The Traditional Informal System of Education in Pre-colonial Ghana,' *Présence Africaine*, no. 95 (1975), pp. 271–272.

For instance, a boy training to be a goldsmith would be apprenticed at about the age of eight or nine and would first learn the names and uses of the tools of his trade. After this, 'the apprentice followed the master-craftsman in his daily routine and learnt from what he did'. This was a process which lasted several years and involved not only learning how to work gold, but also the meanings associated with the objects he would be required to fashion, as well as a working knowledge of the currency used in the region: 'for the products of the goldsmith included gold weights for measuring the gold dust used locally as well as in the external trade with the Europeans on the coast'. If his father was a master-craftsman, then the apprentice would succeed him, taking up his 'tools and weights'. But, if not, 'he had to pass out of the training course'. To do this, his relatives would 'pay the necessary fees for the "passing-out" ceremony' in which the blessing of the gods would be sought for a new craftsman.[6] For girls learning to be potters in Shai society, instruction in preparing clay and the coils for pots began at a very young age, but they were only regarded as being skilled—or even proficient—potters having reached middle and old age. This was a life-long learning process.[7]

Learning from watching and doing, as well as from storytelling, provided skills and information needed by children and young people. But there were more formal institutions of learning too. Kwamena-Poh pays particular attention to the ceremonies which marked girls' and boys' entry to adulthood, at the beginning of puberty. Among the Krobo people, at the onset of menstruation, girls were taken to priestesses and older, post-menopausal women for instruction which

> covers all aspects of motherhood, housekeeping and all other nuances of domestic duties for a period lasting about nine to twelve months. In addition, she is given instruction in handiwork, such as pottery and basket weaving. At the end of the period the young girl is ceremonially bathed, dressed in fine clothes and seated on a white stool in her own home. She then receives gifts and congratulations from visitors. She will then, probably accompanied by other adolescent girls, parade the town in her finery. She will also dance in public to the *Klama* traditional songs and receive public ovation.[8]

Having graduated from her training with older women, the initiated Krobo girl was allowed to consider marriage. Similar schools existed for boys in Krobo and other societies in the region (and across the continent). Writing about her childhood in the 1920s and early 1930s, on the border between South Africa and what was then Basutoland, the anti-apartheid activist and community

---

[6] Kwamena-Poh, 'The Traditional Informal System of Education in Pre-colonial Ghana,' pp. 277–278.

[7] Kwamena-Poh, 'The Traditional Informal System of Education in Pre-colonial Ghana,' pp. 279–208.

[8] Kwamena-Poh, 'The Traditional Informal System of Education in Pre-colonial Ghana,' pp. 272–273.

organiser Ellen Kuzwayo (1914–2006) remembered her curiosity about what took place in similar initiation schools for Basotho girls. As a child in a Christian family, Kuzwayo was barred from participating in the *Lebollo* (initiation schools), despite living among women and girls who taught at or graduated from them:

> Some of the mothers in the community ended up as instructors and supervisors at the girls' *Lebollo* ... The girls ... were peaceful and harmless. On their return they assumed an air of superiority, and openly looked down on those who had not been through this process. In addition to this, they refused to share their experience of the *Lebollo* or give any information related to it with anyone of their age group who had not been there. ... All the same I got to know that for the two to three months that the girls were there they had female tutors who were themselves graduates of that school; further, that sex education was one of the areas given attention. ... The tutors in the *Lebollo*—who were commonly known as '*basue*'—played a very important role in building up the moral standards and personal stability of young girls of that time; a very important role, regardless of the low opinion educated Christian people had about Lebollo.[9]

Kuzwayo's reminiscences point to the tensions between converted and unconverted groups within African societies and also to the value of the information transmitted in initiation schools. As she notes later in her memoir, as a Christian child she received no information at all about sexual reproduction, a significant lacuna in her schooling. In contrast, she lauds the women of the *Lebollo* for providing this vital knowledge to young women—emphasising that sex education actually contributed to 'building up the moral standards and personal stability' of youth, instead of undermining morals and modest behaviour, as was argued by many missionaries at the time.

Of course, there were precolonial forms of schooling provided by religious authorities too. Rudolph T. Ware has described the long history of Quran schooling in West Africa, in which 'children memorise and recite the Holy Book of Islam and learn to read and write the Arabic script'.[10] Writing about Senegambia—the region composed largely of contemporary Senegal and the Gambia—he makes the point that Islamic education was 'firmly established' in the region by the fifteenth century, although it may well have taken root 200 or 300 years earlier, closer to the introduction of Islam to West Africa. He argues that these schools, which were attended by both girls and boys (although often for different periods of time), were a 'stimulus' for the expansion of Islamic religious culture across this part of the continent.[11] Similarly, in much of what is contemporary Ethiopia, the Orthodox Christian Church—whose

---

[9] Ellen Kuzwayo, *Call Me Woman* (Johannesburg: Picador Africa, [1985] 2005), p. 81.

[10] Rudolph T. Ware, *The Walking Qurʾan: Islamic Education, Embodied Knowledge, and History in West Africa* (Chapel Hill, NC: University of North Carolina Press, 2014), p. 1.

[11] Rudolph T. Ware, 'The Longue Durée of Quran Schooling, Society, and State in Senegambia,' in *New Perspectives on Islam in Senegal: Conversion, Migration, Wealth, Power, and Femininity*, eds. Mamadou Diouf and Mara A. Leichtman (Basingstoke: Palgrave Macmillan, 2009), pp. 22–23.

Photograph 5.1 A Quran school in Tabora, Tanzania, the Moravian Archives Herrnhut

deep history in the region reaches back at least to the fourth century CE—provided some schooling to boys. However, the modernising Emperor Menelik II (1844–1913) oversaw the opening of the first two Western-style schools in 1908. Having sent some students to Europe to be educated, Menelik understood the link between this form of schooling and the creation and maintenance of the bureaucratic nation-state. Similar to Japan under the Meiji Restoration during the second half of the nineteenth century, Ethiopia's emperors sought to modernise the state partly through the institution of Western schools. Following Menelik's example, Emperor Haile Sellasie opened a number of schools in the 1920s and 1930s, including an institution for girls, a teachers' training school, a school of art, and a technical school.[12]

These examples demonstrate, firstly, that education in precolonial Africa looked very similar to the forms of education available elsewhere in the pre-industrial world: most of it provided at home to raise children to assist in maintaining the household and to be equipped to set up their own households in adulthood. Vocational training produced new generations of skilled craftspeople, and religious authorities made available some schooling. As a result, and

---

[12] Richard Pankhurst, 'Education in Ethiopia during the Italian Fascist Occupation (1936–1941),' *The International Journal of African Historical Studies*, vol. 5, no. 3 (1972), p. 361.

secondly, colonial conquest did not introduce education to Africa, but, rather, Christian mission and colonial schools in the nineteenth and early twentieth centuries overlaid already existing forms of education. This colonial education was also inextricably bound up with the purposes and contradictions of nineteenth- and twentieth-century imperialism.

Education Under Colonial Rule: Missionaries and Colonial States

The previous chapter described some of Magema Fuze's experiences at Bishop John William Colenso's Ekukhanyeni Institution in colonial Natal in the late 1850s and early 1860s. Colenso had taught mathematics at the elite, private Harrow School in the United Kingdom between 1838 and 1842, and he intended his Natal school to serve a similar purpose: educating another elite to become or to join a colonial ruling class. As a result, the African pupils at Ekukhanyeni were taught a range of subjects which he believed would fit them for this future role, beyond only reading, writing, arithmetic, and religious instruction. But Colenso did not confine his approach to colonial education to his mission school, as historian Rebecca Swartz explains:

> Colenso published eighteen books for the use of missionaries and African scholars over the course of his career, including Zulu and English readers, introductions to science, translations of the Bible and tracts dealing with African life and customs. In spite of a context in which there was an increasing drive to pull Africans into the colonial economy as labourers, Colenso was committed to creating a different kind of pupil, one capable of scientific reasoning as much as hard labour.[13]

As Swartz notes, Colenso's approach to colonial education went contrary to those of the majority of the white settlers in the Natal Colony (and settlers across the British Empire) and many colonial officials, who believed that this intellectually focused schooling would not prepare Africans to be useful colonial subjects, primarily as labourers. Although Colenso advocated for teaching indigenous and African pupils in their home languages and incorporated information about African societies into his curricula, he was part of a broader movement which understood that education could be used to assimilate Africans and other colonial subjects into colonial society. Perhaps the best-known proponent of this stance was the British historian and politician Thomas Babbington Macaulay (1800–1859) who, in 1835, published his Memorandum on Indian Education, in which, among other things, he argued for the provision of English-medium schooling to elite Indian men, inculcating in these pupils a knowledge of British and European culture, history, and values. As he wrote, the purpose of this education was to produce Indian gentlemen 'in

---

[13] Rebecca Swartz, *Education and Empire: Children, Race, and Humanitarianism in the British Settlers Colonies, 1833–1880* (Basingstoke: Palgrave, 2019), p. 155.

blood and colour, but English in tastes, in opinions, in morals and in intellect'. In other words, Macaulay's project was an integrationist one, bringing into the fold of British civilisation—in the language of the time—an Indian upper class.

Macaulay was not the only politician to argue for the use of education to Anglicise and to civilise colonial subjects. Sir George Grey (1812–1898)—explorer and Governor of South Australia, New Zealand, and the Cape Colony—sponsored the opening of industrial schools for Maori and African children in those colonies. What constituted industrial education—which had originated in Europe in the late eighteenth century—changed over time and place, but usually had at its core training in practical subjects and was often aimed at poor or working-class children. Grey believed that industrial schools could function as a humanitarian intervention, civilising African or other indigenous children, a view which Colenso shared. As a result, Grey sponsored the founding of Ekukhanyeni. Clearly, in this and other South African examples, the institution was intended for an African elite, and Colenso modified the vision for vocational training—children at Ekukhanyeni were taught to plough, for instance—by including more scholarly instruction too. This was as much the product of Colenso's focus on pedagogical philosophy, as outlined above, as it was a practical response to circumstances where teachers proficient in vocational subjects were difficult to hire. Ekukhanyeni closed after only five years of operation and had faced significant opposition from Natal's settler society. The assimilationist position's power diminished as the nineteenth century wore on and especially after the Indian Rebellion in 1857 which was blamed partly on support for integration.

The story of Ekukhanyeni helps to reveal one of the key tensions within the provision of education under colonial rule: while figures like Macaulay, Colenso, Grey, and many others argued for making available education in various forms to African or other indigenous children on humanitarian grounds, hoping that schooling would serve to civilise these colonial subjects, their opponents believed that education would be the undoing of colonial rule. White settlers, colonial officials and politicians, and others insisted that African subjects were intended to function as labourers within colonial societies. Any education that did not prepare them specifically for this work was both unnecessary and even dangerous. Well-educated Africans might challenge white youth for skilled positions and might use their education to oppose colonial rule. This position was bolstered in the second half of the nineteenth century by race science, which posited that Africans were intellectually inferior to Europeans and other race groups.

This was not the only contradiction inherent to the project of colonial education. Another pertains to the role of the state. Although missionaries were largely responsible for the introduction of Western education to Africa initially and concerted state involvement in education occurred after the First World War, this did not mean that colonial governments were not at all interested in the question of schooling. Although her focus is on settler colonies, Swartz's point that 'local officials, the imperial government and settlers were all interested in what they termed "native education"' can be extrapolated broadly.[14] Grey's dispensing of funds to industrial schools is not the only example of colonial officials or European governments being willing to devote money to education in the colonies—something which will be discussed in further detail, below. It is little wonder that interest in education was so widespread—as historian Peter Kallaway explains, the form that education took reflected the overall purpose of the colonial endeavour:

> Was colonial education to be about creating African Christians/African workers/African subject/citizens who were to be the vanguard of social, economic and political modernisation and perhaps Westernisation (assimilation for the French) or was the role of the school and missions to prevent such modernisation and radicalisation by facilitating more productive life on the land for peasant farmers and contented 'tribesmen' or educated indigenes who would not threaten the colonial order?[15]

Mission and state aims were frequently at odds, and it was usually the case that there was no single 'state' or 'missionary' stance as regards colonial education. What constituted colonial education was under constant revision and, in Swartz's words, 'was always subject to negotiation'.[16] Colenso modified Grey's original vision for industrial education in a desire to create a new kind of Christian African subject, and missionaries and teachers adjusted curricula to suit what resources were available to them and to what parents and children were willing to tolerate.

Much of the debate over what should constitute colonial education stemmed from the fact that it occurred in the midst of a radical overhaul of education more broadly in Europe, as Kallaway explains:

> The influence of humanism, the legacy of the French Revolution, the impact of the Industrial Revolution and the movements for political and social reform, the challenges of mass education for a newly urbanised working class, the advent of vocational and technical education, the impact of the vast changes in the nature of science and technology...[17]

were all important for shaping shifting state and missionary education policies. In the nineteenth century, especially, there was no widely agreed-upon template for education to be taken from Europe and imposed on Africans. Mass education as it came to exist in the twentieth century did not exist during the partition of Africa, and the wisdom of extending education to

---

[14] Swartz, *Education and Empire*, p. 102.
[15] Peter Kallaway, 'Welfare and Education in British Colonial Africa, 1918–1945,' in *Education and Development in Colonial and Postcolonial Africa: Policies, Paradigms, and Entanglements, 1890s–1980s*, eds. Damiano Matasci, Miguel Bandeira Jerónimo, and Hugo Gonçalves Dores (Basingstoke: Palgrave, 2020), pp. 33–34.
[16] Swartz, *Education and Empire*, p. 133.
[17] Kallaway, 'Welfare and Education in British Colonial Africa,' p. 33.

working-class or otherwise socially marginalised children in Europe was under intense debate. As a result, education in Africa became a place to work out many of the debates over education in Europe. Kallaway notes, for instance, that the key debate in colonial education in Africa—should education be used to 'civilise' Africans or to keep them in their place—was another iteration of similar concerns in Europe:

> the central policy dispute over education in [Europe in] the nineteenth century which was waged between those who wished to explain the provision of mass education as part of an attempt to ward off radical political and economic change by an increasingly organized urban working class, and those who saw the social reforms through education as a means of extending democratic rights, social welfare and human dignity in modern society increasing divided by class divisions.[18]

In the African context, class anxieties were remade into racial anxieties, with the addition of the role of the civilising mission in justifying colonial conquest. Particularly until the interwar era, schooling was inextricably linked to the making of civilised Christian subjects. When African children entered Christian or mission schools opened by missionaries from abroad, they learned not only how to read and write in a European language, but also Christianity and how to *be* Christians. Most missionaries conflated European manners and fashions, diets, social and cultural norms, and labour practices, among other things, with being Christian and thus civilised. As a result, children in mission schools—and especially better resourced mission schools—were taught how to speak, move, and behave like middle-class Europeans. In 'The Education of a British-Protected Child', Achebe describes his mother's education at the turn of the twentieth century at St Monica's Girls' School, which had been founded in 1892 by the Church Missionary Society, a British Protestant missionary organisation. It was the first such institution for young women in Igboland. As the daughter of a 'village ironsmith', she lived with the school's principal and 'performed domestic chores in return for her education and keep'.[19] This arrangement was not an unusual one. Not only did pupils at mission schools often perform domestic labour—from laundry to gardening—but those whose parents could not afford the fees might also be put to work in exchange for their schooling. But what might seem more unusual was the fact that she enrolled after she had been betrothed to her husband, a Christian evangelist. Although Achebe does not provide any explanation for the timing of his mother's entry into Christian schooling, it might have been to prepare her for life as the wife of a Christian preacher. At school she would learn the skills necessary for her future role—reading and writing, some knowledge of history, geography, mathematics, and other subjects—and she would be subject to the school's transformation of her into a Christian woman. She

---

[18] Kallaway, 'Welfare and Education in British Colonial Africa,' p. 33.
[19] Chinua Achebe, 'The Education of a British-Protected Child,' p. 9.

would read and study the Bible, sing hymns and recite palms, listen to sermons, and wear European clothing, speak English, and adopt British manners.

For Achebe's mother, education at St Monica's—which remains one of Nigeria's most prestigious high schools for girls—was intended to transform her from village girl to Christian wife, ready to be a useful helpmeet for her husband. This was not an unusual educational trajectory for girls at missionary institutions which helped to produce an African middle class. Historian Nakanyike B. Musisi describes how elite Ugandan girls were sent to mission schools in the early twentieth century, partly to ensure that a new class of Western educated, Christian African men would find suitable wives to marry and, thus, be able to establish respectable, Westernised households.[20] In this way, the mission school continued the work of the mission station, where conversion to Christianity required that Africans not only confess Christ as their saviour but that they take on the markers of what missionaries believed to be Christian civilisation. Writing about Baptist mission stations in the Belgian Congo in the early decades of the twentieth century, Nancy Rose Hunt refers to the 'knife and fork doctrine' which required that converts living on or employed at mission stations learn to eat cuisine associated with the West, with knives and forks.[21]

The link between education and the civilising mission is particularly evident in the extension of schooling in Senegal. With a presence limited mainly to the Senegalese coast until the 1850s, there was no French policy for education in the region and what European-style schools existed were in the towns of Saint-Louis and Gorée, two major trading posts where French merchants and bureaucrats were well established. But in 1841, the French government requested that the Brothers of Christian Instruction—a Catholic teaching order—take charge of the publicly funded schools in Senegal. Historian Kelly Duke Bryant explains that the decision to hand over education to this religious order was a reflection of the more permanent French presence in Senegal and, as a result,

> these schools more overly pursued a civilising mission. The Brothers designed them to promote French civilisation; to spread French language; to teach academic subjects including mathematics, history, and geography; and to provide vocational training.[22]

---

[20] Nakanyike B. Musisi, 'Colonial and Missionary Education: Women and Domesticity in Uganda, 1900–1945,' in *African Encounters with Domesticity*, ed. Karen Tranberg Hansen (New Brunswick, NJ: Rutgers University Press, 1992), pp. 172–194.

[21] Nancy Rose Hunt, 'Colonial Fairy Tales and the Knife and Fork Doctrine in the Heart of Africa,' in *African Encounters with Domesticity*, ed. Karen Tranberg Hansen (New Brunswick, NJ: Rutgers University Press, 1992), pp. 143–145.

[22] Kelly M. Duke Bryant, *Education as Politics: Colonial Schooling and Political Debate in Senegal, 1850s-1914* (Madison, WI: The University of Wisconsin Press, 2015), p. 14.

Photograph 5.2 A sewing school at a mission, Ghana, c.1885–1895, Special Collections, Yale Divinity School Library

The majority of children and young people who attended were drawn from the métis (or multiracial) and African populations and tended to be from Christian communities, although Muslims did enrol as well. Boys who graduated from these schools went to work in business ('as bookkeepers, clerks, or traders'), and they were 'also prepared … to take up positions with the developing colonial government'. While girls were also provided with some teaching in academic subjects, their schooling focused 'on French, history, sewing, and other domestic tasks'. The overwhelming purpose of these schools, though, 'was to … gain converts to Christianity. Not only was conversion their mission, but [it was] also … critical to the process of civilisation.'[23] As France conquered more of Senegal from the 1850s, so officials 'often rushed to establish schools in newly acquired territories'. In 1892 the colonial government provided funding specifically for education, and by 1895, there were seventeen schools and by 1907 twenty-one schools in Senegal beyond the four Communes (Saint-Louis, Gorée, Dakar, and Rufisque). In the view of these administrators, 'education could, in addition to its practical purpose of training the workforce, engender support for French rule'.[24]

---

[23] Bryant, *Education as Politics*, p. 14.
[24] Bryant, *Education as Politics*, p. 16.

French attitudes towards assimilation in the Communes—where Africans had, potentially, citizenship and the right to vote for representatives in the National Assembly in Paris—were more complex. The colonial state funded and opened a number of schools in each of the four towns—including, among other kinds of institutions, primary, secondary, and vocational schools, most of them Catholic, with some secular—and attendance of those schools increased by the end of the nineteenth century largely, as Bryant makes the point, because parents 'had come to associate colonial schooling with advantages in employment'.[25] Administrators, though, understood the virtue of education to lie in its potential to assimilate. This occurred in a context where 'the French were never willing fully to assimilate the political and administrative structures of the Communes', meaning that what assimilation did happen was in the realms of the cultural and the educational, with schools in the Communes copying the curricula of schools in France, emphasising French language and culture.

In addition to this, new scientific theories arguing that Africans were incapable of becoming as civilised as Europeans, combined with a shift in the nature of French colonial rule as the territory which France governed in Africa massively expanded with the conquest of French West Africa in 1895, meant that the uses of schooling in most of France's African colonies changed at the turn of the twentieth century. The vast majority of African subjects were never promised or granted citizenship as was the case in the Communes, and, so, the 1903 education decree which created an education system for French West Africa 'categorised most schools ... as "village" schools where students would receive "adapted" education. Students would learn primarily spoken French, though reading, writing, arithmetic, agriculture, hygiene, and Arabic (in Muslim areas) would be covered in a more cursory way.' Most teachers would be African, the majority of them with relatively little training. Regional schools, where 'African instructors would assist European directors', in more important areas would offer a greater range of subjects, including classes on agricultural and manual trades. The best resourced institutions were, though, the 'urban schools' in the Communes, and there most métis and Africans deemed to be assimilated would send their children. Nevertheless, as Bryant observes, 'even these schools served a practical purpose—training future clerks, telegraph operators, customs workers, and other low-level employees of the colonial state'.[26]

This educational system was built on relatively little funding, which declined at the turn of the twentieth century, and relied on not particularly well-trained teachers. Skilled instructors—most of them from Europe—were hard to come by. It is worth emphasising how few children attended colonial schools. For primary schools in 1909, there were altogether fewer than a thousand boys and girls in the urban schools; 1733 boys and 74 girls in regional schools; and 1202 boys in rural schools. Including pupils in private schools and adults enrolled in

[25] Bryant, *Education as Politics*, p. 16.
[26] Bryant, *Education as Politics*, pp. 18–19.

education, altogether there were about 5440 people in primary education.[27] The history of colonial education in Senegal demonstrates the limits of colonial power, especially as regards pre-existing educational institutions. Particularly in the Communes, French administrators were keen to encourage Muslim parents to send their children to French schools, rather than to the Quranic schools which had long existed in the region. Through education, it was hoped, Muslims would learn fealty to the new French colonial state. As a result, officials from the 1850s introduced regulations intended to limit the work done by Quranic schools, which were perceived to represent a threat to the French education system. These provisions were all 'designed to bring Muslim children into French colonial schools while also undermining Quranic schooling and giving more oversight to the French'. But these efforts ultimately failed: Quranic schools 'remained popular and cost little to operate' and the marabouts—or religious scholars and teachers—who ran the schools found ways of accommodating or working around the French rules. Parents were not discouraged by the French state's efforts, and, in 1909, in contrast to the relatively low number of people in the French educational system, there were between 11,000 and 12,000 children in Quranic schools.[28] As Ware argues, it is as important to underscore that Quranic schools were themselves also subject to change in this period, with Sufism, for instance, infusing 'Quranic education with new social meanings' during a period of enormous social, political, and economic change as a result of colonial conquest and anti-colonial resistance.[29]

The example of Senegal is useful for understanding how education was coopted by religious organisations, religious scholars, and the colonial state, all for different ends. It demonstrates the degree to which the success of educational schemes depended on the willingness of parents to send their children to those schools—explained in greater detail below—and the willingness of European governments and missionary societies to fund those efforts. The rollout of colonial education was, thus, uneven. This is especially evident in other imperial contexts, where the state intervened in education much longer after conquest, if, indeed, at all. In 1884, Germany seized what became South West Africa—contemporary Namibia—and proceeded to employ genocidal methods to counter African resistance to the region's colonisation, killing tens of thousands of people between 1904 and 1908. In this context, education for the indigenous population remained entirely in the hands of missionaries. From 1902, the colonial state apportioned funds to mission schools which could prove that they taught German 'satisfactorily', and while the state had the right to inspect mission schools, it did not. As a result, for all intents and purposes, the Rhenish Missionary Society was in charge of educating the majority of children in South West Africa. The Rhenish missionaries had operated in the region pre-conquest, and were not the only missionary society

---

[27] Bryant, *Education as Politics*, p. 68.
[28] Bryant, *Education as Politics*, pp. 50–51, 68.
[29] Ware, 'The Longue Durée of Quran Schooling, Society, and State in Senegambia,' p. 29.

there, but they did run most of the schools in the colony.[30] In 1910, the Society held a conference to organise its schools, resulting, as Cynthia Cohen explains, in the first attempt to create a uniform system of education in the colony for the majority of children:

> schooling was to be given on five mornings a week in the following subjects: religion, reading, writing, arithmetic, German, singing, regional and nature studies and handwork of various varieties. The first four were to be taught as the main subjects while the remainder were subsidiary.[31]

Teaching was to be done by missionaries assisted by African instructors, and would be done in both German and the children's own languages. The fact that children were taught mainly to speak—rather than to read and write—German demonstrates the degree to which this schooling was intended to fit children for lives of labour in service of the colonial state and settlers. Most afternoons were taken up by learning practical skills, a task which the Mission's leadership took seriously. By 1912, the Rhenish Mission operated thirty-five primary schools, educating 1585 African children. At the end of German rule in 1919—one of the provisions of the Treaty of Versailles in 1919 was the reallocation of German colonies, mostly to other imperial powers—there were altogether 115 mission schools, teaching only 5490 children in a colony whose African and multiracial populations totalled roughly 200,000.[32]

What state education was provided to children in South West Africa was focused almost entirely on whites, and by 1919 there were seventeen primary schools and three high schools, one of them for girls, exclusively for white children. These were a mix of state and missionary schools, overseen by a school board (constituted in 1906) and an inspector, who began work in 1913. All these schools aimed to replicate the German curriculum in a concerted effort to maintain white supremacy in the colony. Teachers were German, and the curriculum—which included both academically and vocationally oriented subjects—was far more demanding than that taught in African schools. Compulsory education was introduced for white children between the ages of six and fourteen living within a four-kilometre radius of a school in 1906, and in 1911 the requirement was extended to all white children, with boarding houses built for children who lived far from schools. Unsurprisingly, funding was significantly higher for white schools: in 1909, the colonial state devoted 9000 marks to African children's education while, in contrast, in 1914–1915 officials spent 329,000 marks on whites. There were considerably fewer white children in school—only 775 in 1913, for instance.[33]

---

[30] Cynthia Cohen, '"The Natives Must First become Good Workmen": Formal Educational Provision in German South West and East Africa Compared,' *Journal of Southern African Studies*, vol. 19, no. 1 (1993), pp. 124–125.

[31] Cohen, '"The Natives Must First become Good Workmen,"' p. 119.

[32] Cohen, '"The Natives Must First become Good Workmen,"' pp. 119–120, 123.

[33] Cohen, '"The Natives Must First become Good Workmen,"' pp. 125–128.

Photograph 5.3 Boys working in the garden of the Livingstonia Mission in Malawi, 1903, The National Library of Scotland

As a settler colony, education was co-opted in a project of maintaining white rule over South West Africa. Something similar occurred in the Cape Colony—formally a British colony from 1815—from the 1870s, when colonial officials raised the alarm over how few white children were enrolled in school. However, during the first half of the nineteenth century, the Cape had experimented with a form of non-racial, free education funded by the government. The New System was launched in 1839 largely in response to the haphazard, poorly attended system already in place, dominated mainly by schools run by the local Dutch Reformed Church (DRC), but it was also an attempt to reform Cape colonial society. As historian Helen Ludlow explains, the New System 'drew upon a discourse of a late phase of evangelical humanitarian liberalism strongly associated with the abolition of slavery'.[34] Partly as a result of this, the colonial officials who proposed the System were able to secure the support of the Colonial Office. For a system which insisted on the teaching of an academically

---

[34] Helen Ludlow, 'Shaping Colonial Subjects Through Government Education: Policy, Implementation, and Reception at the Cape of Good Hope, 1839–1862', in *Empire and Education in Africa: The Shaping of a Comparative Perspective*, eds. Peter Kallaway and Rebecca Swartz (New York: Peter Lang, 2016), p. 85.

inclined curriculum, in English, by trained teachers, the colony's government needed to raise substantial amounts of money. Herein lay the roots of the System's failure. By the 1860s it had collapsed as a result of a combination of limited funding and poorly maintained bureaucracy. White, middle-class parents had never bought into an experiment in educating children across racial and class divides, either. So when the Cape Colony began to invest in the extension of education for poorer white children in the final decades of the nineteenth century, it did so via churches and, specifically, the DRC. Even more importantly, this willingness to devote resources to white children's education was born out of a fear that rural white poverty would destabilise white control of the Cape, and South Africa more broadly. In other words, education was put in the service of maintaining the settler colony.[35]

The New System and later efforts to encourage white children to attend school foreshadowed changes in other British colonies in Africa. Initially, British administrators had been content to allow missionary societies to found schools and generally take charge of education, dispensing funds periodically to assist in their efforts. Some colonial governments did open schools, but these were relatively few in number and existed side-by-side with mission schools. Only a handful of children attended schools in British colonies, and most of those who did were white or from other minorities or were from elite families. Colonial education in the nineteenth and early twentieth centuries schooled only a minority of children, even in settler colonies. As referred to earlier, in the nineteenth-century Cape Colony, for instance, poor, rural white parents resisted state demands that they send their children to school, and educational institutions were virtually non-existent in the two Boer Republics established by Dutch-Afrikaner white settlers in 1852 and 1854, with the exception of a handful of elite schools in the Republics' capital cities. It was only during the second half of the South African War between the Republics and Britain (1899–1902) that a majority of white youth from the Boer Republics received an education and that was in the schools established in the concentration camps for civilians run by the British. The express purpose of these schools was to encourage Boer children to develop an allegiance to the imperial project and to imagine themselves as subjects within a united South Africa.[36]

It was partly in response to this history of failure to bring Africans into schools (but also to other factors, as will be discussed below) that in the 1920s and the 1930s the Colonial Office sponsored a series of reports and surveys on the state of education in British colonies in Africa. The institution of the League of Nations' Mandates Commission—which was tasked with monitoring the rule of former German colonies—opened up the possibility for self-governance or even independence for those colonies deemed to be suitably advanced. This,

---

[35] SE Duff, *Changing Childhoods in the Cape Colony: Dutch Reformed Evangelicalism and Colonial Childhood, 1860–1895* (Basingstoke: Palgrave, 2015), pp. 88–111.

[36] SE Duff, '"Capture the Children": Writing Children into the South African War, 1899–1902,' *Journal of the History of Childhood and Youth*, vol. 7, no. 3 (Fall 2014), pp. 368–370.

as Kallaway remarks, 'led to tentative attempts to understand Africans as global citizens in a world where fascism and communism were influencing debates about the nature of colonialism, and nationalist movements were rising in the colonial world'.[37] Officials in colonies and in London had in mind both the ideological struggles of the interwar era and the wave of strikes which crashed over much of the continent in the 1930s, in which workers demanded not only better wages and employment conditions but also representative government. Education needed to fit these new circumstances. In the 1920s, a collection of reports (two by the Phelps-Stokes Foundation in 1922 and 1924, and the Colonial Office's *Memo on Education in Tropical Africa* in 1925) recommended greater state involvement in education, as well as the secularisation of schooling. They placed particular emphasis on using education to develop the countryside and encouraged the greater presence of African languages and cultures in the curriculum. In the following two decades, education and the development of African colonies were linked. For instance, the Colonial Office's education policies were led by the 1942 and 1944 Colonial Development and Welfare Acts, which aimed partly to boost the economies of Britain's African colonies in the midst of wartime. After 1945, as Britain began to plan for potential decolonisation—in India and beyond—the Colonial Office's 1948 policy document *Education for Citizenship in Africa* envisaged potential national education systems on the continent after independence.[38]

Even as Britain and, to some degree, France began to shift education policies to accommodate changed political and social landscapes after the Second World War, it cannot be underestimated how few children and young people were enrolled in educational institutions. Minorities of children attended schools in Algeria—a settler colony—and French West Africa. Kallaway explains:

> In Belgian Congo there was no effort to promote postprimary education or to give Africans access to jobs in the state bureaucracy for which they would require higher education. Much the same can be said for the Portuguese colonies of Angola, Mozambique, and Guinea, though for a tiny elite of *assimilados*, such schools provided access to the Portuguese language and limited access to employment.[39]

Ironically, apartheid South Africa was an anomaly under these circumstances. The 1953 Bantu Education Act represented the massification of education especially for African youth. But this legislation—which was, effectively, an attempt to wrest control of African education from missionaries and churches suspected of opposing apartheid—was done explicitly in the service of training

---

[37] Peter Kallaway, 'National Education Systems: Africa,' in *The Oxford Handbook of the History of Education*, eds. John L. Rury and Eileen H. Tamura (Oxford: Oxford University Press, 2019), p. 231.
[38] Kallaway, 'National Education Systems: Africa,' pp. 229–231.
[39] Kallaway, 'National Education Systems: Africa,' p. 232.

African youth as semi-skilled labourers for the apartheid state. Even more than that, Bantu education was anti-assimilationist, aiming to 'retribalise' African youth by providing them with schooling delimited by what apartheid administrators believed African children would find familiar. The Act removed state funding from mission schools, and every church, with the exception of the Roman Catholics, accepted that schools would be taken over by the state. This suspicion that mission schools provided African children with an education befitting settler or white children and youth was neither specific to apartheid South Africa nor to the mid-twentieth century. Since they had begun work, opening schools for African youth, missionaries were routinely accused by colonial administrators and other settlers of being too close, politically, to Africans and African converts and of, thus, working to undermine colonial or settler rule. However, as historian Linda Chisholm has demonstrated, some missionaries—such as the German Lutheran Hermannsburg missionaries in South Africa—were supportive of colonial rule and segregation and, in the case of South Africa, were loath, for reasons ranging from the theological to the political, to criticise apartheid. And some African parents and traditional leaders were supportive of the closure of mission schools, in favour of institutions run under the auspices of the Department of Bantu Education. Regardless, though, even as Bantu education opened up schooling to more African children than could be made available by the combination of mission and government-funded schools before the 1950s, its purpose was never to allow African children—and Indian or multiracial children—the same quality of schooling as that of white youth.[40]

This more complicated history of African responses to mission schools in South Africa undermines a widely held view that all missionary institutions provided excellent education to African pupils. That stereotype is the most true for the handful of mission high schools for children of the elite, many of them the sons and daughters of Christian converts. Schools which accepted girls emphasised their transformation into civilised Christian women, fitting them to become the wives of a new generation of middle-class professionals. Writing about elite girls' schooling in nineteenth-century Sierra Leone, scholar of education Fiona Leach remarks that these girls were part of a project of 'restructuring' African society in an image of middle-class Britain, one of the consequences of which was that, at times, girls' education was domestic and practical in focus, rather than intellectual.[41] There were, though, notable exceptions. For example, the Empress Mänän School in Ethiopia operated between 1931 and 1936 (its closure forced by the brutal Italian invasion of the country), employed French teachers with professional degrees, and emphasised both domestic and scholarly attainments, as historian Pierre Guidi writes:

---

[40] Linda Chisholm, *Between Worlds: German Missionaries and the Transition from Mission to Bantu Education in South Africa* (Johannesburg: Wits University Press, 2017).

[41] Fiona Leach, 'African Girls, Nineteenth-Century Mission Education and the Patriarchal Imperative,' *Gender and Education*, vol. 20, no. 4 (July 2008), p. 345.

Priority was given to language teaching and, in the practical field, to knowledge and skills relating to management of the home. In terms of morality, the school instilled humility, devotion to husband and family and good working habits. The objectives of Madame Garicoïx [the headmistress] were to prepare a refined 'hostess' and a home-maker equipped with technical skills.

In spite of the priority given to domestic skills, however, girls were also prepared for the French *Certificat d'études primaires*. This involved the teaching of academic subjects such as French, arithmetic, history, geography and drawing, which were the compulsory subjects for the examination.[42]

As the future wives of elite men, and the future mothers of an educated, modern Ethiopian upper middle class, these girls needed both the scholarly and practical training to make them skilled managers of households and the intellectual matches of their husbands.

One of the ironies of decolonisation was that anti-colonial movements were led by men and, to a lesser extent, women who were the graduates of these elite institutions. By the interwar period, missionary institutions were augmented by high schools opened by colonial states, with the purpose of moulding a new generation of African leaders. Some of these were sites for experimentation and not simply copies of similar elite schools in Europe. Writing about Achimota, the first state-funded high school in the Gold Coast—what is now Ghana—in the late 1920s, historian Cati Coe explains that it was opened by 'expatriate romantics of African culture and history' who sought to use the school 'to wed the best of Africa and the West to educate African leaders who, for the greater development of their nation, would at once be in touch with "the people" and serve as brokers of Western ideas'.[43] But this idealism soon withered in the face of the 'contradictions', in Coe's words, present at the founding of Achimota: subjects (drumming and dancing) related to the teaching of 'African culture' were made extracurricular; most of the senior teachers were from Europe with little knowledge of the societies of the Gold Coast; and 'there was more of a focus on students' appreciation of "African culture" than on actual competence or knowledge'. 'African culture' was defined, narrowly, as a collection of unchanging traditions 'of a reified "ancient" past' and students were never encouraged to participate actively in analysing, contesting, or re-defining what might constitute 'African culture'. Nevertheless, Achimota represented an attempt by the colonial government at 'guiding the future of the Gold Coast through education', partly in response to increasing pressure from local

---

[42] Pierre Guidi, 'Independence and Influence: Empress Mänän School—An Ethio-French Girls' School in 1930s Ethiopia,' in *Empire and Education in Africa: The Shaping of a Comparative Perspective*, eds. Peter Kallaway and Rebecca Swartz (New York: Peter Lang, 2016), p. 85.
SE Duff, *Changing Childhoods in the Cape Colony: Dutch Reformed Evangelicalism and Colonial Childhood, 1860–1895* (Basingstoke: Palgrave, 2015), p. 307.
[43] Cati Coe, 'Educating an African Leadership: Achimota and the Teaching of African Culture in the Gold Coast,' *Africa Today*, vol. 49, no. 3 (Autumn, 2002), p. 24.

Photograph 5.4 Pupils at the main entrance of the Marist Brothers College, Kisangani, Democratic Republic of Congo, c.1920–1940, Special Collections, Yale Divinity School Library

elites—supporters of anti-colonial nationalism—for better secondary and higher education.[44]

In contrast, the Lovedale Institute—founded in 1841 by the Glasgow Missionary Society—in the Cape Colony was opened initially to educate the children of missionaries as well as some Africans. But its first principal, William Govan, believed in the necessity of providing all the pupils at the institution, regardless of racial identity, with the same education received by middle-class Scottish children, including overtly academic subjects like Latin and Greek. Despite recurrent funding crises and intense settler opposition—including from the Cape's Superintendents for Education—to this scholarly teaching, Lovedale persisted in maintaining its academic standards, offering university-level courses, and training ministers and teachers. Its teachers advocated for the extension of secondary education to Africans more broadly and Lovedale educated generations of anti-colonial, anti-segregationist, and anti-apartheid activists, both men and women. It was also—like the Inanda Seminary, Adams College, and Healdtown, among other missionary schools—one of the major sites for the making of an African middle class.[45] While student activism at Lovedale will be discussed below, it is important to note here that the pupils at the institution—and at other missionary and colonial schools across the

---

[44] Coe, 'Educating an African Leadership,' pp. 25–26.

[45] DE Burchell, 'African Higher Education and the Establishment of the South African Native College, Fort Hare,' *South African Historical Journal*, vol. 8, no. 1 (1976), pp. 60–64.

continent—were not passive recipients of schooling. They spoke back to their teachers, protested, and even rebelled against rules or practices they experienced as unfair or racist. Schools were sites where colonial rule and the ideas which underpinned and justified it were debated—even if the teachers at those institutions had little desire for this to occur.

What this broad overview of education in colonial Africa has shown is that for all the policy documents and colonial discourses about the virtues of assimilation or the necessity of maintaining the purity of African culture (however that might be defined), and of the importance of civilising Africans through education, the extension of schooling across the continent under colonial rule was ad hoc. It is difficult to generalise the content and experience of missionary education, and colonial states' efforts to found schools often fell apart over the practicalities of providing adequate funding, seeking out properly trained teachers, and implementing curricula. This is not to suggest that the rollout of new education systems, particularly after the First and Second World Wars, was incapable of causing harm—the case of Bantu Education (which will be explained further in Chap. 7) exemplified precisely that. Rather, it suggests that colonial education was never a top-down, one-way imposition of European education on Africans. The following section pays closer attention to parents' and children's responses to this schooling.

Parents' and Pupils' Approaches and Responses to Schooling

Chinua Achebe attended a high school and university which were established during the interwar and post-war period of colonial investment in education, welfare, and development. Opened in Umuahia in 1929 (alongside another, similar boarding school in Ibadan) it 'was a byword in Nigeria for excellence' and Government College remains one of the country's best high schools. Umuahia was founded in a similarly utopian spirit as Achimota. Its first headmaster, the Rev. Robert Fisher, designed the school's crest, which included 'a pair of torches, one black, one white, shining together silently'.[46] The institution's purpose was to educate a class of Africans who would serve to translate or mediate cultures and societies, bringing together Western and African intellectual, political, and social traditions and practices. And this despite the fact that most of the content of the teaching related to Europe and to Britain. During Achebe's early years at the school in 1946 or 1947, it was visited by the members of the Elliot Commission, an example of the post-war movement to open up educational and other developmental opportunities to Africans. One of the commissioners was Julian Huxley, the first Director of the United Nations Educational, Scientific and Cultural Organisation (UNESCO), an institution which encapsulated the utopian internationalism of the mid-twentieth century. (During their visit to the school, while most of the commis-

---

[46] Chinua Achebe, 'The Education of a British-Protected Child,' p. 23.

sioners 'came to chapel service on Sunday morning', Huxley 'roamed' the 'extensive grounds' of the school, 'watching birds with binoculars'.)[47] The Elliot Commission recommended that an institution of higher learning be opened in Nigeria, and what is now the University of Ibadan was founded in 1948. Achebe was one of the first students to enrol there. Like his high school, its curriculum was overwhelmingly Eurocentric:

> In my final year at Ibadan, I once had a chance to discuss with Professor [of Religious Studies, James] Welch one of a growing number of disagreements the students were beginning to have with the college. He was then vice principal. In some exasperation he said to me, 'We may not be able to teach you what you want or even what you need. We can only teach you what we know.'[48]

Welch's response—and the frustrated question from Achebe which prompted it—captures something of the friction at schools across the continent: African students demanding to be taught more about the continent, and teachers either ill-equipped or unwilling to do so. Chapter 7 will consider in greater detail the occasional explosions of student protest at mission and colonial schools, events which were produced as much by circumstances specific to each institution (bad or not enough food, crowded living conditions, harsh discipline) as they were by broader political and social contexts. This section, though, is on how parents and young people themselves understood the value of schooling. One of the most profound explorations of one young African woman's desire for education is in *Not Either an Experimental Doll*, a correspondence collected and edited by historian Shula Marks. The book includes letters written between the late 1940s and early 1950s, between an adolescent African girl Marks dubs Lily Moya and the British-born educationalist Mabel Palmer (1876–1958). Sixteen-year-old Moya wrote to Palmer in 1949, in her capacity as the co-ordinator of the University of Natal's division for African, Indian, and other non-white students, asking that she be admitted to study as a college student, even though she had not yet completed her final school examinations (or her Matriculation Certificate). The daughter of migrant workers who was in the care of relatives in the rural Eastern Cape, Moya's family were Christian converts—on the edges of the country's small African middle class—but lacked the funds for her to complete her education:

> I'm still at home not in school, only due to financial embarrassment. My heart aches when I see other children having gone and still going to school.
> I humbly beg you to sympathise with me. The only way you can show your sympathies is by taking me in your College to complete this Matriculation Course this year.

---

[47] Chinua Achebe, 'The Education of a British-Protected Child,' p. 21.
[48] Chinua Achebe, 'The Education of a British-Protected Child,' p. 22.

> Really there is no other way possible for me to carry on my education without your monetary assistance. Don't put me in for the coming year—would die if I stay a whole year out of school.[49]

Palmer arranged for her to attend the prestigious Adams College, a missionary institution in Natal. Although relations between Moya and Palmer eventually soured, a constant in their letters was the intensity of Moya's desire to receive an education, which she conceptualised as a route out of rural poverty. Her and Achebe's experiences demonstrate how education—and also the processes of conversion to Christianity, which often accompanied this education—was not a 'colonisation of consciousness'.[50] Rather, Africans responded to schooling and Christianity in a multitude of ways, sometimes accepting, often rejecting, and also remaking the content of their schooling and the sermons they might have heard.

Historian Carol Summers has described African responses to education in Southern Rhodesia—now Zimbabwe—in the first half of the twentieth century. She makes the point that education was of interest to a range of people in this settler colony—from missionaries to colonial politicians and from settlers to middle-class Africans—all of whom 'had high hopes for education's power to transform and improve individuals, communities, and the region as a whole'. And 'Africans had specific educational expectations and wants' linked to a perception that education might enable access to jobs and other opportunities in the colonial state. As she makes the point, though, that was precisely the lie of colonial schooling. In reality, schools were shaped by 'the dynamics of Southern Rhodesian colonialism' and, as a result, 'created a space for conflict, instead of a simple gateway to opportunities and patrons'.[51] For instance, in Gutu District in the southern part of the colony, in the 1920s and 1930s African parents protested the low quality of education provided by the DRC, the only mission church recognised by the colonial state in the area. Not only did it not provide the kind of schooling African parents found useful—most importantly, English language learning and skills training for jobs—but the schools were also poorly maintained and resourced and teachers were badly trained. Parents accused DRC teachers of hosting dances where adolescents might have illicit sex, something from which missionaries might profit 'since they levied fines in money or cattle on each pupil or mission adherent caught at illicit sex, or with responsibility for an out-of-wedlock pregnancy'.[52] Parents and pupils responded by staying away from school—despite rules which punished truancy—as well as through petitions demanding better education. In 1931, Africans began to

---

[49] Shula Marks, *Not Either an Experimental Doll: The Separate Worlds of Three South African Women* (Bloomington, IA: Indiana University Press, 1988), p. 60.

[50] Jean and John L. Comaroff, *Of Revelation and Revolution: Christianity, Colonialism, and Consciousness in South Africa*, vol. I (Chicago, IL: University of Chicago Press, 1991), p. xi.

[51] Carol Summers, *Colonial Lessons: Africans' Education in Southern Rhodesia, 1918–1940* (Portsmouth, NH: Heinemann, 2002), pp. 3–4.

[52] Summers, *Colonial Lessons*, p. 7.

establish their own schools via the independent Zionist Church, emptying out the DRC schools in the process:

> Independent schools attracted a wide spectrum of students, including some middle-aged men and some women with babies on their backs, but the vast majority of students were men between the ages of 18 and 30. These schools were attended by ex-DRC students who wanted to learn more.[53]

While the independent schools were short lived and strongly opposed by the colonial state, children did not necessarily return to the DRC schools in great numbers. As Summers explains, the DRC schools did eventually improve to some degree, offering better English tuition and curtailing the use of violence to discipline pupils. This was due entirely to pressure from African parents but, as she notes, there were limits to what they could achieve under colonialism: 'African activism in Gutu … did not succeed in developing new standards to which the DRC would be held. It did, however, force the DRC to try to meet standards set and kept by' the colonial state.[54]

One of the reasons why African pressure did manage to exercise some impact in Gutu was that senior men—some of whom held political authority—supported the shift away from DRC schools. Across the continent, schools could

Photograph 5.5 Pupils at a school in Tsévié, Togo, c.1920–1940, Special Collections, Yale Divinity School Library

[53] Summers, *Colonial Lessons*, p. 12.
[54] Summers, *Colonial Lessons*, p. 15.

be powerful tools for chiefs and other African authorities. In early twentieth-century Senegal, for instance, chiefs could 'curry favour' with colonial authorities by cooperating in educational initiatives.[55] At the same time, some chiefs in South Africa viewed mission schools as infringing on their own authority over the communities they governed. Others supported the transformation of mission schools into state schools under Bantu education in the 1950s, in the belief that the shift away from missionary authority would give them greater control over those schools.[56] Schools could, thus, confer significant authority to elites. Writing about interwar Zanzibar—then a British Protectorate, but under the authority of the Sultan of Zanzibar—Corrie Decker describes the founding of the Arab Girls' School in 1927, the first government-funded school for girls on the island. The institution's early success rested on its embrace by Zanzibari elites:

> The Arab Girls' School was the embodiment of elite Arab male discourses on *heshima* ('respectability'). Everything about the school—the building, location, curriculum, and culture—upheld the ruling family's regime of respectability.[57]

But this school also functioned to promote modern Islamic reform and to demonstrate that an embrace of modernity would not prevent the school's pupils from going on to become good Muslim wives and mothers. On the contrary, the school suggested that their modern education fitted them even better to raise future modern Zanzibari elites (echoing, thus, similar justification for elite women's education in Europe, the United States, and elsewhere). The Sultan's endorsement of the school was vital for persuading parents to send their daughters there. But the institution had to appeal to parents directly too: the school's first pupils were the daughters of men who had also been educated in government schools, a schooling which had smoothed the way of some of them into government positions as teachers or officials. Mothers and grandmothers who worried about their daughters' marriage prospects were invited to the Arab School on special Mother's Days to demonstrate to them the value of their daughters' education. One particular area of contention was the practice of *ukungwi* or the initiation that a girl received upon beginning to menstruate. Muslim male reformers held up education as a tool for ending a practice they condemned as barbaric and associated with backward 'African-ness', so when Zanzibari mothers and grandmothers realised '"modern" girls' education was meant to eradicate *ukungwi*, one of the few areas of public life dominated by women, they objected vehemently'.[58]

The Arab Girls' School became, then, a site for a gendered fight over race (the attempted 'Arabisation' of elite girls) and modernity (the relinquishing of

[55] Bryant, *Education as Politics*, p. 10.
[56] Chisholm, *Between Worlds*.
[57] Corrie Decker, *Mobilising Zanzibari Women: The Struggle for Respectability and Self-Reliance in Colonial East Africa* (Basingstoke: Palgrave Macmillan, 2014), p. 21.
[58] Decker, *Mobilising Zanzibari Women*, pp. 37–39.

precolonial custom for modern education). But what of girls' experience of their education? They walked a complicated line between maintaining the respectability that was so valuable for their parents (their mothers especially) and presenting themselves as modern, literate young women. At the same time, it was precisely this literacy which gave these young women access to books, magazines, and popular culture from abroad, and so they could fashion themselves as Modern Girls (a category which includes flappers in the West, for instance), testing the relative freedom that schooling allowed them within Zanzibari society. Although the Modern Girl was accused routinely of superficiality and unseriousness, being able to read about different ways of being a girl in the world permitted many of the pupils at this institution to fashion alternative futures for themselves, although only as far as was possible under the circumstances in which they operated. Decker quotes Muna, who attended the Arab School in the 1950s and was among the second generation of her family to go to government schools and who eventually graduated with a degree from Makerere University in Uganda, one of the most prestigious universities on the continent. Her education gave her the freedom to embrace her tomboyishness, regardless of the comments of her family's neighbours:

> radical families sent their daughters to school... Well, the neighbours are the ones who mind. And they are the ones who published stories. 'So-and-so's daughter put on some trousers. So-and-so's daughters plays rounders in shorts.' But now they're letting up. They know they can't do anything about it. We were the pioneers, so onwards and upwards. Spearheading a movement we had to pierce this and pierce that.[59]

Muna's sense of herself as a pioneer is complicated by her criticism of the school's curriculum: her 'hatred' of subjects like sewing and her dislike of the Eurocentric history textbooks (even if she and her friends made 'fun of the pictures' in their books, 'laughing about whether they would marry the man with or without "whiskers"').[60] Muna and her classmates took what was interesting and useful to them in their education and rejected that which bored or insulted them or which they felt was irrelevant. They transformed their schooling into a tool to fashion themselves and their futures.

Conclusion

Education under colonial rule was unevenly distributed, tending to privilege Christian converts and the politically well connected. It helped to produce a middle-class African elite of mostly men, but also some women, who, ironically, were among the first seriously to criticise colonial rule and to mobilise in

---

[59] Corrie Decker, 'Reading, Writing, and Respectability: How Schoolgirls Developed Modern Literacies in Colonial Zanzibar,' *The International Journal of African Historical Studies*, vol. 43, no. 1 (2010), p. 113.

[60] Decker, 'Reading, Writing, and Respectability,' p. 97.

Photograph 5.6 A kindergarten in Blantyre, Malawi, staffed by African converts and a British missionary, 1926, The National Library of Scotland

favour of decolonisation. One of the main achievements of postcolonial African states—despite the embrace of the project of development by some European governments—was the rollout of mass education during and after the 1960s. On independence in 1963, 900,000 children were enrolled in Kenyan primary schools, a figure which grew to 5.5 million by the 1990s. Across the continent, 'primary enrolments went from 43 percent of the population in 1960 to 77 percent in 1997, secondary from 3 percent to 26 percent, university from practically nil to 4 percent'.[61] Funding for schooling and teacher training remains limited, though, and African educational attainments are some of the lowest in the world. But it is worth noting how exceptionally few children attended school before the early 1960s and how disorganised the provision of education was: often the province of missionary societies and churches and badly funded by colonial states.

Education was also a site of experimentation and of contestation. Schools were accused by settlers and colonial officials of undermining colonial rule by training African students too similarly to white middle-class pupils, and they were used by some European politicians and colonial administrators as laboratories for the making of new African elites who would draw from African tradition and European modernity in the making of new African societies. They were places where colonial elites could remake themselves as modern, even as members of that same class feared the erasure of customs and practices they

---

[61] Frederick Cooper, *Africa Since 1940: The Past of the Present* (Cambridge: Cambridge University Press, [2002] 2009), p. 111.

Photograph 5.7 A Roman Catholic mission school in Bailundo, Angola, c.1920–1940, Special Collections, Yale Divinity School Library

believed to be essential in making young men and women; they were potential routes into employment and patronage, even as Africans resented them for the violence which occurred in classrooms and the intellectual poverty of the curriculum. Education was held up as the most powerful tool in civilising Africans (whether that meant conversion to Christianity, assimilation into European culture, or the imbibing of a particular version of African history and culture) as it was underfunded and badly run.

Achebe's decision to write about his education as a British-protected child from the 'middle ground' makes sense under these circumstances. However, as his experience demonstrates too, through schools, children were aware of how colonial rule tried and failed to mould them into new kinds of colonial subjects. They resisted this, used it strategically, and reflected on it. Like Ellen Kuzwayo, enrolment in a school placed them outside of the worlds of children who still participated in precolonial forms of education—like the initiation schools whose graduates she enjoyed watching as they danced. But this education was always limited to a small group of children. The majority of children worked.

CHAPTER 6

Work and Play

In 1981, eleven-year-old Esnart took up an offer of employment as a domestic worker in Lusaka, the capital of Zambia. Esnart was one of nine children, born to a couple who worked as subsistence farmers in the country's Eastern Province. Her father's alcoholism meant that her mother was responsible for caring for the household as well as performing the vital agricultural labour which would support the family. When the wife of a former teacher of Esnart's approached her parents with news of the position, it was in the awareness that even the low wages she would earn in the capital would make a significant impact on the family's finances. In Lusaka, she worked for a middle-class family, performing similar tasks to that which she had undertaken at home, helping her mother to run the household. Historian Sacha Hepburn—who collected Esnart and other Zambian domestic workers' recollections a few decades after their initial employment as children—remarks that Esnart's remittances became exceptionally important to her family:

> Esnart regularly sent all of her wages home to her mother. This was her family's only source of cash income. She explained, 'even if I send everything I will still have something to eat, somewhere to sleep.' Esnart placed high value on her ability to work so that she could offer this support to her family.[1]

Other girls left home to lighten their parents' financial burden, reducing the numbers of children for whom they had to care. At about the same time that Esnart left for Lusaka, fifteen-year-old Grace travelled from her parents' house in Northern Province to live with her sister in Lusaka. A year previously, Grace had been forced to give up her education because her parents could no longer

---

[1] Sacha Hepburn, '"Bringing a Girl from the Village:" Gender, Child Migration, and Domestic Service in Post-Colonial Zambia,' in *Children on the Move in Africa: Past and Present Experiences of Migration*, eds. Elodie Razy and Marie Rodet (Woodbridge: James Currey, 2016), p. 74.

© The Author(s), under exclusive license to Springer Nature Switzerland AG 2022
SE. Duff, *Childhood and Youth in African History*,
https://doi.org/10.1007/978-3-031-11097-9_6

afford the fees. In Lusaka, she found a position as a live-in domestic worker—like Esnart—but, unlike Esnart, she did not send home her wages:

> Though Grace was acutely aware of her family's difficult financial circumstances, her primary motivation for migrating to Lusaka was to complete her secondary education. Grace's employer supported her ambition to study. For five years Grace worked in her employer's home from 6 am to midday and attended a nearby high school in the afternoon. She then continued with domestic work in the evenings and at weekends. After completing her studies, Grace found employment as a hostess in a local restaurant.[2]

In these two cases, girls' employment shielded one family from absolute destitution, and allowed another young woman to receive an education and to take up better remunerated work. As Hepburn argues, it is vital to understand these two girls' experiences in broader context: in the 1980s, women's participation in Zambia's labour force increased by 155 per cent. This enormous growth included women who had achieved the qualifications to enter white collar and professional positions, as well as those who found jobs in the service industry and in the informal sector. These adult women's entry into the world of work was underpinned, though, by an expansion of the numbers of women domestic workers: 'Zambian women's ability to work outside of the home often depended upon them finding a replacement to care for children and complete other domestic work.'[3] The cases of Priscilla and Jane demonstrate why girls were especially in demand for this work. In the 1980s, Priscilla (a university-educated librarian and archivist) and Jane (a schoolteacher) both sought out girls to assist them after the birth of their first babies. 'Priscilla asked her older sister, who lived in rural Eastern Province, to "bring a girl from the village"' and Jane 'asked her husband's sister to help her find a female child from her village'. In this way, 'professional women balanced work and motherhood by relying on the labour of female children'.[4]

These experiences of girls and women in postcolonial Zambia demonstrate the complexity of writing histories of children's employment. As historian Wiseman Chijere Chirwa explains, 'child labour' is difficult to define. Firstly, the category of 'child' is, as we have seen, malleable and subject to change over time and place. Would, for instance, eleven-year-old Esnart and fifteen-year-old Grace have been treated similarly, one being on the cusp of adolescence, the other nearing the completion of her high school education? Secondly, 'labour' is not necessarily sharply defined either. On the one hand it 'occurs in a variety of disguised forms'. The younger domestic workers in 1980s Lusaka may have looked like younger relatives, and that was part of their appeal to the women who hired them. On the other, the boundaries between 'labour' and other kinds of activities were often difficult to discern. Labour could also 'be a form

---

[2] Hepburn, "'Bringing a Girl from the Village,'" p. 75.
[3] Hepburn, "'Bringing a Girl from the Village,'" pp. 77–78.
[4] Hepburn, "'Bringing a Girl from the Village,'" p. 78.

of socialisation and acculturation' (as girls in pre- and colonial societies cared for younger children in preparation for motherhood); it could be education (as children learned the trades that would support them in adulthood); it could be play. In addition to these questions of definition are complicating factors, such as parents' support for their children's entry into the labour market, and, as the Zambian examples referred to above attest, children and young people's own decisions to go to work. (Although the degree to which they made those choices freely is debatable.) And underpinning all of these complications is the status of child labour as an 'emotive' issue, in Chirwa's words.[5]

The association of children's wage-earning labour with exploitation—the view that childhood is incompatible with work—has driven global campaigns to eradicate child labour from the early twentieth century. But this is a relatively recent notion, and one which has been taken up unevenly around the world. In addition to this, as Hepburn and April Jackson make the point, not all forms of children's employment are necessarily 'harmful to children's physical and mental development'. As a result, historians and other scholars of childhood distinguish between children in employment or at work, and child labour which exploits children.[6] This chapter pays attention, then, both to children's employment and to child labour, seeking to understand why children entered the workforce, the nature of the work they undertook, and their experiences of it. The chapter is also interested in play and in children's leisure. Not only did work and play frequently overlap, but also many of the debates over children's employment in the colonial era encompassed anxieties about how they might use their free time. Concerns about labour and play were two versions of the same debate. However, this chapter begins in the precolonial era, when those categories of play and work were much more difficult to disentangle.

CHILDREN, WORK, AND PLAY IN PRECOLONIAL SOCIETIES

Although child labour was a feature of colonial rule across the continent, as Chirwa argues: 'It is worth noting that the use of children in agriculture and domestic chores was not a creation of the colonial economy.'[7] Perhaps most importantly, children were enslaved in many precolonial societies, and as pawns were required to work for the people into whose care they were loaned. As Chap. 3 demonstrated, most enslaved and pawned people on the continent were children, and many of those transported across the Atlantic or into the Indian Ocean world were children and young people. Political scientist Beverly Grier describes the kinds of labour undertaken by unfree children:

---

[5] Wiseman Chijere Chirwa, 'Child and Youth Labour on the Nyasaland Plantations, 1890–1953,' *Journal of Southern African Studies*, vol. 19, no. 4 (1993), pp. 663–664.

[6] Sacha Hepburn and April Jackson, 'Colonial Exceptions: The International Labour Organization and Child Labour in British Africa, c.1919–1940,' *Journal of Contemporary History* (2021), p. 2.

[7] Chirwa, 'Child and Youth Labour on the Nyasaland Plantations,' p. 664.

Child and adolescent slaves and pawns were used as farm laborers, herders, domestic servants, retainers for royal households, soldiers, porters, miners, and assistants in craft industries (leatherworking, beadmaking, pottery, etc.).[8]

Even as enslavement and pawning were either discouraged or banned outright under colonial rule, those practices endured and occasionally intensified, changing according to shifting social and economic circumstances, and to avoid the colonial state's new legislation. During this period when unfree labour came under increasing pressure, 'it was almost exclusively children who were captured, traded, smuggled, and disguised as adoptees, wards, or child brides or who were given as pawns to creditors'.[9]

Enslaved and pawned children differed from free children not because they worked, but rather as a result of their unfree status. All children worked, and the nature of that work depended on their age and their gender. Writing about early colonial Nyasaland—contemporary Malawi—Chirwa notes:

> The main difference between the boys and girls came by way of the sexual division of labour in the traditional economy. It was the girls' role to prepare food while the boys' role was to forge and maintain the implements for its collection. Girls were therefore more involved in household chores than boys. While the girls collected food items from domestic sources such as gardens, fishing and hunting were generally regarded as male activities hence associated with boys.[10]

Early colonial Pedi boys spent their time herding cattle, during which they learned animal husbandry through instruction and observation. Pedi girls stayed closer to home, looking after younger siblings, cooking, gathering water and firewood, and learning how to cultivate the land from their mothers (a form of labour regarded as being in women's sphere until the colonial era and the introduction of capitalist agriculture).[11] As Godfrey Pitje describes, a young woman entering a communal space carrying 'a pitcher of water, a bundle of wood, or a bowl of porridge' would receive praise from her elders: not only was she contributing to a household, but she also demonstrated her preparation for adulthood.[12] Work was, thus, socialisation, as well as education—as they herded, Pedi boys learned what Pitje calls 'veldcraft' or knowledge of the veld. Apprenticeship—as discussed in Chap. 5—required that children work under the supervision of a skilled craftsperson or trader until they had learned enough to become independent workers on their own. In early twentieth-century Lagos, girls worked as hawkers, linked to a market

---

[8] Beverly Grier, 'Child Labor and Africanist Scholarship: A Critical Overview,' *African Studies Review*, vol. 47, no. 2 (Sept., 2004), p. 7.

[9] Grier, 'Child Labor and Africanist Scholarship,' p. 7.

[10] Chirwa, 'Child and Youth Labour on the Nyasaland Plantations,' p. 665.

[11] G.M. Pitje, 'Traditional Systems of Male education among Pedi and Cognate Tribes,' Part I, *African Studies*, vol. 9, no. 2 (1950), pp. 67–72.

[12] Pitje, 'Traditional Systems of Male education among Pedi and Cognate Tribes,' Part I, p. 73.

Photograph 6.1 Boys cooking outdoors, Malawi, c.1910, The National Library of Scotland

trading system which was dominated by adult women. Although boys worked as hawkers too, the residents of the city regarded 'hawking … as an apprenticeship towards a career in market trading and as a component in the socialisation of girls'. Girls, were, thus, being prepared for entry into a form of work dominated by women.[13]

Work and play also overlapped. Or, put another way, play was serious business. Pitje describes a game played by Pedi boys while out with cattle, the purpose of which was, clearly, to train young herders to observe their stock more carefully:

> Every boy constructs a miniature kraal in which he places miscellaneous objects—pebbles, sticks, grass, stones of fruit, etc. These are called 'cattle'. Each one examines his cattle in order to make sure that he can identify them when they are in another's kraal. One of them closes his eyes, and his neighbour on the right side takes out one cow from his kraal which he places in his own kraal. When he opens his eyes he tries to identify it in his neighbour's kraal, and if he fails, he is called upon to close his eyes once more. Another cow is taken, and he must try and identify it when he opens his eyes again. If he succeeds this time, his neighbour

---

[13] Abosede George, 'Within Salvation: Girl Hawkers and the Colonial State in Development Era Lagos,' *Journal of Social History*, vol. 44, no. 3 (Spring 2011), p. 841.

on the right hand side closes his eyes, and the same thing is done. The game continues until one of them empties their kraals into his own.[14]

In pre- and early colonial Zulu society, boys were initiated into manhood not through circumcision and ceremonies associated with that process, but, rather, 'through cohort-based, rule-bound competitions like stick fighting'. While it is clear why Zulu kings might approve of stick fighting as preparation for young men's entry into the highly trained, well-organised Zulu army, as historians Benedict Carton and Robert Morrell point out, boys used only sticks and were forbidden from accessing more dangerous weapons, and their 'sparring accentuated risk-averse simulations such as parrying blows, exercising "pure" restraint and revering "fair" play'.[15] The purpose of the game was to allow young men space to 'pursue the heroic feats of a martial art' and 'manly vigour' within a carefully delineated space, controlled by older men. The rules of stick fighting reinforced the importance of 'communal respect', the authority of elders, and of honour.[16] Similarly, in Xhosa society where boys were circumcised as a mark of their entry into adulthood, stick fighting was also rooted in this society's perception of itself as being always ready for war, and was associated with an ideal masculine identity. While younger boys were required to devote themselves 'to home chores such as cattle herding', older boys—those closer to leaving their youth behind them—were expected to be interested in rivalries and politics between them, using stick fighting to 'settle scores'. This fighting was governed by rules and, as historian Anne Mager explains, stick fighting 'was a ritual that taught boys the rules of manliness'.[17]

Precolonial societies depended on children's work. Some of this was profoundly exploitative, as enslaved and pawned children laboured in fields, households, and elsewhere for their owners and those who had agreed to care for them. At the same time, though, even free children were expected to contribute to the livelihood of their homestead, depending on both their age and gender. Work blended into play. This had the function of preparing young people for adult roles, both in terms of providing training in practical skills—how to sell goods to customers, how to milk a cow—as well as the values of the society into which they were being socialised. Unsurprisingly, with the coming of colonial rule and, especially, the introduction of capitalism, the nature of this work changed radically. However, understanding the fact and nature of children's employment in the precolonial era helps to explain how and why children were employed as they were under colonialism and after. Many of the structures of children's work and play endured into the colonial and

[14] Pitje, 'Traditional Systems of Male education among Pedi and Cognate Tribes,' Part I, p. 71.

[15] Benedict Carton and Robert Morrell, 'Zulu Masculinities, Warrior Culture and Stick Fighting: Reassessing Male Violence and Virtue in South Africa,' *Journal of Southern African Studies*, vol. 38, no. 1 (2012), p. 40.

[16] Carton and Morrell, 'Zulu Masculinities, Warrior Culture and Stick Fighting,' p. 51.

[17] Anne Mager, 'Youth Organisations and the Construction of Masculine Identities in the Ciskei and Transkei, 1945–1960,' *Journal of Southern African Studies*, vol. 24, no. 4 (1998), p. 658.

Photograph 6.2 Children described as 'Matabelle' by the photographer, but probably in Matabeleland, Zimbabwe, c.1910–1920s, image courtesy of the Melville J. Herskovits Library of African Studies Winterton Collection, Northwestern University Libraries

postcolonial eras, changing to accommodate new circumstances, and also still shaping children's work and play. One key difference of the colonial period (and after) was the growing moral crusade against child labour. The paradox of the increasing number of children labouring in cash economies at the same time as the first efforts were initiated to end or ban child labour is the focus of the following section.

COLONIAL CONQUEST AND CHILD LABOUR

Writing about child labour in Southern Rhodesia—now Zimbabwe—in the late nineteenth and early twentieth centuries, Grier argues:

> As ubiquitous as African children and adolescents were as workers in the towns and mining camps and on white farms, they have been largely invisible in the social and economic history of colonial Zimbabwe. Underresearched and under-

theorised, children and adolescents are the 'invisible hands' whose labour was involved in substantial ways in the capitalist transformation of the colony but who have gone largely unnoticed by scholars.[18]

Grier's now well-known formulation of child labourers as 'invisible hands' in colonial economies is a powerful evocation of the unacknowledged work of children and young people in African colonies, settler and otherwise. Capitalism transformed not only the nature of work within colonial societies, but restructured power relations and social systems, undermining or giving rise to new political formations. This chapter will pay particular attention to the implications of capitalism in relation to age categories—a major vector of power in pre- and colonial societies—and, especially, to children and young people. The application of wage earning to certain age categories either allowed those people more power or diminished that which they already wielded. All of this occurred under colonial rule and laws which sought to re-engineer African societies to the benefit of European powers. For instance, writing about the early twentieth-century Gold Coast (present-day Ghana), historian Emmanuel Akyeampong considers how the emergence of a cocoa industry and the banning of slavery and pawning at the end of the nineteenth century changed the nature of relationships between men and women. As Chap. 3 discussed, as slavery became illegal (in the Gold Coast in 1874 and in 1896 in the nearby Crown Colony of Asante, which also became part of Ghana), so the practice of fostering appeared to become more widespread, and probably because it hid the increased—and illegal—incidence of the pawning of children. Akyeampong adds that more women were pawned, too, because 'women were crucial to the processes of production and reproduction':

> The abolition of pawning coincided with the take-off of the cocoa industry, when labour was in great demand. Men exploited the labour of their immediate family, especially wives and children. Bride price ... became artificially inflated, and male elders cashed in on the 'marriage boom' and exchanged female wards for large sums of money.[19]

Demand for cocoa caused, then, the pawning of women—and probably young women—in greater numbers, and then the transformation of pawning into marriage, effectively, on its abolition. While there were clear similarities to precolonial practices where women and children cultivated land for a patriarch, capitalist production served to change and to intensify these relationships. But as historian Jean Allman adds, in the 1920s and 1930s, women became cocoa

---

[18] Beverly Carolease Grier, *Invisible Hands: Child Labour and the State in Colonial Zimbabwe* (Portsmouth, NH: Heinemann, 2006), p. 2.

[19] Emmanuel Akyeampong, 'Wop e tam won pe ba ("You like cloth but you don't want children"): Urbanization, Individualism, and Gender Relations in Colonial Ghana c.1900–1939,' in *Africa's Urban Past*, eds. David Anderson and Richard Rathbone (Portsmouth, NH: Heinemann, 2000), p. 227.

farmers in their own right too. This relative financial security allowed women to challenge patriarchal norms, often through the new colonial legal system, meaning that

> women ... were quite prepared to divorce a husband who refused to set up a farm for his wife. Others turned to customary courts to challenge matrilineal inheritance, demanding portions of a divorced or deceased husband's cocoa farm in recognition of labour invested. Still others sought to avoid marriage altogether or, at the very least ... to insist on its fluidity and the mutuality of conjugal obligations.[20]

These two examples attest to how a combination of colonial rule and capitalist production served to reshape people's most intimate lives. Under these circumstances, the meaning of childbearing, the value of accumulating a large family, and the value of daughters and sons were all influenced, to some degree, by the effects of cocoa production.

But while Allman demonstrates convincingly that some adult women had the capacity to forge lives of independence for themselves (an independence constantly under threat from colonial officials and African patriarchs), evidence also shows that the forced labour of children—especially of prepubescent girls—was essential to the cash crops grown in the interior, the import-export trade on the coast, and the building of infrastructure, especially roads. As a result, farmers, British and other foreign trading firms, and the colonial state all exploited forced child labourers. As historian Kwabena O. Akurang-Parry explains, the practice was shaped by precolonial circumstances: most of the girls forced into labour were from a region that had supplied enslaved people to trading ports on the Gold Coast (these young women were probably, in his words, 'of servile origin').[21] It is worth noting here the frequent difficulty of discerning enslavement from forced labour (where a wage was paid, although not necessarily to the labourer).

As enslavement and pawning were banned, so employers found new ways of accessing cheap labour. In Soyo in Angola, for instance, the Holy Ghost Fathers established a mission among the Solongo people, intended as a self-sufficient Christian community in the late 1870s and early 1880s. At the centre of the mission was a school, attended by children of local elites—who hoped this education would prepare their offspring for future positions in colonial politics or trade—as well as children freed from enslavement, among others. The Spiritans—as the Fathers were known—bought those children from local markets, in a society in which enslavement and other forms of unfree labour had very deep histories. While many missionaries across the continent bought and

---

[20] Jean Allman, 'Rounding up Spinsters: Gender Chaos and Unmarried Women in Colonial Asante,' *Journal of African History*, vol. 37, no. 2 (1996), p. 210.

[21] Kwabena O. Akurang-Parry, '"The Loads Are Heavier than Usual": Forced Labor by Women and Children in the Central Province, Gold Coast (Colonial Ghana), c. 1900–1940,' *African Economic History*, no. 30 (2002), p. 32.

freed enslaved people as part of their commitment to the abolitionist cause, the Spiritans—and no doubt other missionary societies—had an ulterior motive too: they needed labour on the mission. Historian Jelmer Vos explains their solution:

> Since any type of physical labour was considered servile in Solongo culture and because Soyo children were surrounded by friends and family, the mission struggled to press these local students into a daily routine of work, study, and prayer. In the end, the mission came to employ a division of labour in which redeemed child slaves performed comparatively hard manual tasks and the dependants of local families carried out a variety of lighter domestic duties.[22]

It is important to emphasise here that the Spiritans did not regard labour as being incompatible with African Christian childhood; indeed it would seem they believed the opposite. Enslavement was the foundation on which an apparently 'free' labour regime was built.

Between 1840 and 1870 in the Zuid Afrikaansche Republiek (ZAR, South African Republic), a settler state founded by Dutch-speakers who called themselves 'Boers' and incorporated in the twentieth century into modern South Africa, African children constituted a new class of unfree labour. Called *inboekselings*, these were, as historians Peter Delius and Stanley Trapido explain, 'children and to a much lesser extent young women formally apprenticed—*ingeboek*—to Boer settlers'. They had been captured by Boer commandos during periodic raids of African societies, sold by other settlers or some Africans, or 'handed over' by those African societies 'as tokens of political and diplomatic assurance'. These children worked as domestic servants, as hunters serving Boer homesteads, or, as they aged, became tenants on settler farms. The *inboekseling* system—which was often indistinguishable from enslavement—developed in the form that it did because of the abolition of slavery in the Cape Colony in 1833, one of the several causes of many Boers' trek northwards.[23]

Thus, imperialism facilitated new forms of unfree labour. Under British rule, close to a million Indians signed contracts of indenture to work on sugar plantations, in mining, and building infrastructure (like railways) on Indian Ocean islands, Fiji, the Caribbean, and in East and South Africa. The majority of those indentured workers were men, but women and some children sailed across oceans to lives marked, frequently, by incredible hardship. Babies were also born on and subsequent to those voyages. As historian Uma Dhupelia-Mesthrie explains, children constituted thirteen per cent of the 152,184 indentured

---

[22] Jelmer Vos, 'Child Slaves and Freemen at the Spiritan Mission in Soyo, 1880–1885,' *Journal of Family History*, vol. 35, no. 1 (2010), p. 84.

[23] Peter Delius and Stanley Trapido, '*Inboekselings* and *Oorlams*: The Creation and Transformation of a Servile Class,' *Journal of Southern African Studies*, vol. 8, no. 2 (1982), p. 214.

Photograph 6.3 Girls doing laundry work, Bali Nyonga, Cameroon, c.1908–1911, Basel Mission Archive

Indians recorded as having come to Natal in South Africa between 1860 and 1911, when the system came to an end. She writes:

> We know that children accompanied their indentured mothers to the fields on the sugar estates and often lay unprotected from the elements until a law compelled employers to put up shelters. Many also remained in the barracks being cared for by other women and those off shift. Once children turned 10 years they joined weeding gangs and did other small work. The Natal Government Railways employed children to help with mail, deliver messages and collect tickets.[24]

Unlike the children of enslaved adults, the offspring of indentured labourers did not carry the same status as their parents. However, as Dhupelia-Mesthrie's description suggests, the children of indentured workers—who usually lived in poverty—had little choice as to whether they would work or not.

The forced labour that Akurang-Parry describes on the Gold Coast was not, thus, unusual for the period. It built, too, on a pre-existing gendered division

---

[24] Uma Dhupelia-Mesthrie, 'India-South Africa Mobilities in the First Half of the Twentieth Century: Minors, Immigration Encounters in Cape Town and Becoming South African,' in *Children on the Move in Africa: Past and Present Experiences of Migration*, eds. Elodie Razy and Marie Rodet (Woodbridge: James Currey, 2016), p. 160.

Photograph 6.4 A group of porters, including children, in the Belgian Congo, now the Democratic Republic of Congo, c.1920–1940, Special Collections, Yale Divinity School Library

of labour which 'facilitated the exploitation of female labour'. But colonial rule created the conditions for the increase in girls forced into work. Education and the wealth accrued by farmers in the new cash crop economy tended to favour men, 'leading to the feminisation of menial labour'. Parents and guardians hired out girls to farmers and coastal trading companies (something which would have intensified during periods of economic hardship), as did chiefs who 'supplied female labourers to the colonial authorities to perform various tasks, including cleaning up towns, engaging in porterage labour, building facilities', and other tasks. Aged mainly between nine and fourteen years, overwhelmingly girls worked as porters, carrying 'heavy loads' of cocoa, palm oil, and other goods 'over long distances' often walking quickly, with little rest and food.[25] Yet even under these exceedingly harsh conditions, girls seem to have found ways of resisting their captors:

> The colonial sources do not mention resistance, but oral history suggests that prepubescent female porters sometimes faked illness or took to flight to mitigate or end their bondage. ... Also, desertion and shiftlessness were common features among involuntary labourers who worked on public projects or accompanied colonial officials on trekking duties.[26]

[25] Akurang-Parry, '"The Loads Are Heavier than Usual,"' pp. 32–34.
[26] Akurang-Parry, '"The Loads Are Heavier than Usual,"' p. 34.

The situation that Akurang-Parry describes in the Gold Coast was similar in many ways to other regions of the continent under colonial rule. Writing about Nyasaland, Chirwa explains the changes wrought by the 'coming of capitalist agriculture' to the Shire Highlands at the end of the nineteenth century, a region which encompassed the southern part of the colony, where large-scale plantation agriculture was soon dominated by white settlers. Children were employed on these new plantations. Again, the work they performed 'incorporated some elements of the pre-existing local division of labour' and they 'were often employed in agricultural tasks which they normally performed in their family units: insect-picking, weeding, scaring predators, harvesting', and other activities. Also, the presence of African families on plantations as tenants was due partly to Yao and Mang'anja traditions regarding access to land. Within these societies—which dominated in areas with large plantations—men gained the ability to cultivate land via marriage, and so young men who were not yet married 'easily found their way into wage employment on the European plantations'. But capitalism shaped the conditions under which children and their families laboured. Child labourers had an 'impersonal' relationship with an employer who paid them a wage, and their employment was 'part of the employers' labour mobilisation strategy'.[27] Living on plantations with their parents, children were also 'vulnerable' to being employed by planters—they were 'brought up and cultured in the plantation life' and were perceived as a 'reserve' for labour. Tenancy, thus, 'made child labour easily accessible' to landlords. Plantations made use of child labour from the 1890s, but by the 1920s child labour was essential to the tobacco and tea industries in Nyasaland.

The growing importance of children to Nyasaland's plantations was the product of another major consequence of the capitalist economies of Southern Africa: the creation of a system of migrant labour, in which young men from across the region migrated temporarily to mines in, especially, the Copper Belt in Northern Rhodesia (or contemporary Zambia), and the gold mines in the Witwatersrand in South Africa. Especially during the economic downturn of the late 1920s and 1930s, men left rural areas in search of more lucrative work. In Nyasaland, in the absence of male labourers, European planters turned to women and, particularly, children for the production of tobacco and tea:

> Both crops required a lot of what the planters called 'light work': hoeing, weeding, tending nurseries, watering, pruning, stripping and stemming, and picking and tying of leaves. In the factories, youth and children were employed in a variety of menial jobs: sweeping the floors, running errands, and packing and unpacking of the tea or tobacco leaves. Since the leaves had to be gathered on time for quality to be maintained, the demand for child and youth labour tended to be greater during the harvesting seasons: February to April for tea and March to May for tobacco. A lot more of youth and child labour was also used in processing: spreading, fermenting and curing of the leaves.[28]

[27] Chirwa, 'Child and Youth Labour on the Nyasaland Plantations,' pp. 665–666.
[28] Chirwa, 'Child and Youth Labour on the Nyasaland Plantations,' p. 672.

Working conditions were very bad: children worked long hours with few breaks, with no protection from the weather, and little in the way of available first aid in case of injury. They were fed poorly, and their wages were half of those paid to adults. Because they were children, their employers did not provide them with a weekly food allowance, believing instead that their parents should supply them from adult rations. While some planters did offer children schooling in exchange for working half the day, the overwhelming reason for children's employment was that 'their parents needed money'. Child labour 'was an important source of cash income for the families residing on the plantations and in the villages surrounding them'.[29]

These two examples drawn from the Gold Coast and Nyasaland demonstrate the degree to which children often had little or no say as to the fact of their waged employment: they were either compelled into labour by adults in authority or pushed into it by their parents' straitened circumstances. Echoing the experiences of women in the Gold Coast who entered into cocoa farming or market trading in the early twentieth century and found ways of living less under patriarchal authority, some young people—especially young men—escaped the strictures of rural living by leaving to find waged employment. Historian William Beinart examines why the sugar plantations in Natal in South Africa employed many Xhosa-speaking boys and young men from the Pondoland area of rural Transkei (a region also on South Africa's east coast, but to the south of Natal) in the first half of the twentieth century. Life on the plantations was exceptionally hard, with young labourers—some of them in their early to mid-teens—subject to violent forms of control, disease (malaria especially), and back-breaking labour. The question, then, was why young men travelled to work on the plantations.

As Beinart makes the point, children had long been incorporated into South Africa's economy: a significant proportion of domestic servants were children (in the Cape, one of the legacies of enslavement in the region), and children worked a variety of low-paid jobs in towns and cities (as messengers, newspaper sellers, hawkers of fresh produce, and doing lighter work on the docks). In the countryside—similar to Nyasaland—African labour tenancy gave white farmers access to the labour of the families of the men who settled on those farms: 'herding, domestic service, hoeing and weeding could all be done by African boys and girls or youths.' This situation was undergirded by legislation which allowed African heads of households—men, in other words—'responsibility ... over the labour of their families as a whole'. They could 'bind' their children to a contract up to the age of eighteen by 1932. Both white farmers and African patriarchs could, then, more easily control the movement of African youth, especially young men.[30]

---

[29] Chirwa, 'Child and Youth Labour on the Nyasaland Plantations,' p. 675.

[30] William Beinart, 'Transkeian Migrant Workers and Youth Labour on the Natal Sugar Estates 1918–1948,' *The Journal of African History*, vol. 32, no. 1 (1991), p. 55.

In fact, the 1911 Native Labour Regulation Act forbade mining companies from recruiting young men under the age of eighteen not out of revulsion of child labour but, rather, in order to protect 'the access of landlords and agricultural employers to youth labour'. This was the crux of the issue: Who could control young men and the work that they did? Like many other African societies in the region, Xhosa youth were 'entrusted' with the 'critical task of herding'. Beinart elaborates:

> emergent capitalist agriculture incorporated elements of the established local division of labour. Pre-capitalist and peasant labour relationships were embedded in broader kin relationships and in an ethic which made them part of socialising processes. Herding for boys involved education about the natural world and about custom, the formation of friendship networks, and the learning of fighting skills. The pace of work was also very much shaped and determined by the social practices of the youth: there was time for enjoyment. Work was part of a domestic environment supervised by family members and not an 'impersonal' wage relationship.[31]

The work of herding was certainly different to waged labour for farmers in that it was part of the socialisation of young men into adulthood, but it was work nonetheless and there were harsh penalties for those who either shirked or badly executed their duties. In the interwar period, stocks of cattle and sheep increased, producing more demand for youth labour—from African families and white farmers—and this work became harder with bigger herds needing to be moved more frequently as pasture deteriorated. At the same time, employment options for those young men opened up—including working on sugar plantations further north. Young men sought work harvesting sugar for a range of reasons, including raising money for their schooling or supporting their families, which were also often the result of the increasing social stratification of Pondoland as capitalist agriculture was entrenched.[32]

In Pondoland, Nyasaland, and the Gold Coast—and other places—the transformation of rural living by colonial rule and capitalist agriculture and migrant labour changed the nature of work for children and young people, decoupling it from systems of socialisation, play, and forms of education. Herding, caring for younger siblings, assisting with crop cultivation, and other activities undertaken by children and young people in precolonial societies became wage labour, governed by an impersonal contract between employer and employee. However, while it is true that work for children and young people in pre- or early colonial societies may have been difficult or even exploitative (and much of that work was necessarily exploitative when undertaken by enslaved or pawned children), labour under capitalism was frequently coercive. Forced labour practices or the employment of children and young people under horrible conditions—when they had little choice over whether they

---

[31] Beinart, 'Transkeian Migrant Workers and Youth Labour on the Natal Sugar Estates,' p. 56.
[32] Beinart, 'Transkeian Migrant Workers and Youth Labour on the Natal Sugar Estates,' p. 58.

would work or not—flourished, particularly in the first half of the twentieth century.

Akurang-Parry's point about the silence of the colonial archive as to children and young people's labour is an important one. Scholars of children's work in colonial Africa routinely come up against this challenge, encountering bad record keeping of labourers' ages, few if any references to children or young people, and, perhaps most obviously, little as to the experiences of those labourers. As a result, scholars must 'extrapolate'—as Akurang-Parry writes—from what evidence is available, making use of oral sources, for instance, to fill in the gaps. The movement in opposition to child labour provides a useful archive as well, although inevitably shaped by its own politics and perceptions of Africa and of African children. If child labour was useful to the colonial state, how, then, did businesses, settler employers of this labour, and colonies themselves respond to increasing pressure from the metropole to reduce or eradicate entirely child labour?

In the case of the Gold Coast, where anti-child labour agitation flowed out of the abolitionist movement, the colonial state tried to have things both ways: 'the colonial state adopted ad hoc measures to satisfy the dictates of the anti-slavery societies, while at the same time exploiting female and child forced labour.' It was only in the 1930s that the League of Nations placed greater pressure on both the Colonial Office in London and the government of the Gold Coast to end forced labour and the pawning of girls. In the mid-1930s the Colonial Office proposed some regulations on child labour (including preventing children from being employed at sea), none of which actually applied to the Gold Coast. In 1940, finally, Ordinance 19 outlawed the employment of children under the age of twelve by people other than the child's immediate family. But, as Akurang-Parry discovered, this made little difference to girls: 'with the introduction of schools in the interior, parents, for the most part, sent their male children to school and exploited their female children as porters and farmhands.' It appears that after the 1940s the numbers of children involved in porterage might have grown.[33] Similarly, in Nyasaland, after urging from the Colonial Office, the colonial state did in 1937 introduce legislation intended to improve the working conditions of women and children, but, as in the case of the Gold Coast, this did little to reduce the numbers of children working on plantations. In fact, children continued to work on tea plantations as casual labour well into the postcolonial era.[34]

This foot-dragging was intentional: child labour was important to colonial economies, something colonial governments recognised. As Hepburn and Jackson argue, the work of the International Labour Organisation (ILO)—which was founded in 1919 specifically to protect the rights of workers—was undermined by colonial powers seeking to prevent any serious overhaul of labour conditions in their colonies. In the first three years of its existence, the

---

[33] Akurang-Parry, '"The Loads Are Heavier than Usual,"' p. 43.
[34] Chirwa, 'Child and Youth Labour on the Nyasaland Plantations,' p. 677, 679–680.

ILO adopted seven conventions and three recommendations as regards children in waged employment, becoming 'the key forum where children's rights and employment were discussed and constructed'. But there were loopholes in the ILO's processes: 'member states were expected to apply ILO conventions in their colonies, protectorates and non-self-governing possessions' but were allowed to alter these conventions, or even not implement them at all, if they deemed 'local conditions' to render them 'inapplicable'. This had significant consequences, as Hepburn and Jackson explain: 'the ILO ... constructed a two-tier system of international labour law which rendered colonized children less protected than their Western counterparts.'[35] British and other colonial officials presented a number of arguments in favour of allowing the employment of children in African colonies (and elsewhere, such as India). Many of these rested on a racialised conception of African childhood, which—drawing on racial pseudo-science—posited that African children in warm climates matured more quickly than their European counterparts. They insisted that children enjoyed the work, and it was beneficial to them to spend long periods of time outdoors: work was a tool for the development of societies characterised as backward and prevented children from falling into idleness and mischief. As a result of these interventions, colonial powers were allowed a great deal of leeway in putting into place limitations on the employment of children in their colonies. As the examples cited above show, the Colonial Office did ask that colonial governments implement protections for child labourers, but the measures taken by those colonies—often under pressure from settlers and businesses—were usually watered down:

> For instance, the first laws governing the employment of children in Kenya were introduced in 1933, through the 'Employment of Women, Young Persons and Children Ordinance'. Complying with Convention Five, the Ordinance established a minimum age for the employment of Africans in industry of 14 years. Reflecting the right of colonial powers to modify ILO conventions, however, it also allowed African children's employment in industry from the age of 12 if government approval was secured.[36]

Even if colonial administrators were intent on enforcing legislation, they were hindered by the fact that very few children were registered at birth and possessed identity documents. Occasionally legislation was shaped by this bureaucratic failure, for example requiring that children's ages be identified by appearance and not using chronological ages recorded in official documents: in Angola, a Portuguese colony, 'government officials and employers used children's appearance to judge their "maturity" and suitability for employment in mining'.[37]

---

[35] Hepburn and Jackson, 'Colonial Exceptions,' pp. 2–3.
[36] Hepburn and Jackson, 'Colonial Exceptions,' p. 14.
[37] Hepburn and Jackson, 'Colonial Exceptions,' p. 15.

It should be emphasised that the ILO's inability to curtail child labour on the continent was subject to criticism by African trade unions, missionaries, and non-governmental organisations, like the Save the Children Fund (SCF). At the 1931 International Conference on African Children organised by the Save the Children International Union (which was allied to the SCF), delegates from beyond and within Africa—including Jomo Kenyatta, the future President of independent Kenya—offered criticism of colonial rulers and the ILO, among other international institutions, for not providing better care for African children's health, education, and welfare.[38] But inertia at a local, colonial level was such that these interventions had very little effect. Another point worth emphasising—echoing Beinart—is that African adults were interested in the control of children and young people's labour as well. As historian Jack Lord writes of the persistence of the employment of children in the Gold Coast in the 1940s and 1950s—in the late colonial period, in other words—households depended on children's wages. Equally important, though, was 'the unpaid use of children' in the 'plugging' of 'temporary or permanent shortages of labour, and extending the reach and mobility of household labour, production, and exchange'. While children were undoubtedly exploited by their families—the numbers who ran away from home, usually to work in towns or cities, attests to this—work could also grant them greater autonomy, allowing them to move more, and to have access to some money.[39]

Adult justifications for children's employment rested, often, on the argument that children who had too much time on their hands would become delinquent. More particularly, both patriarchs and administrators worried that with the social changes wrought, especially, by capitalism, young people were less obedient to their elders, and more willing to seek out different kinds of work beyond that which they were expected to perform at home. As a result, managing children's leisure time became an issue of some significance in African colonies in the late nineteenth and twentieth centuries. This is the focus of the following section.

Managing Leisure Time

British anthropologist Jean la Fontaine spent 1962 and 1963 at Lovanium University in Zaire—previously the Belgian Congo and currently the Democratic Republic of the Congo—shortly after the new nation's independence in 1960. Lovanium had been founded in 1954 by the Catholic University of Leuven in Belgium, becoming one of a small handful of institutions of higher education in the then vast colony. La Fontaine carried out research on Kinshasa—the capital of the independent Zaire, previously Léopoldville—and

---

[38] Hepburn and Jackson, 'Colonial Exceptions,' pp. 20–22.
[39] Jack Lord, 'Child Labour in the Gold Coast: The Economics of Work, Education, and the Family in Late-Colonial African Childhoods, c. 1940–57,' *The Journal of the History of Childhood and Youth*, vol. 4, no. 1 (Winter 2011), pp. 102–106.

wrote about the children and, especially, the young men she encountered in the city. Kinshasa was, she observed, a young city, with over half of its population under the age of eighteen in the late 1950s. This was partly a consequence of Kinshasa having been for some time an educational centre for the western part of Zaire. Children were sent by their families to the city to attend school. And yet the majority of young people in Kinshasa were not in school, with educational facilities—from primary to tertiary level—'inadequate'.[40] For instance, in 1962–1963, there were 'about 354,000' people under the age of eighteen in Kinshasa, with 'a round figure of 100,000 boys and girls in school … probably a liberal estimate', meaning that 'only 29 per cent of school-age children were actually going to school.'[41] La Fontaine's interest was in the majority of young people who were not in school. She noted that there was widespread concern about the activities of this group of young people who were not apparently engaged in any sort of productive activity, and who were not under any obvious parental control. (La Fontaine pointed to the high incidence of poverty in most households in Kinshasa, with overworked and frequently absent parents.) What was described as a 'social problem' of unoccupied youth—especially boys and young men—was dealt with in a number of ways, including the institution of youth organisations whose purpose was 'to provide occupation and some instruction for the city's youth', although most of these emphasised overwhelmingly 'moral rather than practical instruction' and were no real substitute for school.[42]

While Chap. 7 considers questions of delinquency, violence, and gangsterism—and La Fontaine wrote about the youth gangs of Kinshasa—it is worth considering her descriptions of the day-to-day activities of young people not occupied by work or by school—those apparently not receiving any form of socialisation at all. It is striking that La Fontaine calls these young people 'teenagers', a term which originated in the United States in the 1930s and globalised over the course of the mid-twentieth century. It applied first to largely white, middle-class young people with the time and disposable income to pursue a range of leisure pursuits out of schooltime. Also, drawing on the child study movement of the period which posited adolescence as a period of hormonal flux and emotional instability and immaturity, teenagers were characterised as moody and irrational, still learning to control their impulses, and in need of adult supervision. The term modified as it was applied to new contexts, but the Congolese teenagers in La Fontaine's writing are strikingly similar to their working-class teenage counterparts in Birmingham or Chicago, for instance. They drew from specifically American popular culture, as 'symbols and mythical figures of the cinema and advertising'—especially a '"Cowboys

---

[40] JS La Fontaine, 'Two Types of Youth Group in Kinshasa (Léopoldville),' in *Socialisation: The Approach from Social Anthropology*, ed. Philip Mayer (London and New York: Routledge, [1970] 2004), p. 193.

[41] La Fontaine, 'Two Types of Youth Group in Kinshasa,' pp. 196–197.

[42] La Fontaine, 'Two Types of Youth Group in Kinshasa,' p. 197.

and Indians" motif'—worked their way into slang and nicknames. In fact, these teenagers used their own slang, *kindoubil*:

> Speaking it has several interrelated meanings: it marks the speaker off as resident of Kinshasa, a sophisticated urbanite rather than a country bumpkin; it serves as a perpetual reminder of the separation between youth and the world of adults; and, by providing the means to talk freely about activities which are frowned on by adult society, it defies the mores of that society.[43]

The 'activities' of which adults disapproved included dating multiple partners before marriage (drawing on a different set of ideas about what should constitute marriage, including love and sexual attraction). Young people embraced fashion and cosmetics, using their appearances to signal their modernity, worldliness, and sophistication.

This example of teenagers in early 1960s, post-independence Zaire picks up on a number of themes in scholars' research on young people's leisure time in colonial and postcolonial Africa: the links between urbanisation, the making of new youth cultures, and adult fears about apparently inadequately socialised youth; shifting attitudes towards sex and sexuality among both young people and adults; and institutional efforts to contain potentially disruptive youth. In addition to these motifs—discussed in greater detail below—as was especially clear in settler colonies, these fears about unproductive youth were heavily racialised and shaped by attitudes towards social class. In the nineteenth- and early twentieth-century Cape Colony, for example, white politicians, missionaries, and social reformers argued that apparently idle working-class white, African, or multiracial youth were prone to delinquent behaviour. While white, middle-class young people attended school during the day, their leisure time—filled with cricket matches, tea parties, boating expeditions, reading, charitable good works, and similar—was understood as vital for preparing them for adulthood. It was during this time that they would meet and court future romantic partners, and constitute the social networks that would sustain their adult lives. In contrast, the free time of working-class and, especially, African and multiracial children and young people was figured as dangerous. As a result, employment was held up as the best means of maintaining control over African and multiracial children and youth—but, even then, not all employment was considered to be a suitable solution. On the one hand, African and multiracial girls employed as domestic servants in white households—where work was unrelenting and almost constantly supervised—were believed to be in little danger of falling into disruptive behaviour. But, on the other, girls of the same class and racial categories who worked in Cape Town's factories making matchsticks, fake flowers, and jam, and who were left fully to their own devices outside of working hours, were the cause of much anxiety for the city's white middle

---

[43] La Fontaine, 'Two Types of Youth Group in Kinshasa,' p. 199.

classes: these were the girls who were believed to fall into sex work and other apparently disreputable activities.⁴⁴

Clearly, much of the concern about unproductive youth was linked to the growth of towns and cities in African colonies from the late nineteenth century onwards. As Marie Rodet and Elodie Razy show, children and young people were among those Africans who moved from the countryside to new urban centres, seeking not only work, but also education. Adult nervousness about the presence of increasing numbers of children and young people in towns and cities was by no means specific to Africa in the twentieth century, but in a colonial context this urbanisation was often understood as posing a threat to the colonial social order.⁴⁵ In addition to this, and echoing Beinart's analysis of young men's employment on sugar plantations, African patriarchal authorities in the countryside objected to their inability to access the labour of young men and women who moved away. As the example of young women factory workers implies, these concerns were often gendered and clustered around a set of anxieties about sexuality: about the presence of sex workers in cities; about young people having sex before or beyond the bounds of marriage; about the possibilities for interracial sex; and about unmarried young women managing unplanned pregnancies. Writing about early twentieth-century South Africa, historian Deborah Gaitskell describes efforts to establish hostels and domestic training schools for unmarried African girls in Johannesburg, Cape Town, and Durban. These were opened and run mainly by missionary or other Christian social welfare organisations, usually with the support of municipal and national labour departments. They were more than a place for women to live, though, offering cookery classes and other opportunities for respectable socialising outside of working hours. African politicians understood precisely that these hostels were intended to reinforce the segregation of South Africa's cities and, moreover, served to 'oil the domestic wheels of white society' by channelling African women into white households.⁴⁶

Concern about young African men and women in cities was not limited to white, middle-class churches, politicians, and social workers. African educators, clergy, journalists, and politicians—the members of the Christian, mission-educated middle class—understood that missionaries' refusal to allow for pre-colonial forms of sex education to be transmitted to young people was one of the reasons for an increase in unplanned pregnancies among young women, especially in urban areas. They produced interventions to encourage what they

---

⁴⁴ SE Duff, '"*Onschuldig vermaak*": The Dutch Reformed Church and Children's Leisure Time in the Nineteenth-Century Cape Colony,' *South African Historical Journal*, vol. 63, no. 4 (2011), pp. 501–502.

⁴⁵ Marie Rodet and Elodie Razy, 'Child Migration in Africa: Key Issues and New Perspectives,' in *Children on the Move in Africa: Past and Present Experiences of Migration* (Woodbridge: Boydell & Brewer, 2016), pp. 13–15.

⁴⁶ Deborah Gaitskell, '"Christian Compounds for Girls": Church Hostels for African Women in Johannesburg, 1907–1970,' *Journal of Southern African Studies*, vol. 6, no. 1, Special Issue on Urban Social History (Oct., 1979), pp. 53–54, 62.

described as moral behaviour and to fill up young men and women's free time. In 1919, the Bantu Purity League was founded at Inanda Seminary, an elite missionary school for African girls. At the League's first meeting 'over a hundred young men and women signed the purity pledge', but its work was always more than discouraging sex before marriage:

> Sibusisiwe Violet Makhanya, the Purity League's Secretary in the 1920s, told the Natal Missionary Conference that in the League's meetings, talks were given not only on bodily purity and abstinence from alcohol and tobacco, but also on anything else that elevated the conduct of youth and made them (in the word she chose) 'respectable.'[47]

There were also games and music at its meetings. Similarly, the meetings of the Pathfinders and Wayfarers—equivalents of the Boy Scouts and Girl Guides for African young people in South Africa—included games, singing, and country dancing, alongside practising the skills members of these organisations would need in order to earn badges.[48] Ironically, given its explicitly pro-imperial politics, the Boy Scout movement enjoyed widespread support among African parents in some parts of the continent. The constitution of Scouting reflected the racial and class politics of Anglophone colonies. In Nigeria and the Gold Coast where there were very small settler populations, the well-funded Scout associations were, by the 1930s, almost entirely African, although Europeans tended to occupy positions of authority. In Uganda, the leadership included Africans who had attended missionary schools. In South Africa, Scouting was segregated, hence the formation of the Pathfinders movement. In Tanganyika, Scouting remained the preserve of elite schools, as Timothy Parsons writes:

> In 1937, Emmanuel Kibira and Julius Nyerere took the lead in introducing Scouting to the Tabora Central School. Nyerere, who would go on to be the first prime minister of independent Tanganyika, read *Scouting for Boys* [by the founder of Scouting, Robert Baden-Powell] on his own, and convinced his headmaster to assign a pair of teachers to serve as Scoutmasters. Nyerere easily mastered the Scouting curriculum and became the senior patrol leader of the troop.[49]

In Kenya, though, Scouting was initially only for white and, to a lesser extent, Indian young men, but as a result of sustained pressure from African parents, the East African Scout Association was integrated in 1935. Interest in Scouting was such that many young people and parents had simply founded

---

[47] Deborah Gaitskell, '"Wailing for Purity": Prayer Unions, African Mothers and Adolescent Daughters, 1912–1940,' in *Industrialisation and Social Change in South Africa: African Class Formation, Culture, and Consciousness*, eds. Shula Marks and Richard Rathbone (London: Longman, 1982), p. 345.

[48] Gaitskell, '"Wailing for Purity,"' p. 346.

[49] Timothy H. Parsons, *Race, Resistance, and the Boy Scout Movement in British Colonial Africa* (Athens, OH: Ohio University Press, 2004), p. 137.

their own troops, occasionally making use of old Scout uniforms. The East African Scout Association realised that the only solution to widespread unauthorised Scouting was simply to allow African boys to join. The question, then, was why the appeal of Scouting. Why did Nyerere—one of the major figures of African decolonisation—found his own troop? For boys themselves, Scouting was 'entertaining' and 'useful' but, as Parsons emphasises, 'they had their own ideas of what it meant to be loyal and disciplined'. Being a Scout 'conferred sophistication, social status, and legitimacy, and demonstrated a mastery of Western cultural norms'. Parsons adds:

> Most important, African Scouts and their communities embraced the movement to claim the rights of full citizenship in colonial society. They used the Fourth Scout Law, which declared that a Scout was a brother to every other Scout, to challenge racial discrimination under what was known as the colour bar. ... Rather than papering over the contradictions of colonialism, Scouting offered Africans another means of contesting their social status. In anglophone Africa, therefore, Scouting was thus both an instrument of colonial authority and a subversive challenge to the legitimacy of the empire.[50]

Scouting—like so many other organised leisure activities for African young people—functioned in a number of ways. While it was intended to instil loyalty to empire and to curb the potentially delinquent activities of young men not in school (and it must be emphasised that Scouting was a largely middle-class pursuit, linked to schools in most cases), it became a tool for contesting empire. And at the same time, it was appealing to boys because it was fun.

CONCLUSION

Child labour did not end with decolonisation. As the lives of the girls employed as domestic workers in 1980s and 1990s Zambia demonstrate, the employment of children and young people remained important to postcolonial African countries' economies. In the case of Zambia, the childcare and housework undertaken by young women like Esnart and Grace allowed educated, middle-class Zambian women to enter the workforce. A lack of state investment and infrastructure which would provide cheap crèches and other forms of childcare, persistent poverty (particularly in the countryside), low rates of enrolment in school, and lackadaisical enforcement of labour legislation which either bans or restricts the employment of children, among other factors, have contributed to the fact that child labour remains the most prevalent in Africa, in contrast to other regions of the world. In 2016, the ILO reported that twenty-seven per cent of children between the ages of five and seventeen in Africa were employed; of these, almost twenty per cent were engaged in child labour (work which

---

[50] Parsons, *Race, Resistance, and the Boy Scout Movement in British Colonial Africa*, p. 6.

undermines their well-being), and nine per cent were in what the ILO describes as 'hazardous' labour.[51]

It is clear that children worked in precolonial societies, and that this work could be exploitative. This was obviously the case for children who were enslaved and pawned, but even for those free children who performed the tasks expected of them by their elders—from childcare to herding—there were significant punishments for not completing their work correctly. Capitalism, though, altered the nature of children's work. No longer largely governed by the rights and obligations of kinship, it became an impersonal transaction between employer and employee. Rural poverty, the legacies of enslavement, the emergence of new forms of unfree labour (like indenture), and the unwillingness of the colonial state to intervene to protect children from exploitation all contributed to the often-appalling conditions in which children worked from the late nineteenth century onwards. And yet—at the same time—employment had the potential to offer children and young people (and particularly young men) new possibilities. Moving to towns and cities to earn a wage allowed some young people to begin or continue their education. The changes wrought to interpersonal relations and family life in some regions as a result of the introduction of cash economies and waged labour disrupted patriarchal control over women and young people. Colonial-era legislation aimed at controlling the labour of young men was frequently approved of by older men because it allowed them to maintain earlier social hierarchies, with younger men providing the manpower for herding livestock.

Understood in this light, the anxiety over the presence of young people in growing towns and cities in colonial Africa was an expression of concern about access to labour, and about what was perceived as the collapse of what was referred to as traditional African society. As La Fontaine demonstrates, city living, where parental control was either distant or weakened, made possible all kinds of experimentation for young people, and for the emergence of a distinct youth culture. This was a culture which was self-consciously outward-looking, drawing on, particularly, American influences. But these were melded with local fashions and social mores, allowing young people to distinguish themselves from their elders, and to engage in new ways of forming relationships, for example. Even the ostensibly staid, rule-bound Boy Scouts opened up possibilities for contesting colonial rule. This boundary testing—even this rebellion—is the focus of the next chapter.

---

[51] International Labour Organisation, *Global Estimates of Child Labour: Results and trends, 2012–2016* (2017), p. 9.

CHAPTER 7

Politics and Violence

In 1956, the practice of clitoridectomy, an important feature of the process of initiation which marked girls' transition to adulthood, was banned in the administrative direct of Meru in Kenya. The ban was introduced by the *Njuri Ncheke*, the local council of male leaders who governed with the approval of the Kenyan colonial state. The majority of adolescent girls in the area responded with defiance. They chose to circumcise themselves, earning for themselves the name '*Ngaitana*' or 'I will circumcise myself'. Referencing interviews with women who were *Ngaitana* or who encountered this movement, historian Lynn Thomas explains:

> Caroline Kirote remembers that, in Mitunguu, girls purchased razor blades and went to the bush to 'circumcise each other' while their parents sat listening to the Headman announce the ban. ... Between 1956 and 1959, *Ngaitana* spread from one area of the District to another. Most areas of the District experienced two or three separate episodes or 'waves' of girls, of increasingly younger ages, 'circumcising themselves'. Charity Tirindi, of the second 'wave', remembers how *Ngaitana* came to her home area of Mwichiune: 'it began from Igoji [to the south] and then went to Mwiriga Mieru [to the north] so we were left in the middle alone. They used to call us cowards, abusing us, and calling us *nkenye* (uncircumcised girls) so we sat down and we decided how we will circumcise ourselves.' This statement reveals how groups of recently excised girls exerted peer pressure, often through song, on unexcised girls in other parts of the District to join *Ngaitana*.[1]

Between 1956 and 1959, 2400 men, women, and girls were charged with defying the ban in the African Courts, and thousands more paid fines to *Njuri* councils and headmen. What renders this movement all the more remarkable

---

[1] Lynn M. Thomas, *Politics of the Womb: Women, Reproduction, and the State in Kenya* (Berkeley, CA: University of California Press, 2003), pp. 89–90.

was the fact that it occurred in the midst of the Mau Mau uprising, a phenomenon which, as Thomas notes, may have originated 'in black Kenyans' longstanding grievances against colonial land polities' but became 'a web of conflicts that pitted black central Kenyans against white settlers, the colonial government, and often each other'. The Kenyan state responded to—and thus fuelled—the Mau Mau by declaring a state of emergency, which lasted between 1952 and 1960. The state of emergency empowered the colonial government to remove over 100,000 Africans from Nairobi and settler farms back to rural areas, held 80,000 in detention camps, and 'forced over a million to live in heavily guarded "villages" meant to prevent them from providing supplies and support for rebels living in the forest'. Security forces killed 11,000 Africans, executed 1000 more, and imprisoned 19,000. The Mau Mau was characterised by Kenyan settlers and administrators as an attack on whites and European civilisation, although just over 100 whites and Asians and roughly 2000 African loyalists were killed by the rebels.[2]

How, then, to understand adolescent girls' refusal to give up clitoridectomy in this context? And especially during a period when they would have been acutely aware of the potentially deadly consequences of challenging state authority? As Thomas observes, 'it is tempting to situate a history of the 1956 ban on excision within the now familiar paradigm of resistance to colonialism'. The ban and opposition to it occurred during the Mau Mau, and the debate over and efforts to eradicate clitoridectomy were linked to anti-colonial politics. But these considerations 'do not explain why so many girls and women challenged' the prohibition.[3] Drawing on conversations with women who engaged in debates over *Ngaitana* in the 1950s, Thomas develops an argument which has at its centre an acknowledgement of the rituals and traditions which allowed women authority within central Kenyan society. Historically, circumcision was carried out by older women on younger women shortly before marriage. This was a communal event in that it was held outdoors and was attended by women and younger children. The initiates might also alter their bodies in other ways, including tattooing and ear piercing. But during the interwar period, clitoridectomy had come under increasing pressure from British feminists and, especially, from missionaries and Christian converts who argued that true African Christians would never allow their daughters to be circumcised and would—if they were girls—resist circumcision. Efforts had been made to reduce the severity of the excision, but the 1956 ruling was the first blanket prohibition of circumcision.

Women were not present at the making of this decision. Rather, it was proposed by the local district commissioner with the support of Christian converts and voted into being by *Njuri Ncheke*. For the district commissioner, the ban demonstrated to his superiors in Nairobi that the district of Meru accepted the rule of the colonial government and was free from support for the Mau Mau.

---

[2] Thomas, *Politics of the Womb*, p. 80.
[3] Thomas, *Politics of the Womb*, pp. 80–81.

For the members of the *Njuri Ncheke*—whose legitimacy was questioned by some in Meru, and especially younger, school-educated men who resented the authority of older men who appeared to be allied to the interests of the colonial state—the ban was a tool for showing their loyalty to the state.[4] Both younger and older women opposed the ban. Because excision needed to be done in secret to avoid arrest and punishment, the nature of the practice changed: it was done by young women themselves (as the moniker '*Ngaitana*' indicated) and no longer in big, open spaces with attendant rituals; they used razor blades bought in shops rather than the traditional iron-wedge knives; and the age of the girls initiated dropped. The ban encouraged rather than discouraged excision, partly because the *Ngaitana* themselves were so influential. They had, too, the support of older women:

> Grandmothers' strong support for excision stemmed from the important roles that older women usually played as the organisers of initiation, as well as from the special relationship which existed between grandparents and grandchildren, enabling them to discuss intimate topics considered inappropriate for discussions between parents and children.[5]

As young women themselves frequently had little knowledge about how to conduct circumcision—or what constituted clitoridectomy—older women intervened in the secret ceremonies. Even mothers and women who had never before conducted excisions were drawn into the rebellion, often risking the wrath of their male relatives. The district commissioner and some of the members of the *Njuri Ncheke* interpreted this intransigence within the framework offered by the Mau Mau: the district commissioner blamed young men who supported the Mau Mau for encouraging the practice, thus weakening the authority of older men; the *Njuri Ncheke* saw women's opposition to the ban as being similar to women's support for the Mau Mau and, thus, an illegitimate refusal of patriarchal power. Yet while the women and girls who participated in the secret excisions—in other words, the *Ngaitana* and their supporters—recognised the parallels between their rebellion and the Mau Mau, they insisted that their movement was different.[6] Thomas writes that the 'girls of *Ngaitana* defied the ban in order to gain respect and become young women', while older women (who 'probably had a better sense of how *Ngaitana* related to past and present struggles against colonial law and order') 'reclaimed responsibility for making immature girls into fertile women'.[7]

This example of a rebellion led by young women against representatives of the colonial state and the authority of older men in 1950s Kenya—in the midst of the Mau Mau—helps to illuminate some considerations to take into account when describing young people's involvement in politics and, especially, violent

---

[4] Thomas, *Politics of the Womb*, pp. 81–89.
[5] Thomas, *Politics of the Womb*, p. 92.
[6] Thomas, *Politics of the Womb*, pp. 91–94.
[7] Thomas, *Politics of the Womb*, pp. 94–95, 102.

politics in colonial and postcolonial Africa. The *Ngaitana* defy the stereotype of African youth politics. Firstly, this was a movement originated by girls and older women around an issue which was specific to the constitution of the identities and power of girls and older women in Meru society. These young women were by no means unusual on the continent: girls offered up resistance to colonial rule and challenged the power of their elders for a multitude of reasons and in a variety of ways. The fact that scholars have tended to attend to boys and young men's involvement in politics is a reflection of, among other things, boys' presence in the archive as the colonial state tended to record their resistance more so than girls'. Secondly, the *Ngaitana* demonstrate the degree to which girls' revolt was not an unthinking, irrational reaction but was, rather, grounded in their opposition to older men—be they African patriarchs or colonial officials—intervening in a tradition which shaped the trajectory of their own lives. Although this revolt over circumcision occurred within the context of the Mau Mau, and many of the *Ngaitana* supported the Mau Mau, not every youth revolt was explicitly against colonial rule. Thirdly, while much of the rebelliousness of African youth in colonial and postcolonial Africa (and to some degree in the precolonial era too) was driven by intergenerational resentment, the *Ngaitana* provide an example of intergenerational solidarity, forged in shared opposition to patriarchal power. Finally, the *Ngaitana* took place in the midst of extraordinary violence, most of it exercised by the agents of the colonial state. While many scholars have been interested in how young people—particularly young men—have used violence to pursue politics, it is important to emphasise that they usually did so in contexts where the colonial or postcolonial state had far greater capacity to terrorise, detain, arrest, torture, kill, or execute than did any protest movement.

This chapter describes how young people's rebellions against parental or other forms of power in colonial and postcolonial Africa were constituted, carried out, and perceived. It begins, though, in the precolonial and early colonial eras, exploring how the age-based structures of many African societies produced tensions between, especially, older and younger men and how those antagonisms changed and intensified under colonial rule. The chapter then turns to colonial anxieties about 'detribalisation' and the rise of what was described as 'delinquency'—including youth gangs. The final two sections are on children and young people's political engagement through schools and other educational institutions and in conflict as child soldiers.

Wealth, Marriage, and Intergenerational Tension

In April 1856 in the war-torn Eastern districts of the Cape Colony, two girls went to frighten birds away from the crops planted by the community's women at the beginning of the growing season. One of the girls, Nongqawuse, was an orphan in her mid-teens and lived with her uncle, Mhlakaza, and the other, Nombanda, was about eight years old and was Mhlakaza's sister-in-law. As they went about their work, they encountered two strangers who entrusted

Nongqawuse with a message for her uncle. When the two girls relayed what they had been told to Mhlakaza, who was a diviner and relatively wealthy, they were ignored. The following day, they returned to the same field and the strangers reappeared, reiterating that Nongqawuse and Nombanda must tell Mhlakaza what they said. This time, though, Nongqawuse succeeded in winning her uncle's attention because he recognised in her description one of the strangers as his deceased younger brother and Nongqawuse's own father. Simply on these grounds it is unsurprising that the girls might have been dismissed by their elders. But what they had been told by the two strange men—ancestors returned to the world of the living, as it transpired—was shocking: the girls were to instruct the leaders of Xhosa society to slaughter 'all the cattle now living'; that the cultivation of grain should cease; new cattle kraals and grain stores should be built. If the Xhosa did this, their ancestors would return—they would rise from the dead and assist 'in driving the white men out of the land'.[8]

What followed was the self-immolation of Xhosa society: around 400,000 cattle were killed, about 40,000 Xhosa people starved to death, and Xhosa resistance to British colonial rule effectively came to an end. When Nongqawuse and Nombanda reported what they had heard to Mhlakaza, Xhosa society was in deep crisis, under enormous stress after successive wars against the British and epidemics of both human and livestock disease. This context helps to account for why so many men were willing to sacrifice their cattle—the signifier of both wealth and adult manhood in Xhosa society—and why Xhosa people more generally destroyed what remained of their food supply. But historian Helen Bradford argues for the importance of taking into account the age and gender of Nongqawuse because 'an adolescent, of marriageable age, had everything to do with cattle'. She had probably been initiated on entering puberty and was regarded as being of marriageable age—she was, thus, 'a sexual being, an *intombi*', who could be married if a suitor was able to pay the requisite bride price in cattle to her uncle. Herein lay the issue that Bradford highlights:

> massive cattle losses from the 1830s—in frontier wars, in drought and in famine, in the lungsickness epidemic from 1854—were presumably wreaking havoc with older ways of regulating sexuality. By 1848, in the heartland of the region later swept by 'cattle-killing', some 80 per cent of households owned fewer than six cattle; nearly a third owned none at all. Furthermore, bridewealth had recently risen to ten oxen: completely out of reach for most homesteads.[9]

In other words, marriage was harder to arrange because of the rising cost of bridewealth as cattle herds shrank. This denial of marriage meant a denial of

---

[8] Jeff Peires, *The Dead Will Arise: Nongqawuse and the Great Xhosa Cattle-Killing Movement of 1856–7* (Johannesburg and Cape Town: Jonathan Ball, 1989), pp. 191–193.
[9] Helen Bradford, 'Women, Gender and Colonialism: Rethinking the History of the British Cape Colony and Its Frontier Zones, C. 1806–70,' *The Journal of African History*, vol. 37, no. 3 (1996), pp. 361–362.

adulthood. Young men—possibly because their 'masculinity was threatened by delayed marriages, defeat, and colonial encroachment'—were 'extensively press-ganging young women' into sexual relationships. The usual penalty for this—a fine paid in cattle—was harder to enforce in a situation where the value of cattle had risen so high. Understood in this light, Nongqawuse's prophecy was an attack on men's (mis)behaviour during a time of widespread crisis: misbehaviour that attacked women and also prevented a younger generation from reaching maturity.[10]

The roles of these two young women in such a cataclysmic event were profoundly unusual and indicate the degree to which the imposition of British colonial rule and years of warfare had turned the world of the Xhosa upside down. But it is an instructive example of how generational tension was exacerbated by—and became a motivator of—resistance against colonial rule and rebellion within African societies under colonialism. Generally speaking, though, while boys and young men may have fought in the armies of precolonial and colonial Africa, politics tended to remain a sphere closed off to children and young people (and most women and unfree people too). The changes caused by colonial conquest fractured African societies, sometimes opening up opportunities for youth to influence politics themselves.

This noted, in the precolonial era the ability to enter into positions of political leadership and to gain power—depending on the society this could take the form of working a large extent of land, having a large kinship group, or owning a lot of livestock—was associated with the formal achievement of maturity. For men, and to some degree women, this meant marrying and starting a family. In many societies—as in the case of the Xhosa, described above—marriage rested on bridewealth paid by the groom's family to that of the bride. Young men needed to have access to wealth in order to marry and thus to attain adulthood. In others—such as in Yao society in what is now Malawi—the men to whom women were betrothed laboured on the bride's land before their marriage, and afterwards would have fuller access to that land. Regardless of how young men accrued the wealth necessary to marry, this process ensured that elders—especially patriarchs—controlled young women's reproductive capacities as well as young men's ability to shift from youth to adulthood via marriage.

For example, Ankole, Buganda, Buhaya, and Bunyoro were gerontocratic societies in the Great Lakes region during the precolonial period. They were built on a structure of men marrying and then gradually accumulating wealth—a home separate from that of the man's family and ownership of land and livestock—over their lifetimes, eventually accruing the property and status which might allow them to wield political power. Marriage signalled full adult maturity for both men and women, and the age of marriage for young men was determined as the time at which they had managed to acquire the property—which could include animals, like goats—they needed to pay as bridewealth. While they could work to accumulate this wealth, they could also enter into

---

[10] Bradford, 'Women, Gender and Colonialism,' p. 362.

client relationships with wealthier kin or borrow property from others. In this way, while marriage certainly caused young men to go into debt, it also built relationships across generations, allowing for a degree of transfer of wealth. The imposition of colonial rule, new forms of wage labour, and the arrival of Christian missionaries transformed marriage in the Great Lakes region and across the continent. In the twentieth century, missionaries observed that the age of marriage for men actually increased in the Great Lakes in the first half of colonial rule. This may have been the result of an unequal distribution of wealth within the colonial economy—privileging older rather than younger men—but it might also indicate that younger men were, in fact, wealthy enough to marry and could grow their wealth without the assistance of others and chose, rather, to delay marriage until their late twenties or older.[11] Many places—including in these four societies—experienced a crisis of marriage in the twentieth century. Historian Shane Doyle explains:

> A crisis of marriage destabilised colonial societies across Africa, as elders fought a rearguard action to preserve their control over wealth and the reproductive power of young women, now threatened by young men's education, experience of the outside world, and paid employment. The frustration of young males propelled colonial change across the continent.[12]

Among the Barolong-Tshidi people in Southern Africa, the transformation of an individual's status within a community, personal relations, and wealth, among other factors, which occurred at marriage, was an ongoing process: marriage was a state 'of "becoming," not "being"'.[13] Being unable to marry and to form a family was, then, a denial not only of status, but also of the opportunity to live fully as a member of a community. The crisis of marriage under colonial rule was produced by a range of factors: it was an attempt by elders to hold on to systems which had entrenched their power historically; young men who had received schooling and who entered into wage earning labour now sought alternative work and life courses other than those demanded by an older generation; young women, too, were increasingly educated and understood towns and cities as spaces where they could fashion forms of freedom for themselves; conflict and capitalist production had varying impacts on the price of cattle and other livestock and the availability of land, rendering familiar relationships with land and livestock different; and all of this occurred within a context where intergenerational tension was increasingly politicised, with elders often seen as being allied to the colonial state.

---

[11] Shane Doyle, 'Premarital Sexuality in Great Lakes Africa, 1900–1980,' in *Generations Past: Youth in East African History*, eds. Andrew Ross Burton and Helene Charton-Bigot (Athens, OH: Ohio University Press, 2010), pp. 240–241, 244.
[12] Doyle, 'Premarital Sexuality in Great Lakes Africa,' p. 245.
[13] Jean Comaroff and John L. Comaroff, 'The Madman and the Migrant: Work and Labour in the Historical Consciousness of a South African People,' *American Ethnologist*, vol. 14, no. 2 (May, 1987), p. 197.

For instance, in Uganda in the early decades of the twentieth century—a state which included largely, but not exclusively, Buganda people—missionaries worried about the apparently increasing numbers of young men who had not married and formed households. Colonial taxes which disincentivised marriage, as well as a rising brideprice—blamed variously on rising prices of cattle, deliberate efforts by older men to raise the brideprice in an attempt to assert their power by keeping young men in the countryside and out of the colonial economy, the rising value of wives with the introduction of cash crops, and a tax on brideprice payments levied by chiefs—meant that fewer young men attained formal adulthood. As a result, many young people rejected brideprice out of hand from the First World War onward, thus also rejecting the authority of elders to make them adults through marriage. Young men seem to have become more sexually free after the Second World War, and young women—with secondary school education more easily available to them and freed to move to cities—also experimented with new forms of relationships. Rates of divorce crept up; many couples simply lived together instead of marrying.[14]

Similar factors caused a revolt of Zulu youth in 1906–1908. What is usually referred to as the Bambatha Rebellion was, superficially, an uprising against the Natal Colony's introduction of a poll tax in 1905. Although named for a minor chief, Bambatha, who constituted and led one of the main fighting forces of Zulu men against the colonial state, the rebellion was far more widespread than its identification with one rebel would suggest. Support for the rebellion cut across Zulu society, terrifying both settlers and the colonial state which poured resources and manpower into stamping it out. After about two years of conflict, between 3000 and 4000 Zulu people were dead, around thirty whites were killed, and many of the leaders and participants gaoled or executed. As historian Benedict Carton explains, this was more complex than a tax revolt. Natal's poll tax was intended to be paid by men who were aged eighteen years or older and who were not married. While the tax applied across racial categories, this legislation was felt especially sharply by 'the first generation of African youths to come of age with expanding access to wage employment, redress of grievances in colonial courts and refuge in Christian missions'.[15] This tax which was not to be paid by older, married adult men was perceived as an effort to undermine the gains made by younger men under colonialism. Moreover, it implied that African patriarchs were working with the colonial state to maintain control over young men's labour, as discussed in Chap. 6.

This dynamic—of increasing youthful resentment of an older generation believed to be in cahoots with colonial administrators, of young people experiencing both possibilities for and constraints on their futures as a consequence of colonial rule, and of older men, settler farmers and other businessmen, and the colonial state attempting to maintain control over young men's

[14] Doyle, 'Premarital Sexuality in Great Lakes Africa,' pp. 244–245.
[15] Benedict Carton, *Blood from Your Children: The Colonial Origins of Generational Conflict in South Africa* (Charlottesville: The University of Virginia Press, 2000), p. 2.

labour—was repeated in different ways, and with differing outcomes, across the continent especially during the first half of the twentieth century. While generational tension was not unique to the colonial era, as historian Richard Waller explains, colonial rule 'altered the terms of the debate between generations'. Firstly, it changed 'the structure of opportunity that made the young patient and their elders more tolerant'. Put another way, social, political, and economic change under colonial rule disrupted the mechanisms which ensured the transmission of wealth to a younger generation, allowing both young men and women to achieve adulthood via marriage. These systems which helped to temper generational conflict were weakened as a result of colonial conquest. Secondly, writes Waller, at the same time, colonial rule made possible 'new models of responsible behaviour which, in some ways, discounted the past'. By this, Waller means that for both young men and young women, colonial rule offered new markers of gendered adulthood. For men, there 'were the ideals of productive masculinity, tamed by work and made responsible through the obligations of marriage and citizenship', while for women, there was 'modern wifehood and motherhood that taught girls the disciplines of a new but still subordinate domesticity'.[16] As noted above, wage labour on farms meant that young men were no longer as dependent on older men for assistance in buying cattle to pay brideprice, while young women learned—especially at mission schools—that as good Christian wives they were expected to remain within the sacred confines of the home, rather than working the land, going to market, or engagement in other forms of work, a conceptualisation of women's roles which ran counter to the gendered division of labour in many African societies. As the example of colonial Uganda demonstrates, young men and women could choose to delay marriage and to reject these new modes of adulthood. The point is that precolonial generational relations and the gendered definition of generation came under strain under colonialism, becoming flashpoints for conflict.

Young people had also changed under colonial rule. A small and largely, but not exclusively, male group of youth had been shaped by mission school education and urbanisation and sought employment in the colonial state or in the businesses which sprang up in response to the opening up of cash economies. These young men and some women spoke the languages of colonial rule, wore Western dress, and both rejected and reworked custom. Their demand for access to resources was not necessarily a desire to return to the precolonial past because of what became possible for them under colonial rule. As Waller makes the point, the emergence of a generation of educated young people in search of different futures was one of the ironic effects of colonial rule:

> Co-opting the young and turning them into productive and responsible citizens alone offered colonialism a future. This required appropriately modern or mod-

---

[16] Richard Waller, 'Rebellious Youth in Colonial Africa,' *Journal of African History*, vol. 47 (2006), p. 78.

Photograph 7.1 The son of a district chief in Pondoland, South Africa, dressed for a beer party, 1931, Monica and Godfrey Wilson Collection, University of Cape Town Libraries

ernised institutions of socialisation—schools, youth organisations, welfare, and, if necessary, penal agencies—and also an agreed upon discourse of modernity and maturity. ... The experiences of conversion, education and migration gave the young confidence and the resources to challenge their elders' authority, thereby undermining an alliance between colonialism and 'tradition'.[17]

In other words, colonial rule allowed young people tools with which to question what was described as 'tradition'—usually, a version of the precolonial order of things—thus frequently becoming the cause of social tension. In her research on societies in Ovamboland, in what is now northern Namibia, from the end of the nineteenth to the middle of the twentieth century, historian Meredith McKittrick considers how young people responded to the disruptions produced by the region's involvement in the trans-Atlantic trade in

[17] Waller, 'Rebellious Youth in Colonial Africa,' p. 79.

enslaved people and then by 'the uncertainties of colonial transformations'. As she writes, in Ombalantu and Ongandjera communities, the 'actions' which young people undertook to 'ensure' their 'economic and social security ... looked like rebellion against kings and elders, and were treated as such'. Historically, young people in Ovambo society 'were dependent on their elders for permission to move ahead with virtually any aspect of their lives', meaning that their ability to attain adulthood hinged almost entirely on older adults. Girls needed parental permission to be initiated and then to marry, while young men needed assistance from patriarchs to accumulate the stock they needed to marry and found their own households. Young people were, thus, in a position of relative vulnerability—which was compounded by bearing the brunt of enslavement and suffering the most during famines as food distribution in most households tended to favour elders. By the end of the nineteenth century, as McKittrick argues, young people were in crisis. Drawing on interviews with people born in the precolonial period, McKittrick observes that a third of the people whom she interviewed had grown up outside of their parents' households. Some had been enslaved or orphaned by famine, while others 'had been "given" to relatives without children' or sent away 'when marriages ended' or when their parents were expelled by Ovambo monarchs. These young people could not draw as easily on the obligations of kinship to allow them into adulthood. During this period the stage of 'youth' was increasingly drawn out 'as the resources necessary to move towards senior status were depleted'. This scarcity was the product of the disruptions of colonial conquest: smaller herds meant that young men were unlikely to be granted cattle in order to marry; young men and young women's labour was also 'often key to household recovery strategies'.[18]

How, then, did young people attempt to address this situation? McKittrick explains that they sought alternative routes to wealth and status, through the accumulation of European goods (which had been markers of status in Obambo societies for some time, especially when limited mainly to monarchs in the region), migrant labour, conversion to Christianity, and literacy. Attending mission schools, wearing European clothing, and churchgoing—among other practices—became markers, thus, of a new youth culture. In this way, young people 'created an alternative cultural sphere independent of and often in opposition to that of their parents—a world with its own set of values and meanings'.[19] Over time, elders in Ovambo society began to pick up on these new symbols of status, as non-Christians began using European names and wearing European clothing. Yet senior men found ways of reasserting their dominance through *omutenge* (or 'burden') in which a young man presented an elder with a gift (such as salt or millet), and in return received a goat or a cow, allowing him, thus, to marry. Because cattle remained expensive and

---

[18] Meredith McKittrick, 'The "Burden" of Young Men: Property and Generational Conflict in Namibia, 1880–1945,' *African Economic History*, no. 24 (1996), pp. 117–118.

[19] McKittrick, 'The "Burden" of Young Men,' p. 119.

overwhelmingly in the hands of patriarchs, young men were obliged to pay them what they wished for livestock, thus cementing their power. Importantly, as McKittrick explains, *omutenge* was 'only a marginal practice in the precolonial era', but by the 1920s it became a useful means of allowing 'older men power to demand more from young men'.[20]

This example from northern Namibia demonstrates how pressures on young people produced new ways of marking status and wealth among the youth—in this case, Christianity, European goods, and migrant labour—and, in so doing, changed broader Ovambo society as well. Young people's attempts to fashion their own routes to adulthood were understood as rebelliousness by their elders—and young men's migrancy did certainly reduce the pool of ready labour to work on older men's homesteads—and gave rise to new attempts to assert elders' power within Ovambo society. Perhaps unsurprisingly, these conflicts spilled into the political arena across the continent during the twentieth century. The first nationalist or anti-colonial organisations had been founded in the early twentieth century, but especially after the Second World War, a younger generation of Africans embraced a more radical and aggressive politics, increasingly demanding not only concessions from colonial states in the form of greater self-government, for instance, but also full independence. The youth leagues and wings of established nationalist political organisations linked their radicalism to the relative youth of their founders (usually young men in their twenties and thirties). As Chap. 4 demonstrated, these activists used metaphors of youth to their advantage in colonies, arguing that they represented the future of those societies and wanted, thus, significant change. In *Long Walk to Freedom*, Nelson Mandela recounts his growing political awareness in Johannesburg in the 1940s and 1950s, recognising that his education—at an elite mission school and at university—had pulled him into a new class of young men and women who were self-consciously modern, with middle-class aspirations. But he was ambivalent about this new identity, understanding it as an attempt to co-opt him and others into the management of colonial rule in Africa:

> I, too, had been susceptible to paternalistic British colonialism and the appeal of being perceived by whites as 'cultured' and 'progressive' and 'civilised'. I was already on my way to being drawn into the black elite that Britain sought to create in Africa. … But it was an illusion. … I came to see the antidote as militant African nationalism.[21]

Membership of this class was an 'illusion' because segregationist South Africa—and colonial rulers elsewhere on the continent—had then little interest in devolving significant power to a group of Africans who had 'proven'

---

[20] McKittrick, 'The "Burden" of Young Men,' p. 120–122.
[21] Nelson Mandela, *Long Walk to Freedom: The Autobiography of Nelson Mandela* (London: Abacus, 1995), pp. 111–112.

themselves to be worthy of self-government. However, Mandela and his generation's support for 'militant African nationalism' ran counter to the established leadership of the African National Congress (ANC) who, many felt, were 'more concerned with protecting their own rights than those of the masses'. As a result, he and a group of likeminded activists decided to form a Youth League 'as a way of lighting a fire' under the ANC.[22]

The case of the ANC Youth League was by no means unique. Writing about the movement for the formation of a Greater Somalia in the wake of the Second World War—when the future of Italian East Africa was uncertain—historian Cedric Barnes focuses on the work of the Somali Youth League. Italy seized what is now Eritrea and Ethiopia in a brutal invasion and conquest in 1935–1936 and amalgamated both with Italian Somalia (which had existed as an Italian protectorate since the 1880s). In 1943, a group of young men founded the Somali Youth Club in Mogadishu. Barnes explains:

> Club membership was restricted to Somalis between the ages of 18 and 32, drawn from what a British report described as the newly emerged 'middle class' of Somali, especially private traders and young men from monthly-salaried groups such as government clerks, servants of Europeans, medical dressers, and members of the Somalia *Gendarmerie* [police force]. By 1947 approximately 75 per cent of the Somalia *Gendarmerie* stationed in Mogadishu were members of the club.[23]

Initially, the Club's purpose—like so many similar self-improvement societies founded across the continent in the first half of the twentieth century—was to make available welfare in a time of wartime disorder, as well as providing English classes and other educational activities. The organisation grew quickly, opening branches in towns across Italian Somalia and, as the example of the Club's appeal to the *Gendarmerie* suggests, attracting a relatively powerful membership of young men. Like the ANC, the Club demanded that members identify as Somali and not primarily in relation to their clan membership. By 1946, though, the Club had changed its name to the Somali Youth League, and its members—which included Somalis beyond the former Italian Somalia—engaged in a far more radical politics, demanding the formation of a Greater Somalia.[24]

This politicisation of generation, as cohorts of young men and women embraced modes of adulthood which differed from those of their parents and demanded both freedom from their elders and colonial rule, was a driving force in anti-colonial struggle. As McKittrick makes the point, young people were interested in forging alternative futures to those on offer to them—often under exceptionally difficult circumstances—and those efforts were interpreted, frequently, by both patriarchs and colonial officials as rebelliousness or, more

---

[22] Mandela, *Long Walk to Freedom*, p. 112.
[23] Cedric Barnes, 'The Somali Youth League, Ethiopian Somalis and the Greater Somalia Idea, c.1946–48,' *Journal of Eastern African Studies*, vol. 1, no. 2 (2007), p. 280.
[24] Barnes, 'The Somali Youth League,' pp. 280–281.

specifically, as delinquency. Much political organising as well as the constitution of new youth cultures occurred in rapidly expanding colonial towns and cities, and urbanisation coupled with changing forms of youth socialisation was figured as a threat to order in colonies across the continent. The following section pays closer attention to the phenomenon of delinquency in twentieth-century Africa.

Urbanisation, Delinquency, and Discipline

African cities grew in the interwar period, as people moved from the countryside for a variety of reasons: while many were in search of wage labour, others sought better prospects based on the skills they might have acquired at school or to become part of new trading or business networks. As Chap. 6 demonstrated, children and young people moved in search of education and work to support themselves and their families. Although there were long-established cities in many African colonies—especially in West and East Africa—colonial authorities viewed this urbanisation with alarm, linking it to growing anti-colonial militancy (much of it connected to the waves of strikes which hit the continent from the 1920s onwards), and sought to find ways of stabilising African populations in urban areas. Administrators were especially concerned about the growing numbers of young people, most of them young men, in colonial cities. But, writing about Dar es Salaam under British rule, historian Andrew Burton points out that Africans shared those anxieties, writing to African newspapers to air their worry about the disorder produced by so many young people in Dar es Salaam:

> Throughout the British colonial period district officials received complaints from Africans about the uncontrolled tide of youngsters flowing into the town. More generally, many Africans shared the European view of the urban arena as an environment in which profligacy and demoralisation abounded. In a society that remained overwhelmingly agricultural, anti-urbanism was a widely held sentiment.[25]

At issue were high levels of unemployment, meaning that a growing number of young people appeared to be drifting into crime and causing disruption in Dar es Salaam. Equally, older Africans and settlers felt discomfort with an emergent youth culture in the city. Burton explains that Dar es Salaam represented opportunities for new ways of living for young people: leisure activities, 'cinemas [which] showed Western, Indian, and later home-produced films', football, gambling, bars, clubs, and dancing all 'threatened the respectability of an emerging African bourgeoisie'.[26] As the previous section showed, mission education, especially, caused a generational divide in the early twentieth

---

[25] Andrew Burton, 'Urchins, Loafers, and the Cult of the Cowboy: Urbanisation and Delinquency in Dar es Salaam, 1919–1961,' *Journal of African History*, vol. 42 (2001), p. 202.

[26] Burton, 'Urchins, Loafers, and the Cult of the Cowboy,' p. 206.

century in many African societies. Youth cultures in cities served to reinforce that generational difference, which was framed—as in the example of Tanganyika—as a kind of crisis for African society: What to do with disrespectful and apparently socially unmoored young people? At the same time, ideas about delinquency, detribalisation, and what should constitute a normative childhood became more important for how settlers and colonial states understood the place of children and young people—and particularly those who were not middle class and in school—in cities. These social and cultural changes—urbanisation, the effects of education, entry into wage labour, and what should constitute the socialisation of young people—produced new attempts to discipline young people, via a range of measures, including institutions like reformatories and new legal regimes.

For instance, social reformers in mid-century Nigeria created a juvenile welfare and reform system which was comprised of juvenile courts, the children's bureau of the police force, and children's homes which were run by the state. Nigeria's first juvenile courts began work in Lagos and in Calabar in 1946, and in the former city, the court was housed in a three-story building, 'a towering physical demonstration of the state as disciplinarian and of the power of the Colony Welfare Office' as Abosede George writes. Perhaps unsurprisingly, this institution contained within such an imposing edifice soon worked itself into the social fabric of Lagos: 'Some parents sought to discipline their children by threatening to send them to "The Welfare," as the Juvenile Court Centre was colloquially called.'[27] The project of reforming juvenile delinquents was a beneficiary of the post-war development funds which Britain and other colonial powers devoted to their empires during a period of growing contestation of imperialism. As George demonstrates, juvenile reform worked 'toward shaping youth in general into appropriately gendered colonial citizens'. Children deemed to be in any way problematic 'were to be removed to purifying homes where they might be exposed and restored to modern modes of childhood, masculinity, and femininity'. Definitions of what constituted a 'normal' child or childhood 'were tied to supposed universal ideas of the child. These were in practice middle-class British cultural ideas of the child.' As a result, apparently delinquent boys were to be taught skills, to set them on 'a path toward the breadwinner form of masculinity', while their female counterparts were placed 'in suitable homes, either as inmates or servants, in preparation for a lifetime of domesticity'.[28]

Around the world, the creation of systems of welfare to care for vulnerable children was one of the consequences of the child saving movement in the nineteenth century. The courts, reformatories, and welfare officers dedicated to children in Nigeria were, then, by no means unique to this colony and were modelled to some degree on similar institutions and processes in Britain. One

---

[27] Abosede A. George, *Making Modern Girls: A History of Girlhood, Labor, and Social Development in Colonial Lagos* (Athens, OH: Ohio University Press, 2015), pp. 476–477.

[28] George, *Making Modern Girls*, p. 471.

of the groups of children targeted by welfare departments and organisations were those defined as 'delinquents'—in historian Laurent Fouchard's words, 'an imprecise, nebulous, legal and social label for a wide variety of norm-violating behaviours'. The malleability of this category meant that it could be used to address conditions and anxieties specific to a range of contexts. In most African colonies, it was only after the Second World War that the term was 'popularised by officials, politicians, welfare officers, academics, and later by international organisations'.[29] This was in response to growing concerns about the social consequences of urbanisation and a phenomenon described as 'detribalisation' in the 1920s and 1930s. Administrators and other supposed experts on colonial or African life argued that distance from patriarchal authorities and the norms governing rural living meant that young people were in danger of becoming socially and morally unmoored in modern city living. Writing about interwar Kenya, historian Chloe Campbell notes that the colonial state and its agents distinguished 'between rural youth conforming to ... tribal ... organization, and a detribalized urban youth' who were believed to be particularly vulnerable to falling into criminal behaviour.[30]

And yet the earliest efforts to address delinquency were in the Cape Colony at the end of the nineteenth century, where, as historian Linda Chisholm explains, a combination of a shift to industrial capitalism and the effects of colonial conquest, which displaced thousands of Africans, gave rise to an apparently rapidly increasing number of children and young people found to be engaged in criminal behaviour. Without compulsory education and as the power of laws to control the labour of rural people waned with men and women seeking work in cities, the colony's white middle class drew on the British reformatory model to found the Porter Reformatory in 1882. The overwhelming majority of the inmates were young men who had been 'apprehended for a variety of crimes against property, such as stock-theft on farms, house-breaking, theft, and pilfering'. Girls were sent to Porter 'for theft and "female crimes" such as concealment of childbirth and prostitution' and for 'crimes considered to be "unnatural" to the female sex—assault, culpable homicide, poisoning, and murder' (boys convicted of murder were sent to gaol). Initially, all the inmates lived together, regardless of racial identity, but from the 1890s—reflecting the broader segregation of colonial life—white youth were kept separate from their African and multiracial fellow inmates.[31] All, though, were apprenticed. As Linda Chisholm writes, the Porter Reformatory differed from those in Britain in that it 'became an important source of domestic and agricultural labour for local dignitaries and farmers'.[32] In the Cape, then, the

---

[29] Laurent Fouchard, 'The Making of the Juvenile Delinquent in Nigeria and South Africa, 1930–1970,' *History Compass*, vol. 8, no. 2 (2010), p. 130.

[30] Chloe Campbell, 'Juvenile Delinquency in Colonial Kenya, 1900–1939,' *The Historical Journal*, vol. 45, no. (2002), p. 131.

[31] Linda Chisholm, 'The Pedagogy of Porter: The Origins of the Reformatory in the Cape Colony, 1882–1910,' *The Journal of African History*, vol. 27, no. 3. (1986), pp. 486–487.

[32] Chisholm, 'The Pedagogy of Porter,' p. 485.

reformatory originated as an instrument for channelling young people's labour towards growing industries and commercial agriculture.

In contrast, in Nigeria British officials became concerned about juvenile delinquency during the Second World War, when Boma Boys—or gangs of young men—were accused of harassing British and African soldiers in Lagos. In response, the British Colonial Office established a subcommittee to investigate colonial juvenile delinquency. In the post-war era, this was renamed the Child and Youth Welfare subcommittee and had a great deal of influence in focusing colonial administrations' interest on young people in urban areas. In Nigeria, the formation of this committee led to the appointment of a social welfare officer who 'opened up youth clubs and youth hostels to remove children from the criminal effect of the street'. He helped to establish the legal system for children described above. Fouchard writes that, ironically, these institutions helped to produce ever greater numbers of 'delinquents' precisely because—as George points out—most children in Lagos, and Nigeria more broadly, did not experience normative European childhoods which were held up by the colonial state as the model for all childhoods:

> The whole service, concentrated in Lagos, identified a recurrent 'youth crime problem' and implemented new policies that dramatically changed the perception of youth. The interdiction of girl street trading ... led to the arrest of several hundred girls a year, despite the protests of market women, and this led to a massive increase of the number of juvenile delinquents, as children 'in need of care' were not distinguished from more serious offenders in crime statistics.[33]

Many of those children were removed to the countryside—away from the 'detribalising' effects of city life. In Kenya during the early 1930s, an increase in crime committed by young people coincided both with the Great Depression (and the majority of youth who were arrested were accused of petty theft) and with the development of government policy on juvenile delinquency and reformatories. In other words, legal and bureaucratic infrastructure brought the category of the delinquent into being, at a time when settlers, especially, were anxious about growing numbers of Africans in the colony's urban areas and the effects of detribalisation on apparently unsupervised youth. As Campbell points out, the absence of compulsory schooling in Kenya—and across the continent—meant that especially children in urban areas were not engaged in the kinds of activities that administrators associated with the management of juvenile delinquency would have regarded as appropriate for children and young people. In Kenya, in 1934 the juvenile delinquency system was reformed and significantly expanded, with reformatories redesigned more closely to resemble those in Britain. However, informed by the view that urban delinquents were detribalised, the training of the inmates at the reformatories especially in agricultural work was 'a deliberate effort to push the ex-inmates into rural areas on

---

[33] Fouchard, 'The Making of the Juvenile Delinquent in Nigeria and South Africa,' p. 133.

release'. Those might be reserves designated for African settlement or onto European farms.[34]

One of the changes instituted by the reforms in Kenya was the abolition of corporal punishment in reformatories. During the 1920s and 1930s in Kenya, the majority of boys convicted of crimes were subjected to caning. Corporal punishment—and specifically beating with whips or other, similar tools—was widespread across the continent under colonial rule. As Paul Ocobock explains, it was a powerful means for colonial governments 'to broadcast their authority' as it was used in 'military barracks, schools, courts, and penal institutions'. Given these institutional contexts, young people—and especially boys and young men—were particularly subject to this form of disciplining. Although efforts to manage or even reduce corporal punishment fluctuated according to time and place in Africa (in Kenya, for instance, as caning was limited to punishing adolescent boys in the mid-twentieth century, its use declined overall), it must be emphasised that violence maintained the colonial racial order.[35] As historian Keith Breckenridge writes about workers on South African gold mines in the first half of the twentieth century, the 'beatings' on the mines 'were constitutive of two enduring categories of men—whites and blacks', those who did the beating, and those who were beaten: 'Even where black men beat each other, the force of the conflict was usually the racial hierarchy'. Breckenridge adds, though, that violence became a tool for the socialisation of young African men on the mines. As explored in Chap. 6, stick fighting was an arena for the socialisation of young men in the rural Eastern Cape—from where many miners originated—as it taught them forms of emotional restraint and adherence to social rules and norms. Drawing on interviews with men who had migrated from the region to the gold mines in the second half of the twentieth century, Breckenridge observes that the *iindlavini*, the youth organisations which young men formed in the Eastern Cape, shaped men's experiences of migrancy and life on the mines:

> These groups ... tended to bind young men from particular districts together. [Breckenridge's] informants all migrated with, or followed, brothers, uncles or other male relatives from their home districts. They played (or more commonly danced) and fought together. And, finally, they enforced powerful and enduring notions of appropriate male behaviour.[36]

While violence was used to enforce the colonial order, so—as Breckenridge notes—under different circumstances it could enforce (masculine) solidarity

---

[34] Campbell, 'Juvenile Delinquency in Colonial Kenya,' p. 145.

[35] Paul Ocobock, 'Spare the Rod, Spoil the Colony: Corporal Punishment, Colonial Violence, and Generational Authority in Kenya, 1897–1952,' *The International Journal of African Historical Studies*, vol. 45, no. 1, Toward a History of Violence in Colonial Kenya (2012), pp. 29–30.

[36] Keith Breckenridge, 'The Allure of Violence: Men, Race, and Masculinity on the South African Goldmines, 1900–1950,' *Journal of Southern African Studies*, vol. 24, no. 4 (1998), p. 678.

and be used in the socialisation of younger generations. Writing about Kenya, Ocobock adds:

> Corporal punishment was not simply an instrument of the British colonial state; it was also a weapon of African parents and elders, used to define age and generational station. It separated men from boys, adults from children … Fathers and elder menfolk in Kenya relied on a diverse disciplinary repertoire, which included violence, to correct the behaviour of young men, negotiate boundaries between generations, and preserve senior authority.[37]

The power of older men was not uncontested, providing, thus, checks to their use of violence. Under colonial rule, though, the state's use of violence was on a much larger scale than what had been experienced in the precolonial era across much of the continent (although those societies caught up particularly in the trans-Atlantic slave trade had been subject to violence over several centuries). Also, forms of precolonial violent disciplining changed. As historian Anne Mager writes, too, about the Eastern Cape, as the nature of young men's organisations changed in the 1940s and 1950s, so did their relationships with girls of their own age. Firstly, premarital sexual relationships which had been tolerated—and even encouraged, if they did not result in pregnancy—in the pre- and early colonial eras were actively preached against by missionaries and African converts, meaning that young people kept their relationships secret. Without the knowledge provided by initiation schools about non-penetrative sex, unplanned pregnancies among unmarried couples rose. Secondly, young men threatened girls with violence: 'in some organisations, to be masculine was to assert male control over females in violent ways, to extract feminine obedience literally through the wielding of sticks'. As Mager explains, girls who were perceived as disobedient or who did not want to engage in sexual activity were at risk of being hit by the same sticks that boys used to fight one another or of sexual assault.[38]

Girls were subject, too, to disciplinary efforts under colonial rule. Chapter 6 describes the work done by organisations to contain urbanised girls' activities and movements and to inculcate in them modesty and good morals (or, at least, as defined by those groups). Schooling—as detailed in Chap. 5—was a particularly important tool for producing, especially, the elite women and girls of colonies. The law was another weapon. Age of consent legislation which was introduced across the British Empire at the end of the nineteenth and beginning of the twentieth centuries was intended by the feminists and other social reformers who campaigned for it to increase the age at which girls could consent to sex as a means of raising women's legal status more broadly. In the colonies, this same legislation was used to shore up white supremacy, by protecting white girls only (or initially), as was the case in colonial Natal and Cape, for

---

[37] Ocobock, 'Spare the Rod, Spoil the Colony,' p. 30.

[38] Anne Mager, 'Youth Organisations and the Construction of Masculine Identities in the Ciskei and Transkei, 1945–1960,' *Journal of Southern African Studies*, vol. 24, no. 4 (1998), pp. 661–663.

example.[39] As historian Elizabeth Thornberry points out, debates over the necessity, or otherwise, of raising the age of consent for African girls, specifically, hinged on definitions of racialised childhood among white activists and politicians: 'were black children ... also innocents in need of protection?'[40]

African, multiracial, and white working-class girls were regarded as more sexually dangerous than their white, middle-class counterparts across the continent, meaning that when those girls experienced sexual assault—especially by white men—they were always far less likely to have their attackers arrested and held to account. Also, those girls who lived in towns and cities were vulnerable to attack from the growing numbers of youth gangs in these areas. At the same time, though, anxieties about violence perpetrated by urban youth were driven by a range of factors unrelated to the actual incidence of crime (or crime as experienced by elites)—in other words, delinquency was produced to some degree by a legal infrastructure designed to curtail it. In 1950s Dar es Salaam colonial officials observed with alarm a growing youth culture shaped by exposure to Westerns, as young men dressed like cowboys and imitated their 'rough' behaviour. As Burton writes, this was a panic similar to that which 'accompanied the emergence of a rebellious youth culture in the West after the Second World War'.[41] However, it is also true that young people in cities formed gangs, many of which did harass and harm other residents.

In his research on the youth gangs of twentieth-century Johannesburg, historian Clive Glaser emphasises that these gangs were found across colonial Africa—and elsewhere—wherever 'a substantial population of poor city-bred youth with limited employment possibilities and deprived of adequate housing, schooling and recreation facilities' lived. Yet the youth gangs of colonial Africa were also formed by circumstances specific to the continent. In the 1930s and 1940s, for instance, there were essentially two types of gangs in Johannesburg: those constituted of migrant men (the same discussed by Breckenridge as regards violence and the formation of solidarity), who 'offered comfort and protection during an apparently temporary sojourn in the city', and the street gangs. The latter were known as *tsotsis* by the 1940s and 'identified powerfully with their urban neighbourhoods' and had 'no meaningful sense of belonging beyond the city'.[42] *Tsotsis* were overwhelmingly young men who, like most African youth, were not enrolled in education and struggled to find steady employment in Johannesburg, and while in contemporary South African

---

[39] Nafisa Essop Sheik, 'Cultures of Sex, Laws of Difference: Age of Consent Law and the Forging of a Fraternal Contract on the Margins of the Nineteenth-Century British Empire,' *Law and History Review*, vol. 38, no. 1 (Feb. 2020), pp. 201–218.

[40] Elizabeth Thornberry, 'The Problem of African Girlhood: Raising the Age of Consent in the Cape of Good Hope, 1893–1905,' *Law and History Review*, vol. 38, no. 1 (Feb. 2020), p. 240.

[41] Burton, 'Urchins, Loafers, and the Cult of the Cowboy,' p. 214.

[42] Clive Glaster, 'Swines, Hazels and the Dirty Dozen: Masculinity, Territoriality and the Youth Gangs of Soweto, 1960–1976,' *Journal of Southern African Studies*, vol. 24, no. 4 (1998), pp. 719–720.

speech, *tsotsi* refers simply to gangsters generally, in the 1940s, as Glaser argues, the term meant someone specific:

> A *tsotsi* was a young man who dressed, spoke, and behaved in a clearly identifiable way. He imitated American 'city slicker' clothing styles, spoke *tsotsitaal* [*tsotsi* language], indulged in some kind of criminal or quasi-legal activity, and generally moved around in gangs. ... it is useful to conceptualise the *tsotsis* of the 1940s and 1950s as a subculture.[43]

As in the case of the 'cowboy' gangs of Dar es Salaam, many African adults viewed *tsotsis* with alarm in the 1940s, describing them as a 'dangerous scourge', while yet others 'argued that the *tsotsis* were essentially harmless youths very concerned with their clothing style'. These were young men who had embraced the sharp dressing, cosmopolitan consumer culture, musical and cinematic tastes, and slang of a transnational black urban class. They had contemporaries across African and North American cities, in particular (and elsewhere). However, over time the link between gangsterism and the *tsotsi* hardened:

> the subculture extended to include urban youths who were neither gang members nor criminals. ... A young male could be a member of the "in-group" if he wore *tsotsis* [long trousers], drank alcohol and smoked dagga [marijuana] freely, spoke *tsotsitaal* well, and demonstrated a familiarity with the township environment. Nevertheless, the criminal gangs constituted the *core* of the subculture.[44]

The criminal aspect of the *tsotsis* grew too, so that by the 1960s and 1970s, big gangs dominated Soweto, the large and predominantly African suburb southwest of Johannesburg. By then, their disruption and criminality—which included fighting each other to defend territory, extorting money from businesses, and harassing residents, especially young women—produced in 1974 the Makgotla, a 'civil guard movement' of middle-aged men who sought, largely unsuccessfully, to curtail younger gangsters' activities. As Glaser notes, the Makgotla 'was in many respects an attempt by older men to reassert patriarchal authority over defiant urban youth'.[45]

Urbanisation under colonial rule or forms of segregation in settler states produced a context in which young African people—especially young men— were regarded with suspicion by colonial administrators and adults, settler, African, or otherwise. This anxiety about unsupervised, apparently unoccupied youth fed into broader colonial concerns about the effects of modernity on African societies (or 'detribalisation') as well as into a growing international discourse on delinquency. The infrastructures created to deal with delinquent children helped, thus, to produce precisely this class. Perhaps the best example

---

[43] Clive Glaser, *Bo-Tsotsi: The Youth Gangs of Soweto, 1935–1976* (Oxford: James Currey, 2000), p. 47.
[44] Glaser, *Bo-Tsotsi*, p. 53.
[45] Glaster, 'Swines, Hazels and the Dirty Dozen,' p. 735.

of this was the transformation of Lagos's girl hawkers from being traders engaged in work—and a form of work which predated colonial conquest—to being delinquent girls in need of saving. Violence was an important feature of efforts to discipline youth, even as it was vital for constituting masculine solidarity in certain settings. Girls, though, and especially those who occupied socially marginal positions, were on the receiving end of male violence, state violence, and the disciplinary efforts of a range of institutions. Even as it opened up opportunities for new ways of living and being, urban living was often harsh for the young men and women who migrated (and who were born) there, with many facing long-term unemployment and navigating overcrowded, unsanitary, and otherwise unsuitable living conditions. That some did turn to forms of criminal behaviour was by no means surprising. Youth gangs functioned both as subcultures—drawing together young people, particularly men, in shared fashion, leisure activities, and language—and as criminal enterprises.

The lines between criminal and anti-colonial or political activity were, though, frequently blurred, with colonial administrators and elders often drawing a sharp distinction between 'respectable' young people in education and those disreputable young people on the streets. However, as the following section demonstrates, schools and universities were also powerful sites for political organising in the colonial and postcolonial eras.

Education, Politics, and Protest

School was no refuge from the world, but, rather, a site in which the struggles of colonial and postcolonial African societies were played out between pupils, parents, and teachers—and also between students and professors at universities. Considering that mission education, especially, was so important for the formation of the first generations of anti-colonial activists, the vital place of schools and universities for political action is unsurprising. As Chap. 5 demonstrated, African parents understood that education could provide routes into employment in the colonial state or in other sectors and—alongside their children—frequently placed pressure on authorities to found high schools and, in some cases, universities, especially in the early twentieth century. It was these institutions which produced an educated elite, who were often highly mobile—travelling abroad, studying in Europe and the United States—and widely read, aware of nationalist movements around the colonial world. As historian Toyin Falola explains, such was the link between education and resistance to colonial rule that the Belgian Congo actively limited secondary and higher education for Africans:

> the Belgian colony of the Congo … allowed the missions to establish elementary schools … The state required the missions to limit severely the purpose of elementary schools, and the majority of African students were instructed in local languages. A few, selected for clerical duties as priests, had the opportunity of learning French. In a highly paternalistic arrangement, the elementary schools

were like convents, and the colleges were like seminaries. The results of the system were that the Belgians occupied all the major technical and administrative jobs, that the brightest Africans were prepared for the priesthood and other for subordinate positions, and that the majority of Africans ended up as workers and producers in the colonial system.[46]

As historian Barbara Yates adds, at independence in 1960, what was then Zaire had some senior-level African administrators, a few dozen college graduates ('the first having obtained his degree in 1956') and 'no black army officers, ... [and] no Congolese physicians, engineers or agronomists'.[47] Zaire's new African leadership—including its first Prime Minister, Patrice Lumumba—were drawn overwhelmingly from the colony's *évolué* class, an upper middle class who had in most cases been able to obtain some education. Members of this elite gained formal *évolué* status by demonstrating the degree to which they had assimilated into European culture by, for example, speaking French, wearing Western dress, and living in Western-style housing. (Lumumba himself had had little formal education, but managed to rise socially, partly through gaining employment in institutions of the colonial state, like the post office.) These colonial elites tended to dominate the leadership of anti-colonial movements, leading African colonies into independence from the late 1950s onwards.

Many of these anti-colonial leaders sharpened their political skills at schools and universities. At Fort Hare University—a South African university founded in 1916 by three churches for African students and which trained several generations of the continent's anti-colonial leaders—Nelson Mandela was expelled in 1940 over the legitimacy of elections for the Student Representative Council. He had enrolled at Fore Hare—itself an impressive feat—because he believed that a degree from a university 'was a passport not only to community leadership but [also] to financial success'. Mandela and his fellow students knew that they 'were the African elite'.[48] But his principled stance on the illegitimacy of the university's governance structures meant that he left without completing a degree there and made his way to Johannesburg instead, following a well-worn path travelled by many young men from his region. Mandela's decision to challenge Fort Hare's white leadership echoed demonstrations in mission schools around South Africa during the 1940s, when students rioted, set fire to buildings, and boycotted classes. Waves of unrest at the country's elite institutions for African youth crested in 1919–1920, 1929, 1944–1946, 1955–1956, 1957, and in the early and mid-1960s, often resulting in the arrest of students by the police, and the temporary closure of some schools. As historian Liz Stanley notes, these protests were produced by a confluence of

---

[46] Toyin Falola, *Nationalism and African Intellectuals* (Rochester, NY: University of Rochester Press, 2004), p. 13.
[47] Barbara A. Yates, 'Educating Congolese Abroad: An Historical Note on African Elites,' *The International Journal of African Historical Studies*, vol. 14, no. 1 (1981), p. 34.
[48] Nelson Mandela, *Long Walk to Freedom: The Autobiography of Nelson Mandela* (London: Abacus, 1995), p. 59.

factors specific to each school, as well as the broader social and political context which allowed for the unrest to spread beyond an initial case. The 1919–1920 protests, for instance, were at Lovedale about 'food shortage and changes in the flour used to make bread'. The rioting and destruction of property which ensued—resulting in the arrest, charging, and expulsion of several pupils—spread over more than twenty institutions, during a period of strikes and opposition to segregationist politics in South Africa more widely.[49] As historian Jonathan Hyslop argues, South African students developed a tradition of militancy where protest at school became a strategy for protesting wider political developments.[50] During the late 1960s, after the banning of anti-apartheid organisations, schools, theological seminaries, teacher training colleges, medical schools, and universities became sites where activists could gather to discuss strategies for opposing the state. Ironically, too, the Bantu Education Act of 1953 had massively expanded access to education for African youth, meaning that increasingly overcrowded schools were sites for politicising a new generation of activists. The Black Consciousness Movement (BCM) had its origins in the founding South African Students' Organisation (SASO) in 1969. Led primarily by Steve Biko and Barney Pityana, both of them students too, SASO aimed to unite black—meaning African, Indian, and multiracial—students in a struggle for black liberation. Their work encompassed consciousness raising and encouraging black university students—many of them at the African-, Indian-, or coloured-only universities founded under apartheid—to engage in community building.[51]

Biko—who was murdered in detention by the South African police in 1977—was acutely aware of BCM as a youth-oriented organisation and intellectual project. Yet he argued for intergenerational solidarity, insisting that BCM's embrace of a more confrontational politics was 'a useful weapon in merging the young and the old. Before then there was a difference in the outlooks of the old generation and the younger generation. The younger generation was moving too fast for the old generation.' Many of the latter, Biko suggested, were still in the thrall of then-banned political organisations like the ANC.[52] The BCM did certainly represent a younger generation's anti-apartheid politics and frustration with elders who seemed to remain loyal to resistance organisations in exile and not as present in South African activism. BCM strongly influenced the student organisations in some Soweto high schools which planned the protests against the imposition of Afrikaans in African schools on 16 June 1976. Police opened fire on the students as they marched,

[49] Liz Stanley, 'Protest and the Lovedale Riot of 1946: "Largely a Rebellion against Authority"?', *Journal of Southern African Studies*, vol. 44, no. 6 (2018), pp. 1043–1044.

[50] Jonathan Hyslop, 'Food, Authority, and Politics: Student Riots in South African Schools, 1945–1976,' unpublished paper, University of the Witwatersrand African Studies Institute, September 1986, p. 4.

[51] Ian MacQueen, 'Black Consciousness,' in *The Routledge Handbook of Pan-Africanism*, ed. Reiland Rabaka (London and New York: Routledge, 2020), pp. 136–145.

[52] Steve Biko, *I Write What I Like* (San Francisco: Harper & Row, 1979), p. 146.

killing up to an estimated seven hundred unarmed protestors. The Soweto student uprising ignited protests across South Africa and helped to reinvigorate the anti-apartheid movement.

Even as many young activists associated with the 1976 protests fled into exile to join South African liberation organisations based in other, newly independent African countries, school-age youth and student organisations remained vital to the growing resistance to apartheid within South Africa during the 1980s and early 1990s. These young people—often dubbed 'comrades'—bore the brunt of state violence, experiencing detention, imprisonment, and torture. Anthropologist Pamela Reynolds estimates that 'between 1976 and 1987, some twenty-four thousand children under the age of eighteen were imprisoned, and many (or most) were tortured or severely ill treated'.[53] As historian Emily Bridger notes, although 'comrades' in popular culture and memory were gendered male, young women certainly 'participated in both non-violent and violent forms of political action, including attending marches and rallies, throwing stones or petrol bombs at police vehicles or homes, punishing suspected informers and other offenders, and even joining underground guerrilla armies'.[54] This was at considerable risk to themselves—from representatives of state authority, but also from within the movement. Anthropologist Isak Niehaus has documented how in some areas, the 'Comrades movement was inspired by a very strong sense of gender and generational consciousness. The predominant ethos was one of youthful masculinity that valued fearless bravery.' Girls—who had long been preyed upon by teachers—were, thus, potential victims of assault from members of their own movement.[55] Schools remained central to the struggle, as school boycotts in the 1980s were one strategy which pulled even young children into the movement.

Young people—and especially those who were black—were at the core of South Africa's liberation struggle, comprising a fractious anti-apartheid movement which (like anti-colonial movements elsewhere) reflected the powerful relations and social dislocations of South African society more broadly. In postcolonial African states, young people continued to question and challenge the status quo. After independence, student protest endured, echoing also the global youth movements of the 1960s. As historian Mamadou Diouf notes, young people 'played a crucial role in the configuration of nationalist coalitions' (or, put another way, were important for constituting anti-colonial nationalist movements) but were also often 'the first group in society' to demonstrate 'hostility' towards 'the authoritarian drift of the postcolonial powers'. In many contexts, young people were 'swept aside' in the postcolonial order,

---

[53] Pamela Reynolds, *War in Worcester: Youth and the Apartheid State* (New York: Fordham University Press, 2012), p. 13.

[54] Emily Bridger, *Young Women against Apartheid: Gender, Youth, and South Africa's Liberation Struggle* (Oxford: James Currey, 2021), p. 4.

[55] Isak Niehaus, 'Towards a Dubious Liberation: Masculinity, Sexuality and Power in South African Lowveld Schools, 1953–1999,' *Journal of Southern African Studies*, vol. 26, no. 3 (2000), p. 396.

Photograph 7.2 Student Protest, Durban, 1986, Omar Badsha, University of Cape Town Libraries

'through invocations of African traditions that uphold rules of deference and submission' between 'juniors and seniors'.[56] Writing about Ghana—the first former British colony to gain independence in 1957—historian Emmanuel Asiedu-Acquah points out that the country's first President, Kwame Nkrumah, acknowledged that the 'political triumph' of his Convention People's Party (CPP) 'was largely the work of the country's youth'. Yet after independence, the CPP viewed young people warily, realising that they retained the potential for causing social and political unrest. The CPP introduced a range of interventions intended to produce the ideal Ghanaian youth, 'a disciplined, productive, and revolutionary patriot with a pan-Africanist outlook' who would be 'an important agent in the mobilisation and development of the country'. The Builder's Brigade and Ghana Young Pioneers Movement were founded—the latter especially in schools and tertiary institutions—to mould these citizens.[57] But students remained critics of the new, independent state, and especially as the CPP consolidated power and turned authoritarian. For instance, in 1963 and 1964, students—often speaking through the National Union of Ghanaian Students—condemned the government's dismissal of the Chief Justice effectively for demonstrating insufficient loyalty to Nkrumah and the CPP and

[56] Mamadou Diouf, 'Urban Youth and Senegalese Politics: Dakar 1988–1994,' in *Cities and Citizenship*, ed. James Holston (Durham, NC: Duke University Press, 1998), p. 42.
[57] Emmanuel Asiedu-Acquah, '"We Shall Be Outspoken": Student Political Activism in Post-Independence Ghana, c.1957–1966,' *Journal of Asian and African Studies*, vol. 54, no. 2 (2019), p. 172.

'protested the government's detention and deportation of Ghanaian and expatriate academics at the universities for unspecified acts of subversion'. In response, the government closed universities in early 1964 during the national referendum on Ghana becoming a one-party state. Clearly, the postcolonial state 'saw the universities and student political activism as the last bastions of opposition to CPP dominance of Ghanaian politics' and those students who protested risked intimidation and arrest.[58]

Similarly, in Tanzania—which became independent in 1961—youth were at the centre of one of the state's early crises. As historian Andrew Ivaska explains, like Ghana (and elsewhere), the anti-colonial movement in what was then Tanganyika was a youth movement as the 'young nationalists of the late 1940s and 1950s' who led the Tanganyika (later Tanzania) African National Union (TANU) successfully eclipsed 'the "elders"' of earlier organisations, empowered by 'access to formal education and wage-labour jobs'. By the 1960s this generation of nationalist leaders was in power and, thus, 'faced with the task of renegotiating their own relationship with "youth"'. On the one hand, the state—as in Ghana—celebrated the political activism of young people, creating a cabinet portfolio for youth, and providing resources to a National Service, the governing party's Youth League, and annual youth festivals. But, on the other, officials 'moved to marginalise youth who potentially posed challenges to that vision'. Like the colonial state, the new Tanzanian state was concerned about unemployed young people in Dar es Salaam, but it was also suspicious of 'teenagers' who were 'perceived to be identifying with "decadent" trends in cosmopolitan style' (it must be emphasised that Tanzania was a socialist state) and of students.[59] In 1960s Tanzania, 'teenager' signalled an unserious and consumerist orientation towards the world. In 1968, the TANU Youth League launched Operation Vijana, which 'prohibited the use of a range of items—mini-skirts, wigs, skin-lightening creams, tight pants or dresses, and short skirts—as "indecent", "decadent" and antithetical to Tanzania's "national culture"'. As Ivaska points out, the Operation was as much an attempt to fashion a new national culture for the socialist state as it was an attempt to discipline urban youth—especially young women.[60]

The University College of Dar es Salaam was opened shortly before independence in 1961 and was the first university in Tanganyika. It was of enormous significance to the new national project, having to produce graduates to Africanise the civil service and the professional class (in 1961, there were fewer than 150 university graduates in Tanganyika). Thus, while students were reminded of 'their obligation to serve the nation' and that they 'were indebted

---

[58] Asiedu-Acquah, '"We Shall Be Outspoken,"' p. 178.

[59] Andrew M. Ivaska, 'Of Students, "Nizers," and a Struggle over Youth: Tanzania's 1966 National Service Crisis,' *Africa Today*, vol. 51, no. 3, Youth and Citizenship in East Africa (Spring, 2005), pp. 84–85.

[60] Andrew M. Ivaska, '"Anti-Mini Militants Meet Modern Misses": Urban Style, Gender and the Politics of "National Culture" in 1960s Dar es Salaam, Tanzania,' *Gender & History*, vol. 14, no. 3 (Nov. 2002), pp. 584–587.

to the country's peasants and workers for enabling their education through taxation', at the same time students at University College understood the power they could wield in a state desperate for skilled workers.[61] The volunteers for the National Service programme were held up as the opposite to the student elite: young men and women who volunteered to 'undergo political, military, and agricultural or vocational training as a prelude to nearly two years spent working on "nation-building" projects'. The programme began in 1963, and it soon became clear that students were profoundly uninterested in joining its ranks and, as a result, in 1965 the government announced that National Service would be compulsory for university and high school graduates.[62] This proposal produced both intense public debate and a backlash from the university and its students. While the state forced the expulsion of the students who protested and slashed academics' salaries, on campus left-wing students and academics formed the United African Students Revolutionary Front, which 'posed uncomfortable questions pointing to the "hidden class struggles" ... of Tanzania's limited experiment with democracy', a criticism precisely of the generation—including Julius Nyerere, the President of Tanzania—which held political power after independence. As Ivaska writes, this stand-off between postcolonial state and university students demonstrates an attempt to 'manage' young people in the making of nation after independence.[63]

Student protests against newly independent African nations endured beyond the 1960s and African students were acutely aware that their contemporaries around the world were engaged in similar generational struggle. As Diouf discusses especially as regards West Africa, students in the 1970s and 1980s aimed their anger often at 'the destruction of the places and monuments of postcolonial munificence' or the symbols of postcolonial power.[64] He adds:

> this new generation felt excluded from the postcolonial munificence and its sites of sociability (e.g., recognition, the rights to free speech, work, and education), and although a numerical majority, as youth, they were reduced to political silence.[65]

In Senegal, neither state repression nor *encadrement* (or pulling young people into state-sponsored youth organisations or other institutions) succeeded in making young people feel integrated into postcolonial society, a feeling exacerbated by high rates of unemployment especially among the youth. As a result, young people became increasingly critical of 'political, economic, social, and cultural institutions'. They created 'autonomous organisations with strong religious or ethnic connotations'—contrary to the spirit of nation-building in postcolonial Senegal. Both rural and urban youth were drawn into protests,

---

[61] Ivaska, 'Of Students, "Nizers," and a Struggle over Youth,' p. 89.
[62] Ivaska, 'Of Students, "Nizers," and a Struggle over Youth,' p. 91.
[63] Ivaska, 'Of Students, "Nizers," and a Struggle over Youth,' p. 102.
[64] Diouf, 'Urban Youth and Senegalese Politics,' p. 44.
[65] Diouf, 'Urban Youth and Senegalese Politics,' p. 46.

and particularly via cultural and athletic associations, and alliances between high school and university students.[66] During and after the 1988 elections, young people took to the streets of Dakar, attacking both people and property, although the 'principal targets' of the rioters were 'symbols of the state' and, such was the magnitude of the riots, the new government agreed to a programme aimed specifically at the uplift of young people in Senegal.[67]

The idea of 'youth' and young people themselves were vital forces within anti-colonial and postcolonial politics on the continent. A generation of young activists—mostly mission-educated young men, like Nyerere, Mandela, and Nkrumah—were the youth who challenged an older generation of African politicians and colonial states in demanding greater political freedom. But once in power, the men of this generation not only ceased being 'youth', but they were also in an ambivalent relationship as regards what constituted 'youth'. Many African states attempted to institute programmes and organisations to manage young people into becoming the 'pioneers' who would drive national development. However, these plans were often undone by young people's resistance (their unwillingness to tolerate political repression, for instance) and desire to embrace different fashions, tastes, and ways of living. But as Diouf also alerts us, the marginalisation of young people—the largest segment of Africa's population—from social, political, and economic spheres after the 1960s had real consequences, both for young people struggling to making a living and for states more broadly as the youth no longer bought into the project of nation-building. Also, young people were co-opted into the conflicts which bedevilled much of postcolonial Africa.

Children at War

Since the early 2000s, a steady stream of memoirs written by former child soldiers who fought in conflicts in Sierra Leone, Uganda, the Sudan, and elsewhere in Africa has found an enthusiastic audience in the West. Perhaps the best known of these are Ishmael Beah's *A Long Way Gone: Memoirs of a Boy Soldier* (2007) and Emmanuel Jal's *Warchild: A Boy Soldier's Story* (2009). Beah was a member of the government's forces in Sierra Leone, while Jal fought for the Sudan People's Liberation Army. These, though, are only two of several such narratives, which recount both boys' and girls' experiences of fighting in postcolonial conflicts across the continent. While children's accounts of war in Africa have, historically, been relatively marginalised, as historian Stacey Hynd points out, ironically, 'these African child soldier memoirs ... have been, if anything, over-privileged in the creation of globalised, collective memories of contemporary conflict in Africa'.[68] Their popularity is due partly to the

---

[66] Diouf, 'Urban Youth and Senegalese Politics,' p. 51.
[67] Diouf, 'Urban Youth and Senegalese Politics,' p. 56.
[68] Stacey Hynd, 'Trauma, Violence, and Memory in African Child Soldier Memoirs,' *Culture, Medicine, and Psychiatry*, vol. 45 (2021), p. 78.

fact that most of these memoirs were purposefully crafted for Western audiences, following a familiar narrative of 'innocence disrupted by war, violence, and trauma, then humanitarian salvation and recovery, with a corresponding disavowal of violence'. They present these readers with a simple moral framework for understanding child soldiering, drawing on 'humanitarian discourses' which 'code children's involvement in war as an adult-perpetrated human rights abuse caused by social breakdown and hyper-violent, non-rule bound contemporary conflict, and which reject child agency and culpability'.[69]

Historians Michelle Moyd, Frances Clarke, and Rebecca Jo Plant point out that the extensive Western coverage of child soldiers since 2000 is certainly a reflection of 'an actual rise in the use of children by rebel groups and state militaries in the late twentieth- and early twenty-first centuries'. But it is also a product of 'the increasing power of human rights ideology, which only in the 1970s began to identify "the child soldier" as a subject for humanitarian intervention'.[70] So while these memoirs do provide readers with narratives of individual young people's experiences of war, it is important to understand their publication within this broader political and cultural context, as well as the fact that the portrait they provide of child soldiering is by no means a complete one.

Before turning to children's involvement in recent African conflicts, it is important to acknowledge that children have long been involved in wars in Africa. Enslaved children were frequently war captives, and pawning increased during and after conflict. In the colonial era, one of the most powerful images used to indict the cruelty of British imperialism was a 1901 photograph of emaciated Lizzie van Zyl, a Boer child incarcerated in a concentration camp established by British forces during the South African War (1899–1902). These camps for Boers as well as the separate camps for black civilians were populated overwhelmingly by women and children. Children died in their numbers, as a result of the camps' poor provisioning and bad management, which were partly responsible for the epidemics of diseases which swept through them. Historians agree that eighty per cent of deaths in the camps were children: the 14,154 officially recorded deaths in the camps specifically for black people were almost certainly an undercount, with the true number being closer to 20,000. An estimated 25,000 to 34,000 died in the Boer camps, but these statistics are also probably inaccurate, as they did not include the many people, most of them children, who died en route to the camps. Children, though, had varied experiences of the conflict: many African children worked through the war, as forced labourers or as servants in Boer camps. Boer boys joined commandoes. They were treated in much the same way as

---

[69] Hynd, 'Trauma, Violence, and Memory in African Child Soldier Memoirs,' pp. 80–81.

[70] Michelle Moyd, Frances M. Clarke, and Rebecca Jo Plant, 'Moral Panic versus Moral Blindness: Responses to Children's Militarization in Uganda and the US,' in *Panic, Transnational Cultural Studies, and the Affective Contours of Power*, ed. Micol Seigel (London and New York: Routledge, 2018), p. 45.

adult prisoners of war when captured, being sent to gaol in South Africa, to concentration camps, and also to prison camps on the islands of St Helena and Ceylon and elsewhere in the British Empire.[71]

The majority of Africans who participated in both colonial and the First and Second World Wars on the continent experienced these conflicts as conscripted labourers. The tens of thousands of Africans who served as porters (on a continent with relatively undeveloped transport infrastructure), as food producers, and as miners to increase export revenue during wartime were men, but a significant proportion of these were also women and children. To be sure, much of this labour was forced labour and, thus, on a continuum with already existing forced labour regimes on the continent. Although writing specifically about African soldiers—or *askaris*—fighting for Germany in East Africa during the First World War, Moyd's account of the work undertaken by women and children can be applied more widely, to other wars in other locales: they 'cooked, cleaned, nursed sick soldiers, gathered food, water, and firewood, and carried equipment'. She points out that the families of soldiers accompanied them on campaign, providing, as a result, unpaid logistical support for the German war effort.[72]

Understood in this longer history, it is unsurprising that children and young people fought in wars of liberation and in postcolonial civil wars. Anthropologist Alcinda Honwana has researched children's participation in the Mozambican and Angolan civil wars, both of which were Cold War conflicts beginning shortly after these states' independence from Portugal in 1975. The Mozambican civil war lasted between the late 1970s and 1992 and was fought between the socialist FRELIMO (Frente de Libertação de Moçambique, or Mozambique Liberation Front), which had led the anti-colonial struggle and controlled the state, and RENAMO (Resistência Nacional Moçambicana, or Mozambique National Resistance), which received funding from the apartheid state and the white-controlled government of Rhodesia (before Zimbabwe's independence in 1980 under majority rule). The latter organisation used the majority of child soldiers—between 8000 and 10,000 children fought in the civil war altogether. About a quarter of a million children were orphaned or separated from their families, and children were included in the more than a million refugees who fled Mozambique.[73] The civil war in Angola lasted between that country's independence—also after an anti-colonial war—and 2002, and for most of its trajectory was, broadly speaking, a struggle between the socialist MPLA (Movimento Popular Nacional de Libertação de Angola, or the Popular and National Movement for the Liberation of Angola), which held the state, and the anti-Marxist, pro-Western UNITA (União Nacional para a

---

[71] S.E. Duff, '"Capture the Children": Writing Children into the South African War, 1899–1902,' *Journal of the History of Childhood and Youth*, vol. 7, no. 3 (Fall 2014), pp. 355–376.

[72] Michelle Moyd, 'Centring a Sideshow: Local Experiences of the First World War in Africa,' *First World War Studies*, vol. 7, no. 2 (2016), p. 119.

[73] Alcinda Honwana, *Child Soldiers in Africa* (Philadelphia, PA: University of Pennsylvania Press, 2007), p. 11.

Independência Total de Angola, or the National Union for the Total Independence of Angola). This was a devastating civil war:

> About half of the displaced population [of approximately 1.2 million people] were children under fifteen years of age. As many as one million children were directly exposed to war as civilians and combatants. More than half a million children died, tens of thousands were orphaned or separated from their parents, and many more were kidnapped during military incursions. Even very young children were dragged into armies and militias. UNITA was most active in abducting and recruiting children, but the government forces also used children as soldiers although to a lesser extent. Children carried weapons and other equipment, fought on the front lines, served on reconnaissance missions, laid landmines, and conducted espionage.[74]

In addition to these children killed, orphaned, and displaced, were those—in both Angola and Mozambique—whose education was disrupted, who struggled to access basic healthcare and adequate nutrition, and who in a range of ways experienced the everyday traumas of wartime.

But Honwana notes that 'the conditions of these civil wars, while extreme, were more visible than they were unusual'. By this she means that children were and are used as soldiers across the continent—in Algeria, Liberia, Sierra Leone, Uganda, and in the Great Lakes region—and Latin America, Asia, and Eastern Europe from the second half of the twentieth century onwards.[75] The growing numbers of child soldiers from roughly the 1970s is due to a range of factors, including the wider availability of lighter, simpler to use, and cheaper weapons; the shifting nature of post-Cold War conflict, where the distinctions between civilians and soldiers are blurred, and where fighters are not necessarily professional soldiers; and the duration of these conflicts, which produces a social context where children might join or be sent to join armies to alleviate poverty. At the same time, there was a global shift in thinking about children and war: the emergence of the category of the 'child soldier' in the 1970s drew attention precisely to this category of person as an example of profound humanitarian failure.

It is difficult to identify a single experience of being a child soldier in Africa—contrary to what popular memoirs might imply. Moyd, Clarke, and Plant explain:

> a majority are aged 15–17, and, by some estimates, nearly 40 percent are girls. Moreover, most children attached to foreign militaries and rebel groups do not serve as combatants but rather as porters, cooks, guards, or 'wives,' whose roles might include domestic labour as well as sex. Finally, in the majority of conflicts, abduction has been the exception rather than the rule. ... as many as two-thirds

---

[74] Honwana, *Child Soldiers in Africa*, p. 14.
[75] Honwana, *Child Soldiers in Africa*, pp. 30–31.

of all child soldiers 'exercise some (at times considerable) initiative in coming forward to enrol.'[76]

None of these factors—the range of activities that child soldiers might perform or the reasons for how and why they might sign up in the first place—mitigate the horror of children's involvement in war, but they do help to describe the constrained and dangerous conditions under which children (and their guardians) are forced to act and make choices. As Honwana observes for the civil wars in Mozambique and Angola, while some were kidnapped and forced into becoming soldiers, many entered armies under far more ambiguous circumstances. She writes: 'young men were pressured to "volunteer"'. This pressure came from adults—themselves acting in fear—as well as from more material concerns ('insecurity, vulnerability, and lack of food').[77] Similarly, in their initiation into fighting, young men were 'agents and victims ... simultaneously', as they learned to kill other people.[78] She suggests that these combatants exercised 'tactical agency': seizing opportunities when they presented themselves to improve the conditions under which they lived. This meant that they might commit atrocities out of self-preservation, as well as enter into a range of behaviours (running away, lying, feigning illness) precisely to avoid killing.[79]

For girls, the 'fundamental feature' of their experience of being held by armies or rebel groups was sexual violence. This is not to suggest that boys were—and are—not subject to sexual abuse in wartime but rather to emphasise that the vast majority of girls who were abducted were raped and enslaved to provide sex. While they 'were used as domestic labour and performed tasks such as carrying water, searching for firewood, cooking, cleaning, and other daily chores', they were under constant threat from soldiers' sexual demands. Some did train as combatants, but relatively few—in comparison to boys—fought actively, instead guarding camps, and participating in reconnaissance and looting missions.[80] (Girls have, though, fought actively in conflicts, for instance in Sierra Leone.) Living mainly in the civilian section of camps in Mozambique, girls risked death and danger from men who were purportedly on the same side: many fell pregnant and might suffer injury or death in childbirth, childcare under these conditions was exceptionally difficult, and many were killed in disputes between soldiers.[81] In this context, girls found solidarities among one another, some managed to constitute enduring relationships with soldiers, and others who managed to remain in the camps for longer periods of time could wield power within these rigidly hierarchical societies. Life outside the army and the camps was dangerous too, with food shortages,

---

[76] Moyd, Clarke, and Plant, 'Moral Panic versus Moral Blindness,' p. 46.
[77] Honwana, *Child Soldiers in Africa*, p. 58.
[78] Honwana, *Child Soldiers in Africa*, p. 59.
[79] Honwana, *Child Soldiers in Africa*, p. 71.
[80] Honwana, *Child Soldiers in Africa*, pp. 78–79.
[81] Honwana, *Child Soldiers in Africa*, p. 85.

vulnerability to attack, absence of healthcare, and a range of other factors frequently causing girls to choose to join armies.

Even this brief overview of child soldiering in Angola and Mozambique demonstrates the difficulty of assisting demobilised child soldiers to reintegrate into societies which, usually, lack the resources and institutions to provide these young people with the material and psychological support they need to constitute lives as adults. Honwana observes that war and the army socialised these children into adulthoods which did not prepare them for peacetime living. She adds:

> In both Mozambique and Angola, many young soldiers were initiated into the military when they had not yet entered their teens. When they returned home after the war, they were seventeen or eighteen, and some were in their early twenties. For many families, boy children went away, but young men came back. These were not young men like their fathers and grandfathers had been; they had missed the training and initiation into adult male roles that their communities normally offer and had, instead, transgressed the boundaries of acceptable adult male behaviour.[82]

Honwana argues that reintegration was even more challenging for girls because of the stigma associated with rape and sexual assault—while those women who returned with children often struggled to support those babies too. While she points to the cleansing rituals in Mozambique performed by both traditional healers and priests from Zionist churches which offered both communities and demobilised child soldiers—girls and boys, combatant and non-combatant—affirmation, support, and social acceptance, Honwana points, too, to the necessity of providing skills training, jobs, and further medical care and psychological counselling, all forms of aid frequently beyond the means of two countries impoverished by civil war.[83] Echoing Diouf's analysis of youth protest in 1980s and 1990s Senegal, Honwana adds that one—of many—strategies both for including former child soldiers and preventing children's participation in future wars is political involvement.[84] Or, put another way, understanding young people as having a stake in the political processes of Angola and Mozambique and emphasising their status as citizens—as adults—with an important contribution to make to the nation. If children could fight for competing visions of national futures, then in peacetime they should be counted as participants in national politics too.

Conclusion

Writing about efforts to reintegrate child soldiers into Sierra Leonian society after a vicious civil war (1991–2002), anthropologist Susan Shepler traces the longer history of children fighting in precolonial and colonial wars in the region

---

[82] Honwana, *Child Soldiers in Africa*, pp. 143–144.
[83] Honwana, *Child Soldiers in Africa*, pp. 146–147.
[84] Honwana, *Child Soldiers in Africa*, p. 164.

and observes that recent work to understand the place of demobilised child combatants must acknowledge 'youth' as a political identity: young people in Sierra Leone (and elsewhere) have long, and especially in the colonial and postcolonial eras, participated in politics, often in violent ways. Making child soldiers part of societies once more requires not an embrace of an understanding of youth as inherently depoliticised, but, rather, as having a role in the exercise of power, and especially state power.[85] This move would require the recognition that, firstly, generational conflict has always been part of African societies. As patriarchal societies, these conflicts have tended to involve and to privilege men, but—as the example from 1950s Meru which opens this chapter suggests—girls have, too, found ways to navigate the double hierarchies of age and gender. Colonial rule exacerbated that tension, as elites frequently formed closer relationships with the state (and elders, settlers, and the state fought for access to young people's labour), and capitalist production served both to enrich older men and, in other places, better serve younger men and women. Colonialism opened up new avenues for becoming adults: through education, urbanisation, and new kinds of wage-earning labour. It is little wonder, then, that young people were so important to anti-colonial political struggle.

Secondly, it would also require the acknowledgment of how young people have been discriminated against on the grounds of their youth. The malleable yet powerful category of the delinquent suggested that it was partly young people's youth which rendered them so dangerous to the social order. Efforts to contain young people in reformatories, as well as postcolonial projects to train young people into becoming the leaders of the nation, all tried to curb potentially disruptive behaviour, political or otherwise. But as youth protests from independence onwards have shown, the increasing political, social, and economic marginalisation of young people—despite being numerically dominant—has significant consequences for ruling parties and the cohesion of African societies more broadly.

---

[85] Susan Shepler, 'Are "Child Soldiers" in Sierra Leone a New Phenomenon?' in *The Powerful Presence of the Past: Integration and Conflict along the Upper Guinea Coast*, eds. Jacqueline Knörr and Wilson Trajano Filho (Leiden: Brill, 2010), pp. 316–317.

CHAPTER 8

Conclusion

This book was begun and completed during the COVID-19 pandemic. As was the case with the HIV/AIDS epidemic—whose victims in Africa were mainly young—the nature of this most recent pandemic in Africa has been shaped by what scholars have described as the continent's 'youth bulge'. As infant and child mortality rates have lowered and fertility rates have remained high, so the proportion of the continent's population which is young has grown. In 2020, Africa was the world's youngest continent, with half of its population aged nineteen years old or younger. The median ages of the next-youngest continents—Latin America and Asia—are thirty-one and thirty-two years, respectively. Europe's population divides evenly at forty-two, making it the oldest continent. Trying to account for what has been dubbed the 'Africa paradox'— the fact that the globe's poorest and infrastructurally least developed continent appears to have suffered least from the virus—some epidemiologists have explored the possibility that the youth of the continent's population is one of the factors which has contributed to consistently low reported infections and deaths, among other reasons (including underreporting of statistics).[1] This framing of Africa's youth bulge as a benefit is in sharp contrast to reporting which tends to emphasise the threat it poses both to the continent and to regional stability. For instance, the software developer turned billionaire philanthropist Bill Gates has warned that in not addressing the youth bulge, Africa risks increasing inequality, falling into greater poverty, and more political upheaval.[2] Concern about Africa's young population is entangled with broader

---

[1] Laura Spinney, 'What can we learn from Africa's experience of Covid?' *The Observer*, 28 Feb. 2021, https://www.theguardian.com/world/2021/feb/28/what-can-we-learn-from-africa-experience-of-covid-death-toll-paradox.

[2] Polly Toynbee, 'The African Youth Boom: What's Worrying Bill Gates,' *The Guardian*, 18 Sept. 2018, https://www.theguardian.com/global-development/2018/sep/18/the-african-youth-boom-whats-worrying-bill-gates.

© The Author(s), under exclusive license to Springer Nature Switzerland AG 2022
SE. Duff, *Childhood and Youth in African History*,
https://doi.org/10.1007/978-3-031-11097-9_8

anxieties about overpopulation, which have long been shot through with eugenic ideas about race: the fear that white or European people might be supplanted by Africans or others deemed to be less advanced or civilised.[3]

This binary understanding of the youth bulge as an opportunity or as a danger elides a more nuanced understanding of the functioning of societies dominated demographically by young people. For instance, the political scientist Diane Singerman developed the concept of 'waithood' to describe one of the consequences of the youth bulge in contemporary Egypt and the Middle East:

> "waithood" ... [is] a liminal position between childhood, adolescence, and adulthood, which is socially equated with marriage. Adolescence no longer falls between the ages of ten and nineteen, but for many it can extend into a young man's thirties, or mid-twenties for educated, urban women.[4]

A collection of factors, including high unemployment (or underemployment) despite ever-increasing rates of education among the young, high costs of marriage, unaffordable housing, and the fact that this large demographic remains mostly excluded from political decision-making, all contribute to a growing frustration among young people over not being able to achieve the milestones which would allow them entry into adulthood.[5] Although Singerman's interest is in the Middle East and, specifically, the youth unrest which caused the Arab Spring, it is clear that 'waithood' has broader relevance beyond this region. Scholars of Africa have applied it to the continent too, pointing out its contradictory nature. Nancy J. Smith-Hefner and Marcia C. Inhorn comment that while some young men and women might find waithood to be a period of frustration and missed opportunity, for others it opens up 'a space for personal exploration and self-improvement'. It is also experienced differently by men and by women—for the latter, delayed marriage and childbearing allows both for new ways of living and working as adults, but also demands rethinking of what constitutes marriage, love, and relationships.[6] Waithood echoes into Africa's colonial past, where young people's ability to marry and establish their own families was slowed or hampered by the social, political, and economic effects of colonial conquest and capitalist production.

This scholarly research on waithood helps to capture the textures of everyday life of the young people caught up in a context neither of their own making nor of their own choosing. Writing a few years after the turn of the millennium, sociologist Jeremy Seekings complained that, too frequently, children and

---

[3] Matthew Connelly, 'To Inherit the Earth: Imagining World Population, from the Yellow Peril to the Population Bomb,' *Journal of Global History*, vol. 1 (2006), pp. 299–319.

[4] Diane Singerman, 'Youth, Gender, and Dignity in the Egyptian Uprising,' *Journal of Middle East Women's Studies*, vol. 9, no. 3 (Fall 2013), pp. 9–10.

[5] Singerman, 'Youth, Gender, and Dignity in the Egyptian Uprising,' pp. 10–13.

[6] Nancy J. Smith-Hefner and Marcia C. Inhorn, 'Waithood: Gender, Marriage, and Global Delays in Marriage and Childbearing,' in *Waithood: Gender, Education, and Global Delays in Marriage and Childbearing*, eds. Marcia C. Inhorn and Nancy J. Smith-Hefner (New York: Berghahn, 2021), pp. 3–5.

young people are figured either as heroes or villains, as they negotiate political and other struggles on the continent. Instead, he writes, scholars should address themselves to the task of 'identifying the "normal" for the young subjects of their study'.[7] Seekings's argument echoes a 1986 essay by the South African writer Njabulo S. Ndebele: 'The Rediscovery of the Ordinary'. In it, Ndebele argues that in seeking to illuminate the viciousness of apartheid, many South African authors fall into a 'spectacular' mode, reducing characters to racial stereotypes. Instead, he suggests, authors might turn to an attempt to write the 'ordinary'. His point is not that this would be an apolitical literature, but, rather, one which is more closely engaged with the struggle against apartheid: 'the ordinary day-to-day lives of people … constitute the very content of the struggle, for the struggle involves people not abstractions'.[8] The literary scholar Christopher Ouma has remarked that recent African fiction and memoir—by authors based on the continent and in the diaspora—often observes Africa through young protagonists precisely because they allow for an exploration of what might constitute the 'ordinary'. Veering away from depictions of Africa which emphasise its soaring victories or crushing catastrophes, novels like Chimamanda Ngozi Adichie's *Purple Hibiscus* (2003) and memoirs such as Binyavanga Wainaina's *One Day I Will Write About This Place* (2011) sketch the everyday lives of young Africans who regard themselves as 'ordinary'. In doing so, they interrogate what, precisely, constitutes an 'ordinary' family, household, or childhood on the continent in the twenty-first century.[9]

Focusing on the ordinary rather than the spectacular—rather than on heroes or villains—is not to suggest that there is a normative, 'ordinary' way of life that exists for all people across time in the same way. Rather, it is to consider how everyday life is constituted and how it changes over time and place—and that it usually exists in tension with how societies define what 'normality' should be. This helps us to understand how bigger political, economic, social, and cultural forces shape lives and how people respond to them; as this book has shown, how children and young people—who are often the least powerful people in societies—have their lives made and remade by these processes and find ways of understanding, living with, accommodating, or occasionally resisting them. 'Waithood' is a useful means of working out how neoliberal economic policies and demographic change, for instance, remake life courses and how those alterations are perceived and experienced. Thinking histories of childhood and youth through the ordinary—beyond the binaries frequently associated with children and young people in Africa—helps historians to approach three key ideas.

[7] Jeremy Seekings, 'Heroes and Villains: The Rediscovery of the Ordinary in the Study of Childhood and Adolescence in South Africa, *Social Dynamics*, Childhood and Adolescence in Southern and East Africa, vol. 32, no. 1 (2006), pp. 1–3.

[8] Njabulo S. Ndebele, 'The Rediscovery of the Ordinary: Some New Writings in South Africa,' *Journal of Southern African Studies*, vol. 12, no. 2 (1986), p. 156.

[9] Christopher E. W. Ouma, *Childhood in Contemporary Diasporic African Literature: Memories and Futures Past* (Basingstoke: Palgrave, 2020), pp. 39–70.

The first is that multiple definitions of childhood and youth could and did exist at the same time, and all of these were subject to change and to contestation. In the precolonial era, African societies' understanding of who was a child or a young person changed over time and place—there was no universal 'African childhood'—and both young people and adults patrolled and asserted, redefined, and questioned what constituted these categories. As Africans came into contact with societies from elsewhere—as they were drawn into commercial networks which spanned the Indian Ocean, the Mediterranean and the Sahara, and the Atlantic—so these connections, too, remade the meanings of childhood and youth. In this way, while European conquest in the nineteenth century brought with it a new set of ideas about childhood and youth, this was by no means the first time that Africans encountered people who considered age differently to how they did. Also, European notions of normative childhood were in a state of flux and changed as missionaries, traders, explorers, and administrators came into contact with Africans over a long period of time. Children and young people negotiated these changing expectations of childhood and youth, frequently being on the frontier of colonial conquest: encountering new ideas at mission schools or in churches, at the receiving end of new efforts to address 'delinquency', or in new forms of labour (coerced or otherwise).

Secondly, while the category of 'youth'—in particular—is linked usually to a specific, biological phase of development (in most cases, the onset of puberty), it can be detached from its biological referent. Or, put another way, 'youth' also describes social status and can exist as a political category. A person can be defined as a 'youth' even if they are not young but, rather, because they have not gained the markers of status necessary to enter into adulthood. The African Union defines 'youth' as ending at the age of thirty-five, gesturing perhaps to the long history of youth engagement in politics, where younger—often more radical—politicians claimed the title of 'youth' as they jostled for power with their elders. Youth can work in intersection with race and gender to determine who can and who cannot leave this phase: in settler societies on the continent, adult African men and women were perpetual 'boys' and 'girls' in the perception and language of whites. Colonial officials argued in the nineteenth and early twentieth centuries over when adulthood—defined as sexual maturity—was truly attained by African girls, believing that their bodies and warm climates made them sexually available to men far younger than their white counterparts. The scholarship on 'waithood' demonstrates that this condition of lengthened youth cuts across class barriers in many contexts, as both middle- and working-class youth struggle to find the well-paying jobs that would support married life.

Thirdly, age is crucial for writing social history. As a key vector of power in African societies, age has long been one of the most important forces in determining social hierarchies, the wielding of political power, and the constitution and maintenance of economic systems—in the precolonial, colonial, and postcolonial eras. This insight draws our attention, then, to the fact that all age categories are subject to change over time—in Africa and beyond. A history of childhood relies on a history of adulthood: these categories are mutually constituted. To produce a full account of how societies change over time requires, then, an attentiveness to how all people inhabit age categories over the course of their lifetimes. Age categories—from infancy to old age—are among the very few categories of identity which most people will inhabit, fitting themselves to, modifying, or refusing the shifting expectations and behaviours associated with those categories. These are all shaped by gender, class, race, and other factors. But all people remember how they moved from one to the next and might anticipate or fear those that lie in their future. It is to this human history of ageing that historians might turn to understand how societies have imagined their futures.

BIBLIOGRAPHY

Achebe, Chinua. *The Education of a British-Protected Child: Essays.* New York: Anchor Books, 2010.
Achebe, Chinua. *Arrow of God.* New York: The John Day Company, [1964] 1967.
Achebe, Nwando. *Female Monarchs and Merchant Queens in Africa.* Athens, OH: Ohio University Press, 2020.
Aderinto, Saheed. 'Colonialism and the Invention of Modern Nigerian Childhood.' In *Children and Childhood in Colonial Nigerian Histories.* Ed. Saheed Aderinto. New York: Basingstoke, 2015, pp. 1–18.
Akínyemí, Akíntúndé. 'Yoruba Oral Literature: A Source of Indigenous Education for Children. *Journal of African Cultural Studies.* Vol. 16, no. 2 (Dec. 2003), pp.161–179.
Akurang-Parry, Kwabena O. '"The Loads Are Heavier than Usual": Forced Labor by Women and Children in the Central Province, Gold Coast (Colonial Ghana), c. 1900-1940.' *African Economic History.* No. 30 (2002), pp. 31–51.
Akyeampong, Emmanuel. '"Wop e tam won pe ba ("You like cloth but you don't want children"): Urbanization, Individualism, and Gender Relations in Colonial Ghana c.1900-1939.' In *Africa's Urban Past.* Eds. David Anderson and Richard Rathbone. Portsmouth, NH: Heinemann, 2000, pp. 222–234.
Akyeampong, Emmanuel and Pashington Obeng. 'Spirituality, Gender, and Power in Asante History.' *The International Journal of African Historical Studies.* Vol. 28, no. 3 (1995), pp. 481–508.
Alanamu, Temilola. 'Yoruba Childhood.' *Transition.* No. 121, Childhood (2016), pp. 92–106.
Allen, Richard B. 'Children and European Slave Trading in the Indian Ocean during the Eighteenth and Early Nineteenth Centuries.' In *Children in Slavery through the Ages.* Eds. Gwyn Campbell, Suzanne Miers, and Joseph C. Miller. Athens, OH: Ohio University Press, 2009, pp. 69–85.
Allman, Jean. 'Fathering, Mothering and Making Sense of "Ntamoba": Reflections on the Economy of Child-Rearing in Colonial Asante.' *Africa.* Vol. 67, no. 2 (1997), pp. 296–321.

© The Author(s), under exclusive license to Springer Nature Switzerland AG 2022
SE. Duff, *Childhood and Youth in African History,*
https://doi.org/10.1007/978-3-031-11097-9

Allman, Jean. 'Rounding up Spinsters: Gender Chaos and Unmarried Women in Colonial Asante.' *Journal of African History*. Vol. 37, no. 2 (1996), pp. 195–214.

Alpers, Edward A. 'The Story of Swema: Female Vulnerability in Nineteenth-Century East Africa.' In *Women and Slavery in Africa*. Eds. Claire C. Robertson and Martin A. Klein. Portsmouth, NH: Heinemann, 1997, pp. 185–200.

Amadiume, Ifi. *Male Daughters, Female Husbands: Gender and Sex in an African Society*. London: Zed Books, 1987.

Arsan, Andrew, *Interlopers of Empire: The Lebanese Diaspora in Colonial French West Africa*. Oxford: Oxford University Press, 2014.

Asiedu-Acquah, Emmanuel. '"We Shall Be Outspoken": Student Political Activism in Post-Independence Ghana, c.1957–1966.' *Journal of Asian and African Studies*. Vol. 54, no. 2 (2019), pp. 169–188.

Barnes, Cedric. 'The Somali Youth League, Ethiopian Somalis and the Greater Somalia Idea, c.1946-48.' *Journal of Eastern African Studies*. Vol. 1, no. 2 (2007), pp. 277–291.

Bastian, Misty L. '"The Demon Superstition": Abominable Twins and Mission Culture in Onitsha History.' *Ethnology*. Vol. 40, no. 1, Special Issue: Reviewing Twinship in Africa (Winter, 2001), pp. 13–27.

Baughan, Emily. '"Every Citizen of Empire Implored to Save the Children!" Empire, Internationalism and the Save the Children Fund in Inter-War Britain.' *Historical Research*. Vol. 86, no. 231 (Feb. 2013), pp. 116–137.

Beecher Stowe, Harriet. *Uncle Tom's Cabin, or, Life among the Lowly*. Cambridge, MA: Belknap Press of Harvard University Press, 2009.

Beinart, William. 'Transkeian Migrant Workers and Youth Labour on the Natal Sugar Estates 1918-1948.' *The Journal of African History*. Vol. 32, no. 1 (1991), pp. 41–63.

Bernstein, Robin. *Racial Innocence: Performing American Childhood from Slavery to Civil Rights*. New York and London: New York University Press, 2011.

Berry, Sara. 'Social Institutions and Access to Resources.' *Africa*. Vol. 59 (1989), pp. 41–55.

Biko, Steve. *I Write What I Like*. San Francisco: Harper & Row, 1979.

Bleek, Wolf. 'Did the Akan Resort to Abortion in Pre-Colonial Ghana? Some Conjectures.' *Africa*. Vol. 60, no. 1 (1990), pp. 121–131.

Bradford, Helen. 'Women, Gender and Colonialism: Rethinking the History of the British Cape Colony and Its Frontier Zones, C. 1806-70.' *The Journal of African History*. Vol. 37, no. 3 (1996), pp. 351–370.

Brantlinger, Patrick. 'Victorians and Africans: The Genealogy of the Myth of the Dark Continent.' *Critical Inquiry*. Vol. 12, no. 1, 'Race,' Writing, and Difference (Autumn, 1985), pp. 166–203.

Breckenridge, Keith. 'The Allure of Violence: Men, Race, and Masculinity on the South African Goldmines, 1900-1950.' *Journal of Southern African Studies*. Vol. 24, no. 4 (1998), pp. 669–693.

Bridger, Emily. *Young Women against Apartheid: Gender, Youth, and South Africa's Liberation Struggle*. Oxford: James Currey, 2021.

Burchell, D.E. 'African Higher Education and the Establishment of the South African Native College, Fort Hare.' *South African Historical Journal*. Vol. 8, no. 1 (1976), pp. 60–83.

Burgess, G. Thomas and Andrew Burton. 'Introduction.' In *Generations Past: Youth in East African History*. Eds. Andrew Burton and Helene Charton-Bigot. Athens, OH: Ohio University Press, 2010, pp. 9–32.

Burton, Andrew. 'Urchins, Loafers, and the Cult of the Cowboy: Urbanisation and Delinquency in Dar es Salaam, 1919-1961.' *Journal of African History*. Vol. 42 (2001), pp. 199–216.

Burton, John W. 'Atuot Age Categories and Marriage.' *Africa*. Vol. 50, no. 2 (1980), pp. 146–160.

Campbell, Chloe. 'Juvenile Delinquency in Colonial Kenya, 1900-1939.' *The Historical Journal*. Vol. 45, no. (2002), pp. 129–151.

Campbell, Gwyn, Suzanne Miers, and Joseph C. Miller. 'Children in European Systems of Slavery: Introduction.' *Slavery and Abolition*. Vol. 27, no. 2 (Aug. 2006), pp. 163–182.

Campbell, Gwyn. 'Slavery in the Indian Ocean World.' In *The Routledge History of Slavery*. Eds. Gad Heuman and Trevor Burnard. London: Routledge, 2011, pp. 52–63.

Carretta, Vincent. *Phillis Wheatley: Biography of a Genius in Bondage*. Athens, GA: University of Georgia Press, 2011.

Carton, Benedict and Robert Morrell. 'Zulu Masculinities, Warrior Culture and Stick Fighting: Reassessing Male Violence and Virtue in South Africa.' *Journal of Southern African Studies*. Vol. 38, no. 1 (2012), pp. 31–53.

Carton, Benedict. *Blood from Your Children: The Colonial Origins of Generational Conflict in South Africa*. Charlottesville: The University of Virginia Press, 2000.

Chapdelaine, Robyn P. *The Persistence of Slavery: An Economic History of Child Trafficking in Nigeria*. Amherst and Boston: University of Massachusetts Press, 2021.

Chijere Chirwa, Wiseman. 'Child and Youth Labour on the Nyasaland Plantations, 1890-1953.' *Journal of Southern African Studies*. Vol. 19, no. 4 (1993), pp. 662–680.

Chisholm, Linda. 'The Pedagogy of Porter: The Origins of the Reformatory in the Cape Colony, 1882-1910.' *The Journal of African History*. Vol. 27, no. 3. (1986), pp. 481–495.

Chisholm, Linda. *Between Worlds: German Missionaries and the Transition from Mission to Bantu Education in South Africa*. Johannesburg: Wits University Press, 2017.

Coe, Cati. 'Educating an African Leadership: Achimota and the Teaching of African Culture in the Gold Coast.' *Africa Today*. Vol. 49, no. 3 (Autumn, 2002), pp. 23–44.

Coe, Cati. 'How Debt became Care: Child Pawning and its Transformations in Akuapem, the Gold Coast, 1874-1929.' *Africa*. Vol. 82, no. 2 (2012), pp. 287–311.

Cohen, Cynthia. '"The Natives Must First become Good Workmen": Formal Educational Provision in German South West and East Africa Compared.' *Journal of Southern African Studies*. Vol. 19, no. 1 (1993), pp. 115–134.

Cohen, William B. 'Literature and Race: Nineteenth Century French Fiction, Blacks, and Africa 1800-1880.' *Race and Class*. Vol. 16, no. 2 (1974), pp. 181–205.

Cohen, William B. 'The Colonized as Child: British and French Colonial Rule.' *African Historical Studies*. Vol. 3, no. 2 (1970), pp. 427–431.

Comaroff, Jean and John Comaroff. 'Reflections on Youth: From the Past to the Postcolony.' In *Frontiers of Capital: Ethnographic Reflections on the New Economy*. Eds. Melissa S. Fisher and Greg Downey. Durham, NC: Duke University Press, 2006, pp. 267–281.

Comaroff, Jean and John Comaroff. 'The Madman and the Migrant: Work and Labour in the Historical Consciousness of a South African People.' *American Ethnologist*. Vol. 14, no. 2 (May, 1987), pp. 191–209.

Comaroff, Jean and John Comaroff. *Of Revelation and Revolution: Christianity, Colonialism, and Consciousness in South Africa*. Vol. I. Chicago, IL: University of Chicago Press, 1991.

Comaroff, John L. 'The Closed Society and Its Critics: Historical Transformations in African Ethnography.' *American Ethnologist*.' Vol. 11, no. 3 (Aug., 1984), pp. 571–583.

Connelly, Matthew. 'To Inherit the Earth: Imagining World Population, from the Yellow Peril to the Population Bomb.' *Journal of Global History*. Vol. 1 (2006), pp. 299–313

Cook Anderson, Margaret. *Regeneration Through Empire: French Pronatalists and Colonial Settlement in the Third Republic*. Lincoln, NE, and London: University of Nebraska Press, 2015.

Cooper, Barbara. *Countless Blessings: A History of Childbirth and Reproduction in the Sahel*. Bloomington, IA: Indiana University Press, 2019.

Cooper, Frederick. 'Conflict and Connection: Rethinking Colonial African History.' *The American Historical Review*. Vol. 99, no. 5 (Dec., 1994), pp. 1516–1545.

Cooper, Frederick. 'The Problem of Slavery in African Studies.' *The Journal of African History*. Vol. 20, no. 1 (1979), pp. 103–125.

Cooper, Frederick. *Africa Since 1940: The Past of the Present*. Cambridge: Cambridge University Press, [2002] 2009.

Cunningham, Hugh. 'Histories of Childhood.' *The American Historical Review*. Vol. 103, no. 4 (Oct. 1998), pp. 1195–1208.

De Almeida Mendes, António. 'Child Slaves in the Early North Atlantic Trade in the Fifteenth and Sixteenth Centuries.' In *Children in Slavery through the Ages*. Eds. Gwyn Campbell, Suzanne Miers, and Joseph C. Miller. Athens, OH: Ohio University Press, 2009, pp. 19–34.

De Luna, Kathryn M. 'Affect and Society in Precolonial Africa.' *The International Journal of African Historical Studies*. Vol. 46, no. 1 (2013), pp. 123–150.

Decker, Corrie. 'A Feminist Methodology of Age-Grading and History in Africa.' *The American Historical Review*. Vol. 125, no. 2 (Apr. 2020), pp. 418–426.

Decker, Corrie. 'Reading, Writing, and Respectability: How Schoolgirls Developed Modern Literacies in Colonial Zanzibar.' *The International Journal of African Historical Studies*. Vol. 43, no. 1 (2010), pp. 89–114.

Decker, Corrie. *Mobilising Zanzibari Women: The Struggle for Respectability and Self-Reliance in Colonial East Africa*. Basingstoke: Palgrave Macmillan, 2014.

Delius, Peter and Clive Glaser. 'Sex, Disease, and Stigma in South Africa: Historical Perspectives.' *African Journal of AIDS Research*. Vol. 4, no. 1 (2005), pp. 29–36.

Delius, Peter and Stanley Trapido. '*Inboekselings* and *Oorlams*: The Creation and Transformation of a Servile Class. *Journal of Southern African Studies*. Vol. 8, no. 2 (1982), pp. 214–242.

Dhupelia-Mesthrie, Uma. 'India-South Africa Mobilities in the First Half of the Twentieth Century: Minors, Immigration Encounters in Cape Town and Becoming South African.' In *Children on the Move in Africa: Past and Present Experiences of Migration*. Eds. Elodie Razy and Marie Rodet. Woodbridge: James Currey, 2016, pp. 159–174.

Diouf, Mamadou. 'Urban Youth and Senegalese Politics: Dakar 1988-1994.' In *Cities and Citizenship*. Ed. James Holston (Durham, NC: Duke University Press, 1998, pp. 42–66.

Diptee, Audra A. 'African Children in the British Slave Trade during the Late Eighteenth Century.' *Slavery and Abolition*. Vol. 27, no, 2 (2006), pp. 183–196.

Doyle, Shane. 'Premarital Sexuality in Great Lakes Africa, 1900-1980.' In *Generations Past: Youth in East African History*. Eds. Andrew Ross Burton and Helene Charton-Bigot. Athens, OH: Ohio University Press, 2010, pp. 245–269.

Duff, S.E. '"Capture the Children": Writing Children into the South African War, 1899-1902.' *Journal of the History of Childhood and Youth*. Vol. 7, no. 3 (Fall 2014), pp. 355–376.

Duff, S.E. '"*Onschuldig vermaak*": The Dutch Reformed Church and Children's Leisure Time in the Nineteenth-Century Cape Colony.' *South African Historical Journal*. Vol. 63, no. 4 (2011a), pp. 495–513.

Duff, S.E. 'Saving the Child to Save the Nation: Poverty, Whiteness and Childhood in the Cape Colony, c.1870–1895.' *Journal of Southern African Studies*. Vol. 37, no. 2 (2011b), pp. 229–245.

Duff, S.E. *Changing Childhoods in the Cape Colony: Dutch Reformed Evangelicalism and Colonial Childhood, 1860-1895*. Basingstoke: Palgrave, 2015.

Duke Bryant, Kelly M. 'A "Sentiment of Humanity"? Child Protection, Surveillance, and State Guardianship in Senegal, 1895-1910.' In *Diverse Unfreedoms: The Afterlives and Transformations of Post-Transatlantic Bondages*. Eds. Sarada Balagopalan, Cati Coe, and Keith Michael Green. New York and London: Routledge, 2020.

Duke Bryant, Kelly M. *Education as Politics: Colonial Schooling and Political Debate in Senegal, 1850s-1914*. Madison, WI: The University of Wisconsin Press, 2015.

Durham, Deborah. 'Youth and the Social Imagination in Africa: Introduction to Parts 1 and 2,' *Anthropological Quarterly*. Vol. 73, no. 3, Youth and the Social Imagination in Africa, Part I (Jul., 2000), pp. 113–120.

Equiano, Olaudah. *The Interesting Narrative of the Life of Olaudah Equiano, of Gustavus Vassa, the African, Written by Himself*. Ed. Werner Sollors. New York and London: W.W. Norton, 2001.

Essop Sheik, Nafisa. 'Cultures of Sex, Laws of Difference: Age of Consent Law and the Forging of a Fraternal Contract on the Margins of the Nineteenth- Century British Empire.' *Law and History Review*. Vol. 38, no. 1 (Feb. 2020), pp. 201–218.

Falola, Toyin and Matthew M. Heaton. *A History of Nigeria*. Cambridge: Cambridge University Press, 2008.

Falola, Toyin and Paul E. Lovejoy. 'Pawnship in Historical Perspective.' In *Pawnship, Slavery, and Colonialism in Africa*. Eds. Paul E. Lovejoy and Toyin Falola. Trenton, NJ: Africa World Press, 2003, pp. 1–26.

Falola, Toyin. *Nationalism and African Intellectuals* Rochester, NY: University of Rochester Press, 2004.

Field, Corinne T. and Nicholas L. Syrett. 'Introduction: Chronological Age: A Useful Category of Historical Analysis.' *The American Historical Review*. Vol. 125, no. 2 (April 2020), pp. 371–384.

Fouchard, Laurent. 'The Making of the Juvenile Delinquent in Nigeria and South Africa, 1930-1970.' *History Compass*. Vol. 8, no. 2 (2010), pp. 129–142.

Gaitskell, Deborah. '"Christian Compounds for Girls": Church Hostels for African Women in Johannesburg, 1907-1970.' *Journal of Southern African Studies*. Vol. 6, no. 1, Special Issue on Urban Social History (Oct., 1979), pp. 44–69.

Gaitskell, Deborah. '"Wailing for Purity": Prayer Unions, African Mothers and Adolescent Daughters, 1912-1940.' In *Industrialisation and Social Change in South Africa: African Class Formation, Culture, and Consciousness*. Eds. Shula Marks and Richard Rathbone. London: Longman, 1982, pp. 338–357.

George, Abosede A. 'Within Salvation: Girl Hawkers and the Colonial State in Development Era Lagos.' *Journal of Social History*. Vol. 44, no. 3 (Spring 2011), pp. 837–859.

George, Abosede A. *Making Modern Girls: A History of Girlhood, Labor, and Social Development in Colonial Lagos*. Athens, OH: Ohio University Press, 2015.

Geschiere, Peter. '"The African Family is Large, Very Large": Mobility and the Flexibility of Kinship, Examples from Cameroon.' *Ethnography*. Vol. 21, no. 3 (2020), pp. 335–354.

Getz, Trevor R. 'British Magistrates and Unfree Children in Early Colonial Gold Coast, 1874-1899.' In *Child Slaves in the Modern World*. Eds. Gwyn Campbell, Suzanne Miers, and Joseph C. Miller. Athens, OH: Ohio University Press, 2011, pp. 157–172.

Glaser, Clive. 'Swines, Hazels and the Dirty Dozen: Masculinity, Territoriality and the Youth Gangs of Soweto, 1960-1976.' *Journal of Southern African Studies*. Vol. 24, no. 4 (1998), pp. 719–736.

Glaser, Clive. *Bo-Tsotsi: The Youth Gangs of Soweto, 1935-1976*. Oxford: James Currey, 2000.

Gleason, Mona. 'Avoiding the Agency Trap: Caveats for Historians of Children, Youth, and Education.' *History of Education*. Vol. 45, no. 4 (2016), pp. 446–459.

Grier, Beverly Carolease. *Invisible Hands: Child Labour and the State in Colonial Zimbabwe*. Portsmouth, NH: Heinemann, 2006.

Grier, Beverly. 'Child Labor and Africanist Scholarship: A Critical Overview.' *African Studies Review*. Vol. 47, no. 2 (Sept., 2004), pp. 1–25.

Guidi, Pierre. 'Independence and Influence: Empress Mänän School—An Ethio-French Girls' School in 1930s Ethiopia.' In *Empire and Education in Africa: The Shaping of a Comparative Perspective*. Eds. Peter Kallaway and Rebecca Swartz. New York: Peter Lang, 2016, pp. 299–320.

Guyer, Jane I. and Samuel M. Eno Belinga. 'Wealth in People as Wealth in Knowledge: Accumulation and Composition in Equatorial Africa.' *The Journal of African History*. Vol. 36, no. 1 (1995), pp. 91–120.

Hepburn, Sacha and April Jackson. 'Colonial Exceptions: The International Labour Organization and Child Labour in British Africa, c.1919-1940.' *Journal of Contemporary History*. (2021), pp. 1–24.

Hepburn, Sacha. '"Bringing a Girl from the Village:" Gender, Child Migration, and Domestic Service in Post-Colonial Zambia.' In *Children on the Move in Africa: Past and Present Experiences of Migration*. Eds. Elodie Razy and Marie Rodet. Woodbridge: James Currey, 2016, pp. 434–451.

Honwana, Alcinda. *Child Soldiers in Africa*. Philadelphia, PA: University of Pennsylvania Press, 2007.

Hunt, Nancy Rose. '"Le Bebe en Brousse": European Women, African Birth Spacing and Colonial Intervention in Breast Feeding in the Belgian Congo.' *The International Journal of African Historical Studies*. Vol. 21, no. 3. (1988), pp. 401–432.

Hunt, Nancy Rose. 'Colonial Fairy Tales and the Knife and Fork Doctrine in the Heart of Africa.' In *African Encounters with Domesticity*. Ed. Karen Tranberg Hansen. New Brunswick, NJ: Rutgers University Press, 1992, pp. 143–171.
Hynd, Stacey. 'Trauma, Violence, and Memory in African Child Soldier Memoirs.' *Culture, Medicine, and Psychiatry*. Vol. 45 (2021), pp. 74–96.
Hyslop, Jonathan. 'Food, Authority, and Politics: Student Riots in South African Schools, 1945-1976.' Unpublished paper. University of the Witwatersrand African Studies Institute. September 1986.
Iliffe, John. 'Poverty in Nineteenth-Century Yorubaland.' *The Journal of African History*. Vol. 25, no. 1 (1984), pp. 43–57.
Iliffe, John. *Africans: The History of a Continent*. Second ed. Cambridge: Cambridge University Press, 2007.
International Labour Organisation. *Global Estimates of Child Labour: Results and trends, 2012-2016*. (2017).
Ivaska, Andrew M. '"Anti-Mini Militants Meet Modern Misses": Urban Style, Gender and the Politics of "National Culture" in 1960s Dar es Salaam, Tanzania.' *Gender & History*. Vol.14, no.3 (Nov. 2002), pp. 584–607.
Ivaska, Andrew M. 'Of Students, "Nizers," and a Struggle over Youth: Tanzania's 1966 National Service Crisis.' *Africa Today*. Vol. 51, no. 3, Youth and Citizenship in East Africa (Spring, 2005), pp. 83–107.
James, Allison. 'Giving Voice to Children's Voices: Practices and Problems, Pitfalls and Potentials.' *American Anthropologist*. Vol. 109, no. 2 (2007), pp. 261–272.
Kallaway, Peter. 'National Education Systems: Africa.' In *The Oxford Handbook of the History of Education*. Eds. John L. Rury and Eileen H. Tamura. Oxford: Oxford University Press, 2019, pp. 228–239.
Kallaway, Peter. 'Welfare and Education in British Colonial Africa, 1918-1945.' In *Education and Development in Colonial and Postcolonial Africa: Policies, Paradigms, and Entanglements, 1890s-1980s*. Eds. Damiano Matasci, Miguel Bandeira Jerónimo, and Hugo Gonçalves Dores. Basingstoke: Palgrave, 2020, pp. 337–356.
Kiragu, Susan. 'Conceptualising Children as Sexual Beings: Pre-Colonial Sexuality Education among the Gĩkũyũ of Kenya.' *Sex Education: Sexuality, Society and Learning*. Vol. 13, no. 5 (2013), pp. 585–596.
Klein, Martin A. and Richard Roberts. 'The Resurgence of Pawning in French West Africa during the Depression of the 1930s.' *African Economic History*. No. 16 (1987), pp. 23–37.
Klein, Martin. 'Children and Slavery in the Western Sudan.' In *Child Slaves in the Modern World*. Eds. Gwyn Campbell, Suzanne Miers, and Joseph C. Miller. Athens, OH: Ohio University Press, 2011, pp. 124–139.
Kuzwayo, Ellen. *Call Me Woman*. Johannesburg: Picador Africa, [1985] 2005.
Kwamena-Poh, Michael A. 'The Traditional Informal System of Education in Pre-colonial Ghana.' *Présence Africaine*. No. 95 (1975), pp. 269–283.
La Fontaine, J.S. 'Two Types of Youth Group in Kinshasa (Léopoldville).' In *Socialisation: The Approach from Social Anthropology*. Ed. Philip Mayer. London and New York: Routledge, [1970] 2004, pp. 191–214.
Last, Murray. 'Toward a Political History of Youth in Muslim Northern Nigeria, 1750-2000.' In *Vanguard or Vandals: Youth, Politics, and Conflict in Africa*. Eds. Jon Abbink and Ineke von Kessel. Leiden and Boston: Brill, 2005, pp. 37–54.
Lawrance, Benjamin N. *Amistad's Orphans: An Atlantic Story of Children, Slavery, and Smuggling*. New Haven and London: Yale University Press, 2014.

Leach, Fiona. 'African Girls, Nineteenth-Century Mission Education and the Patriarchal Imperative.' *Gender and Education*. Vol. 20, no. 4 (July 2008), pp. 335–347.

Lee, Christopher J. 'Do Colonial People Exist? Rethinking Ethno-Genesis and Peoplehood through the *Longue Durée* in South-East Central Africa.' *Social History*. Vol. 36, no. 2 (May 2011), pp. 169–191.

Lord, Jack. 'Child Labour in the Gold Coast: The Economics of Work, Education, and the Family in Late-Colonial African Childhoods, c. 1940-57.' *The Journal of the History of Childhood and Youth*. Vol. 4, no. 1 (Winter 2011), pp. 88–115.

Lovejoy, Paul E. 'Autobiography and Memory: Gustavus Vassa, alias Olaudah Equiano, the African.' *Slavery and Abolition*. Vol. 27, no. 3 (2006a), pp. 317–347.

Lovejoy, Paul E. 'Slavery in Africa.' In *The Routledge History of Slavery*. Eds. Gad Heuman and Trevor Burnard. London: Routledge, 2011, pp. 35–51.

Lovejoy, Paul E. 'Slavery in the Colonial State and After.' In *The Palgrave Handbook of African Colonial and Postcolonial History*. Eds. Martin S. Shanguhyia and Toyin Falola. Basingstoke: Palgrave Macmillan, 2018, pp. 103–122.

Lovejoy, Paul E. 'The Children of Slavery—the Transatlantic Phase.' *Slavery and Abolition*. Vol. 27, no. 2 (Aug. 2006b), pp. 197–217.

Lovejoy, Paul E. and David Richardson. 'The Business of Slaving: Pawnship in Western Africa, c.1600-1810.' *Journal of African History*. Vol. 42 (2001), pp. 67–89.

Lovejoy, Paul E. *Transformations in Slavery: A History of Slavery in Africa*. Cambridge: Cambridge University Press, 2012.

Ludlow, Helen. 'Shaping Colonial Subjects Through Government Education: Policy, Implementation, and Reception at the Cape of Good Hope, 1839-1862.' In *Empire and Education in Africa: The Shaping of a Comparative Perspective*. Eds. Peter Kallaway and Rebecca Swartz. New York: Peter Lang, 2016, pp. 81–110.

MacQueen, Ian. 'Black Consciousness.' In *The Routledge Handbook of Pan-Africanism*, ed. Reiland Rabaka. London and New York: Routledge, 2020.

Mager, Anne. 'Youth Organisations and the Construction of Masculine Identities in the Ciskei and Transkei, 1945-1960.' *Journal of Southern African Studies*. Vol. 24, no. 4 (1998), pp. 653–667.

Marks, Shula. *Not Either an Experimental Doll: The Separate Worlds of Three South African Women*. Bloomington, IA: Indiana University Press, 1988.

Mayer, Philip and Iona. 'Socialization by Peers: The Youth Organization of the Red Xhosa.' In *Socialization: The Approach from social Anthropology*. Ed. Philip Mayer. London: Tavistock, 1967, pp. 159–190.

Mbembe, Achille. *On the Postcolony*. Berkeley, CA: University of California Press, 2001.

McKittrick, Meredith. 'The "Burden" of Young Men: Property and Generational Conflict in Namibia, 1880-1945.' *African Economic History*. No. 24 (1996), pp. 115–129.

McNee, Lisa. 'The Languages of Childhood: The Discursive Construction of Childhood and Colonial Policy in French West Africa.' *African Studies Quarterly*. No. 4 (2004), pp. 20–32.

Meer, Fatima. 'From *The (mis)Trial of Andrew Zondo*.' In *Fatima Meer: A Free Mind*. Ed. Shireen Hassim. Cape Town: HSRC Press, 2019.

Memoir and Poems of Phillis Wheatley, A Native African and a Slave. Boston: Geo. W. Light, 1834.

Mhike, Ivo. 'Intersections of Sexual Delinquency and Sub-Normality: White Female Juvenile Delinquency in Southern Rhodesia, 1930s–c.1950.' *Settler Colonial Studies*. Vol. 8, no. 4 (2018), pp. 575–593.

Miller, Joseph C. 'The World according to Meillassoux: A Challenging but Limited Vision.' *The International Journal of African Historical Studies.* Vol. 22, no. 3 (1989), pp. 473–495.
Miller, Joseph C. *Way of Death: Merchant Capitalism and the Angolan Slave Trade, 1730-1830.* Madison, WI: University of Wisconsin Press, 1988.
Moitt, Bernard. 'Slavery and Guardianship in Postemancipation Senegal: Colonial Legislation and Minors in *Tutelle*, 1848-1905.' In *Child Slaves in the Modern World.* Eds. Gwyn Campbell, Suzanne Miers, and Joseph C. Miller. Athens, OH: Ohio University Press, 2011, pp. 140–156.
Mokoena, Hlonipha. 'Christian Converts and the Production of Kholwa Histories in Nineteenth-Century Colonial Natal: The Case of Magema Magwaza Fuze and his Writings.' *Journal of Natal and Zulu History.* Vol. 23, no. 1 (2005), pp. 1–42.
Mokoena, Hlonipha. 'The Queen's Bishop: A Convert's Memoir of John W. Colenso.' *Journal of Religion in Africa.* Vol. 38, no. 3 (2008), pp. 312–342.
Mokoena, Hlonipha. *Magema Fuze: The Making of a* Kholwa *Intellectual.* Scottsville: University of KwaZulu-Natal Press, 2011.
Morton, Fred. 'Small Change: Children in the Nineteenth-Century East African Slave Trade.' In *Children in Slavery through the Ages.* Eds. Gwyn Campbell, Suzanne Miers, and Joseph C. Miller. Athens, OH: Ohio University Press, 2009, pp. 55–70.
Moyd, Michelle, Frances M. Clarke, and Rebecca Jo Plant. 'Moral Panic versus Moral Blindness: Responses to Children's Militarization in Uganda and the US.' In *Panic, Transnational Cultural Studies, and the Affective Contours of Power.* Ed. Micol Seigel. London and New York: Routledge, 2018.
Moyd, Michelle. 'Centring a Sideshow: Local Experiences of the First World War in Africa.' *First World War Studies.* Vol. 7, no. 2 (2016), pp. 111–130.
Murray, Stephen O. and Will Roscoe. 'Africa and African Homosexualities: An Introduction.' In *Boy-Wives and Female Husbands: Studies in African Homosexualities.* Eds. Stephen O. Murray and Will Roscoe. Albany, NY: SUNY Press, 1998, pp. 38–53.
Musisi, Nakanyike B. 'Colonial and Missionary Education: Women and Domesticity in Uganda, 1900-1945.' In *African Encounters with Domesticity.* Ed. Karen Tranberg Hansen. New Brunswick, NJ: Rutgers University Press, 1992, pp. 172–194.
Ndebele, Njabulo S. 'The Rediscovery of the Ordinary: Some New writings in South Africa.' *Journal of Southern African Studies.* Vol. 12, no. 2 (1986), pp. 143–157.
Nelson Mandela, *Long Walk to Freedom: The Autobiography of Nelson Mandela.* London: Abacus, 1995.
Niane, Djibril Tamsir. *Sundiata: An Epic of Old Mali.* Revised ed. London: Pearson, 2006.
Niehaus, Isak. 'Towards a Dubious Liberation: Masculinity, Sexuality and Power in South African Lowveld Schools, 1953-1999.' *Journal of Southern African Studies.* Vol. 26, no. 3 (2000), pp. 387–407.
Nwokeji, G. Ugo. 'Slavery in Non-Islamic West Africa, 1420-1820.' In *The Cambridge World History of Slavery.* Vol. 3: 1420-1804. Eds. David Eltis and Stanley L. Engerman. Cambridge: Cambridge University Press, 2011, pp. 81–110.
Nyanzi, Stella. 'Dismantling Reified African Culture through Localised Homosexualities in Uganda.' *Culture, Health & Sexuality.* Vol. 15, no. 8 (2013), pp. 952–967.
Ocobock, Paul. 'Spare the Rod, Spoil the Colony: Corporal Punishment, Colonial Violence, and Generational Authority in Kenya, 1897-1952.' *The International*

Journal of African Historical Studies. Vol. 45, no. 1, Toward a History of Violence in Colonial Kenya (2012), pp. 29–56.

Ocobock, Paul. *An Uncertain Age: The Politics of Manhood in Kenya.* Athens, OH: Ohio University Press, 2017.

Oroge, E. Adeniyi. 'Iwofe: An Historical Survey of the Yoruba Institution of Indenture.' *African Economic History.* No. 14 (1985), pp. 75–106.

Ouma, Christopher E. W. *Childhood in Contemporary Diasporic African Literature: Memories and Futures Past.* Basingstoke: Palgrave, 2020.

Pankhurst, Richard. 'Education in Ethiopia during the Italian Fascist Occupation (1936-1941).' *The International Journal of African Historical Studies.* Vol. 5, no. 3 (1972), pp. 361–396.

Parsons, Timothy H. *Race, Resistance, and the Boy Scout Movement in British Colonial Africa.* Athens, OH: Ohio University Press, 2004.

Peires, Jeff. *The Dead Will Arise: Nongqawuse and the Great Xhosa Cattle-Killing Movement of 1856-7.* Johannesburg and Cape Town: Jonathan Ball, 1989.

Pitje, G.M. 'Traditional Systems of Male education among Pedi and Cognate Tribes.' Part I. *African Studies.* Vol. 9, no. 2 (1950), pp. 53–76.

Reid, Richard J. *A History of Modern Africa, 1800 to the Present.* Second ed. Chichester: John Wiley & Sons Limited, 2012.

Renne, Elisha P. and Misty L. Bastian. 'Reviewing Twinship in Africa.' *Ethnology.* Vol. 40, no. 1, Special Issue: Reviewing Twinship in Africa (Winter, 2001), pp. 1–11.

Reynolds, Pamela. *War in Worcester: Youth and the Apartheid State.* New York: Fordham University Press, 2012.

Rodet, Marie and Elodie Razy. 'Child Migration in Africa: Key Issues and New Perspectives.' In *Children on the Move in Africa: Past and Present Experiences of Migration.* Eds. Marie Rodet and Elodie Razy. Woodbridge: Boydell & Brewer, 2016, pp. 1–29.

Seekings, Jeremy. 'Heroes and Villains: The Rediscovery of the Ordinary in the Study of Childhood and Adolescence in South Africa.' *Social Dynamics.* vol. 32, no. 1, Childhood and Adolescence in Southern and East Africa (2006), pp. 1–20.

Shepler, Susan. 'Are "Child Soldiers" in Sierra Leone a New Phenomenon?' In *The Powerful Presence of the Past: Integration and Conflict along the Upper Guinea Coast.* Eds. Jacqueline Knörr and Wilson Trajano Filho. Leiden: Brill, 2010, pp. 297–322.

Singerman, Diane. 'Youth, Gender, and Dignity in the Egyptian Uprising.' *Journal of Middle East Women's Studies.* Vol. 9, no. 3 (Fall 2013), pp. 1–27.

Smith-Hefner, Nancy J. and Marcia C. Inhorn. 'Waithood: Gender, Marriage, and Global Delays in Marriage and Childbearing.' In *Waithood: Gender, Education, and Global Delays in Marriage and Childbearing.* Eds. Marcia C. Inhorn and Nancy J. Smith-Hefner. New York: Beghahn, 2021, pp. 1–30.

Smith, Mary Felice. *Baba of Karo, a Woman of the Muslim Hausa.* New Haven and London: Yale University Press, 1981.

Spear, Thomas. 'Neo-Traditionalism and the Limits of Invention in Colonial Africa.' *Journal of African History.* Vol. 44 (2003), pp. 3–27.

Spencer, Paul. 'Becoming Maasai, Being in Time.' In *Being Maasai: Ethnicity and Identity in East Africa.* Eds. Thomas Spear and Richard Waller. London: James Currey, 1993.

Spencer, Paul. *Youth and Experiences of Aging among Maa: Models of Society Evoked by the Maasai, Samburu, and Chamus of Kenya.* Warsaw and Berlin: De Gruyter, 2014.

Spinney, Laura. 'What can we learn from Africa's experience of Covid?' *The Observer*, 28 Feb. 2021, https://www.theguardian.com/world/2021/feb/28/what-can-we-learn-from-africa-experience-of-covid-death-toll-paradox.

Stanley, Liz. 'Protest and the Lovedale Riot of 1946: "Largely a Rebellion against Authority"?' *Journal of Southern African Studies*. Vol. 44, no. 6 (2018), pp. 1039-1055.

Stephens, Rhiannon. 'Lineage and Society in Precolonial Uganda.' *The Journal of African History*. Vol. 50, no. 2 (2009), pp. 203-221.

Stephens, Rhiannon. *A History of African Motherhood: The Case of Uganda, 700-1900*. Cambridge: Cambridge University Press, 2013.

Stilwell, Sean. *Slavery and Slaving in African History*. Cambridge: Cambridge University Press, 2014.

Summers, Carol. 'Youth, Elders, and Metaphors of Political Change in Late Colonial Buganda.' In *Generations Past: Youth in East African History*. Eds. Andrew Burton and Hélène Charton-Bigot. Athens, OH: Ohio University Press, 2010, pp. 184-203.

Summers, Carol. *Colonial Lessons: Africans' Education in Southern Rhodesia, 1918-1940*. Portsmouth, NH: Heinemann, 2002).

Swartz, Rebecca. *Education and Empire: Children, Race, and Humanitarianism in the British Settlers Colonies, 1833-1880*. Basingstoke: Palgrave, 2019.

Tallie, T.J. *Queering Colonial Natal: Indigeneity and the Violence of Belonging in Southern Africa*. Minneapolis and London: University of Minnesota Press, 2019.

Thomas, Lynn M. '"*Ngaitana* (I will circumcise myself)": The Gender and Generational Politics of the 1956 Ban on Clitoridectomy in Meru, Kenya.' *Gender & History*. Vol.8, no.3 (Nov. 1996), pp. 338-363.

Thomas, Lynn M. 'Historicising Agency.' *Gender & History*. Vol. 28, no. 2 (Aug. 2016), pp. 324-339.

Thomas, Lynn M. 'Imperial Concerns and "Women's Affairs": State Efforts to Regulate Clitoridectomy and Eradicate Abortion in Meru, Kenya, c.1910-1950.' *Journal of African History*. Vol. 39 (1998), pp. 121-145.

Thomas, Lynn M. *Politics of the Womb: Women, Reproduction, and the State in Kenya*. Berkeley, CA: University of California Press, 2003.

Thornberry, Elizabeth. 'The Problem of African Girlhood: Raising the Age of Consent in the Cape of Good Hope, 1893-1905.' *Law and History Review*. Vol. 38, no. 1 (Feb. 2020), pp. 219-240.

Timbs, Liz. 'An In(ter)vention of Tradition: Medical Male Circumcision in KwaZulu-Natal, 2009-2016.' *Journal of Natal and Zulu History*. Vol. 32 (2018), pp. 55-77.

Toynbee, Polly. 'The African Youth Boom: What's Worrying Bill Gates.' *The Guardian*. 18 Sept. 2018, https://www.theguardian.com/global-development/2018/sep/18/the-african-youth-boom-whats-worrying-bill-gates.

Vansina, Jan. *How Societies are Born: Governance in West Central Africa before 1600*. Charlottesville, VA: The University of Virginia Press, 2004.

Vasconcellos, Colleen A. *Slavery, Childhood, and Abolition in Jamaica, 1788-1838*. Athens, GA: University of Georgia Press, 2015.

Vos, Jelmer. 'Child Slaves and Freemen at the Spiritan Mission in Soyo, 1880-1885.' *Journal of Family History*. Vol. 35, no. 1 (2010), pp. 71-90.

Waller, Richard. 'Rebellious Youth in Colonial Africa.' *Journal of African History*. Vol. 47 (2006), pp. 77-92.

Ware, Rudolph T. 'Slavery in Islamic Africa, 1400-1800.' In *The Cambridge World History of Slavery*. Vol. 3: 1420-1804. Eds. David Eltis and Stanley L. Engerman. Cambridge: Cambridge University Press, 2011, pp. 47–80.

Ware, Rudolph T. 'The Longue Durée of Quran Schooling, Society, and State in Senegambia.' In *New Perspectives on Islam in Senegal: Conversion, Migration, Wealth, Power, and Femininity*. Eds. Mamadou Diouf and Mara A. Leichtman. Basingstoke: Palgrave Macmillan, 2009, pp. 21–50.

Ware, Rudolph T. *The Walking Qur'an: Islamic Education, Embodied Knowledge, and History in West Africa*. Chapel Hill, NC: University of North Carolina Press, 2014.

White, Owen. *Children of the French Empire: Miscegenation and Colonial Society in French West Africa, 1895-1960*. Oxford: Clarendon Press, 1999.

Wilson, Monica. 'Nyakyusa Age-Villages.' *The Journal of the Royal Anthropological Institute of Great Britain and Ireland*. Vol. 79, no. 1/2 (1949), pp. 21–25.

Yates, Barbara A. 'Educating Congolese Abroad: An Historical Note on African Elites.' *The International Journal of African Historical Studies*. Vol. 14, no. 1 (1981), pp. 34–64.

Index[1]

A
Aba Women's War, 85
Abolitionism, 73, 82
Abolition of slavery, 51, 73–75, 117, 140
Abolition of the slave trade, 53, 83, 89
Achebe, Chinua, 101, 102, 104, 111, 112, 123–125, 130
Achimota College, 121, 123
Adams College, 122, 125
Adolescent, 2, 16, 26, 90, 105, 124, 125, 134, 137, 138, 155, 156, 159
Adult, 2, 4, 6–9, 11–13, 15, 16, 18, 24–27, 29, 31, 32, 35, 38–40, 43, 44, 47, 55, 58, 59, 62, 65, 67, 73, 75, 77–81, 87–89, 93, 97, 99, 103, 104, 114, 132, 135, 136, 139, 141, 144, 148–151, 160, 162, 165, 173, 175, 185, 187–189, 192, 194
Adulthood, 4, 7–9, 15, 25–28, 32, 36–38, 40, 42–44, 55, 57, 81, 88–93, 100, 104, 105, 107, 133, 134, 136, 145, 150, 155, 159, 160, 162, 163, 165–167, 188, 192, 194, 195

African, 1–16, 1n1, 18–20, 23–26, 28–44, 46–49, 51–54, 60–66, 68–71, 73, 74, 76–78, 80–104, 106, 108–116, 118–130, 137–140, 143–148, 150–154, 156, 158, 160, 162, 163, 166, 168–180, 182–185, 189, 192–194
African child, 1, 12, 13, 15, 62, 66, 70, 73, 78, 81, 82, 88, 91–97, 99, 102, 109, 111, 116, 120, 137, 140, 146–148, 183, 184
African National Congress (ANC), 1, 2, 167, 178
African National Congress Youth League, 167
Age, 2–44, 47, 54, 61, 62, 70, 74, 80, 81, 86, 89, 92, 93, 100, 104–106, 116, 126, 134, 136, 138, 144–147, 149, 153, 155, 157, 159–162, 167, 173, 179, 186, 189, 191, 192, 194, 195
Age grade, 7, 24–26, 38
Agency, 8, 10, 11, 13, 28, 91, 164, 184
Age of consent, 4, 173, 174

[1] Note: Page numbers followed by 'n' refer to notes.

Age-set, 24, 25, 38, 39
Akan, 32, 38, 42
Angola, 29, 85, 119, 130, 139, 147, 185–188
Anthropologist, 3, 7–9, 19, 24, 25, 33, 39, 50, 75, 95, 148, 179, 185, 188
Anti-apartheid struggle, 179
Anticolonialism, 103
Apartheid, 1n1, 2, 6, 119, 120, 178, 179, 185, 193
Apprentice, 47, 105
Apprenticeship, 73, 97, 103, 134, 135
Arabisation, 127
Archive, 10–14, 146, 158
Ariès, Philippe, 6
Asante, 59, 84, 138
Assimilation, 57, 72, 85, 110, 114, 123, 130
Atlantic world, 14, 15, 23, 55, 61, 70
Atwot, 27

B
Baby, 2, 3, 9, 11, 16, 17, 31–37, 64, 126, 132, 140, 188
Bambatha Rebellion, 162
Bantu Education, 120, 123, 127
Bantu Education Act, 119, 178
Bantu migrations, 22, 30
Bantu Purity League, 152
Belgian Congo, 85, 95, 112, 119, 142, 148, 176
Benin, 22
Berlin West Africa Conference, 48, 84
Biafra, 55, 56, 63
Biko, Steve, 178
Birth, 4, 17, 30, 32–37, 58, 95, 132, 147
Birth spacing, 95
Black Consciousness Movement (BCM), 1n1, 178
Boer Republics, 118
Boyhood, 6
Boys, 3, 15, 25, 26, 31, 35–37, 40–42, 63, 65, 79, 80, 91, 92, 94, 100, 105–107, 113, 114, 117, 134–136, 144, 145, 149, 153, 158, 160, 169, 170, 172, 173, 183, 184, 187, 188, 194
Boy Scouts, 15, 152, 154

Breast feeding, 95
Bride price, 33, 34, 138, 159, 162, 163
Bridewealth, 27, 29, 32, 159, 160
British Empire, 53, 63, 73, 101, 108, 173, 185
Buganda Kingdom, 84–85
Bureaucratic state, 88
Burkina Faso, 32
Burundi, 22

C
Cape Colony, 53, 72, 80, 97, 109, 117, 118, 122, 140, 150, 158, 170
Capitalism, 136, 138, 143, 145, 148, 154, 170
Caribbean, 66, 67, 140
Cattle, 15, 21, 23, 35, 40, 81, 92, 125, 134–136, 145, 159–163, 165
Cattle-killing, 159
Central Africa, 3, 14, 21, 46, 51, 53, 60, 63, 67
Ceremony, 8, 18, 24, 32, 33, 38, 40, 43, 52, 57, 81, 92, 105, 136, 157
Chibok girls, 2
Childbearing, 30, 99, 139, 192
Childhood, 2–6, 9–12, 14–16, 18, 19, 23, 24, 30, 31, 35–41, 43, 44, 47, 55, 56, 58, 79–101, 103, 105, 133, 140, 147, 169, 171, 174, 192–195
Child labour, 88, 132, 133, 137–148, 153
Childlike, 73, 78, 82, 86–92, 100, 101
Childrearing, 6, 36, 95, 96
Children, 1–18, 22–38, 40, 43–48, 51–67, 70, 73–82, 85, 87–107, 109–111, 113–120, 122–124, 126, 129–151, 153, 154, 156–158, 160, 165, 168–171, 173–176, 179, 183–189, 191–194
Child soldier, 158, 183–189
Christian, 1, 15, 44, 54, 58, 62, 68, 70, 79–81, 83, 87, 88, 93, 101–103, 106, 108, 111–113, 120, 124, 128, 139, 151, 156, 161–163
Christian evangelicalism, 83
Christianity, 21, 54, 62, 69, 80, 81, 83, 93, 103, 104, 111–113, 125, 130, 165, 166

INDEX 211

Church Missionary Society, 101, 111
Cinema, 1, 149, 168
Circumcision, 40, 42, 43, 136, 156–158
Civilising mission, 83, 111, 112
Class, 3, 4, 6, 7, 12, 13, 15, 18, 50, 88, 93, 99, 108–112, 114, 118, 121–124, 129, 140, 150–152, 166, 167, 169, 170, 175, 177, 181, 194, 195
Clothing, 45, 59, 112, 165, 175
Cocoa, 75, 138, 139, 142, 144
Cold War, 185
Colenso, John W., 79–82, 99, 100, 104, 108–110
Colonial conquest, 3, 6, 8, 10, 19, 20, 24, 43, 67, 75, 81–83, 85–92, 98, 100, 108, 111, 115, 137–148, 160, 163, 165, 170, 176, 192, 194
Colonialism, 48, 82, 86, 91, 119, 125, 126, 136, 153, 156, 160, 162–164, 166, 189
Colonial Office (UK), 117–119, 146, 147, 171
Colonial rule, 8–10, 15, 19, 25, 43, 48, 53, 79, 81, 84–86, 89–91, 93, 95, 97, 98, 100–102, 108–123, 128–130, 133, 134, 136, 138, 139, 142, 143, 145, 154, 158–164, 166, 167, 172, 173, 175, 176, 189
Colonisation, 20, 83, 100, 103, 115
Colony Welfare Office, Nigeria, 169
Coloured, 1n1, 96, 102
Comrades, 38, 179
Concentration camp, 118, 184, 185
Congo Free State, 53, 84, 95
Convention People's Party (CPP), 180, 181
Conversion, 69, 80, 81, 102, 112, 113, 125, 130, 164, 165
Corporal punishment, 172, 173
COVID-19, 191
Cowboys, 174, 175

D
Dahomey, 53
Dar es Salaam, 168, 174, 175, 181
Debt, 27, 45–47, 51, 52, 59, 60, 68, 70, 71, 75, 161

Debt bondage, 51, 58, 68
Decolonisation, 3, 10, 12, 16, 86, 100, 102, 121, 129, 153
Delinquent, 13, 97, 148, 150, 153, 169–171, 175, 176, 189
Democratic Republic of the Congo, 148
Detribalisation, 7, 158, 169–171, 175
Domestic work, 132
Drought, 63, 159
Dutch Reformed Church (DRC), 117, 118, 125, 126

E
East Africa, 3, 20, 22–24, 54, 72, 168, 185
Education, 1–3, 6, 12, 15, 28, 34–37, 41, 44, 59, 61, 62, 75, 79, 80, 85, 88, 96, 97, 99–134, 139, 142, 145, 148, 151, 154, 161–164, 166, 168–170, 174, 176–183, 189, 192
Ekukhanyeni, 79–82, 99, 108, 109
Emotion, 6, 17, 18, 30, 31
Encadrement, 182
Equiano, Olaudah, 55–57, 63–65, 67, 68, 77, 81
Ethiopia, 2, 21, 52, 106, 107, 120, 167
Europe, 6, 20, 52, 53, 62, 83, 87, 90, 94, 100, 103, 107, 109–111, 114, 121, 123, 127, 176, 191
Extra-marital pregnancy, 33

F
Family, 1, 6, 9, 11–13, 18, 20–24, 26–32, 37, 40, 45, 46, 49, 50, 55–57, 59, 60, 62, 67, 70, 76, 77, 79, 95, 97–99, 102, 104, 106, 118, 121, 124, 127, 128, 131, 132, 138–140, 143–146, 148, 149, 154, 160, 161, 168, 185, 188, 192, 193
Famine, 2, 23, 56, 60, 63, 68, 70, 91, 159, 165
Fashion, 25, 99, 105, 111, 128, 150, 154, 161, 166, 176, 181, 183
Father, 1, 2, 17, 25, 28, 30–33, 39, 40, 45, 46, 52, 59, 76, 79–81, 98, 99, 101, 104, 105, 131, 139, 159, 173, 188

Feminist, 4, 43, 94, 156, 173
First World War, 15, 25, 74, 86, 109, 162, 185
Folktales, 13, 35
Forced labour, 53, 139, 141, 145, 146, 185
Fort Hare University, 177
Fosterage, 75
Freedom, 2, 3, 47, 50, 52, 55, 58, 60, 62, 65, 68, 73, 75, 77, 87, 128, 161, 167, 183
French Empire, 69, 74
French West Africa, 74, 76, 98, 114, 119
Frente de Libertação de Moçambique, Mozambique Liberation Front (FRELIMO), 185
Fuze, Magema Magwaza, 79–82, 91–93, 99, 100, 104, 108

G
Games, 13, 31, 36, 37, 41, 135, 136, 152
Gangs, 141, 149, 158, 171, 174–176
Gangsterism, 149, 175
Gender, 3, 4, 6–8, 19, 25–27, 31, 38, 39, 43, 46, 61, 63, 100, 104, 134, 136, 159, 179, 189, 194, 195
Generation, 2, 8, 12, 14, 17–44, 77, 96, 102, 107, 120–122, 128, 160–163, 166, 167, 173, 176–178, 181–183
Germany, 83, 84, 94, 115, 185
Gerontocratic, 27, 160
Ghana (empire), 22
Ghana, 22, 32, 60, 75, 84, 104, 113, 121, 138, 180, 181
Gĩkũyũ, 38
Girl Guides, 6, 15, 152
Girlhood, 6, 10, 15, 94, 97
Girls, 2, 3, 8, 10, 15, 25, 33, 35–37, 39, 40, 42–44, 47, 52, 54, 59–61, 63, 65, 71, 72, 74, 76, 94, 95, 97, 105–107, 112–114, 116, 120, 121, 124, 127, 128, 131–135, 139, 141, 142, 144, 146, 149–153, 155–159, 163, 165, 170, 171, 173, 174, 176, 179, 183, 186–189, 194
Goats, 160, 165

Gold Coast, 63, 64, 75, 84, 121, 138, 139, 141, 143–146, 148, 152
Grandmother, 35, 127, 157
Great Depression, 76, 86, 97, 171
Great Lakes region, 22, 53, 160, 161, 186
Grey, George, 109, 110
Griot, 17, 18
Guinea, 18, 119

H
Hall, G. Stanley, 91
Hausa, 26, 32, 48
Hawking, 15, 94, 135
Herding, 15, 20, 35, 71, 80, 91, 103, 134, 136, 144, 145, 154
HIV, 42, 191
Holy Ghost Fathers, 139
Humanitarianism, 93
Husband, 32, 39, 45, 111, 112, 121, 132, 139

I
Ibadan, 101, 123, 124
Igbo, 22, 37, 55, 85, 101, 104
Imperialism, 69, 73, 78, 94, 108, 140, 169, 184
Inanda Seminary, 122, 152
Inboekselings, 140
Indenture, 140, 154
Independence, 27, 36, 79, 86, 90, 100, 118, 119, 129, 139, 148, 166, 177, 179–182, 185, 189
Indian, 1n1, 69, 77, 96, 97, 108, 109, 120, 124, 140, 141, 152, 168, 178
Indian Ocean slave trade, 77
Indian Ocean world, 7, 45, 53, 68, 69, 72, 133
Indirect rule, 79, 85
Industrialisation, 83, 87, 88
Industrial school, 109, 110
Infancy, 36, 195
Infant, 12, 17, 32–34, 37, 64, 71, 94, 95, 98, 191
Infantilisation, 89

Initiation, 7, 25–27, 31, 40–42, 47, 57, 81, 106, 127, 130, 155, 157, 173, 187, 188
Innocence, 15, 16, 47, 55, 88, 94, 184
International Labour Organisation (ILO), 146–148, 153, 154
Islam, 21, 22, 42, 71, 106

J
Jamaica, 65, 66
Johannesburg, 151, 166, 174, 175, 177

K
Kenya, 28, 38, 42, 43, 51, 84, 85, 94, 147, 148, 152, 155, 157, 170–173
Kenyatta, Jomo, 148
Kidnapping, 52, 55, 56, 61
Kingdom of the Kongo, 53
Kinshasa, 148–150
Kinship, 14, 22–24, 29, 35, 47, 49, 50, 54, 57, 59, 66, 67, 77, 154, 160, 165
Kuzwayo, Ellen, 106, 130

L
La Fontaine, Jean, 7, 148, 149, 154
Labour, 3, 4, 6, 8, 12, 15, 17, 22, 29, 32, 36, 43, 44, 46–53, 57–59, 61, 63, 65, 68, 69, 73–77, 85, 93, 95, 104, 108, 111, 116, 131–134, 137–148, 151, 153, 154, 161–163, 165, 166, 170, 171, 185–187, 189, 194
Lagos, 15, 94, 95, 97, 134, 169, 171, 176
Land ownership, 160
Lebanese, 96, 99
Liberia, 51, 86, 186
Life stage, 18, 24, 26, 62
Lineage, 23–30, 36–38, 40, 41, 44, 46, 49, 56–58, 77
Literacy, 128, 165
Livestock, 22, 27, 29, 40, 45, 104, 154, 159–161, 166
Lovedale Institute, 122
Lusaka, 131, 132

M
Macaulay, Thomas Babbington, 108, 109
Madagascar, 95
Madrasa, 103
Malawi, 98, 129, 134, 135, 160
Mali (Empire), 17, 18
Mali (modern nation-state), 18
Mandela, Nelson, 40, 166, 167, 177, 183
Marriage, 4, 8, 24, 26, 27, 29–33, 36, 38–40, 59, 75, 98, 105, 127, 138, 139, 143, 150–152, 156, 158–168, 192
Mau Mau, 156–158
Mauritania, 62
Mauritius, 69
Mayer, Iona, 7, 33, 39
Mayer, Philip, 7
Mediterranean trade, 53
Meer, Fatima, 1, 2
Menstruation, 42, 44, 105
Meru, 155–158, 189
Middle Passage, 61, 64–66
Midwife, 34
Migrant labour, 16, 143, 145, 165, 166
Miscegenation, 98
Missionaries, 12, 13, 15, 37, 41, 43, 44, 55, 70, 82–85, 87, 90, 91, 93–95, 97, 100, 102, 103, 106, 108–123, 125, 127, 129, 139, 148, 150–152, 156, 161, 162, 173, 194
Missionary schools, 116, 152
Missionary societies, 104, 115, 118, 129, 140
Modernity, 4, 7, 87, 103, 127, 129, 150, 164, 175
Mombasa, 86
Mossi, 32
Mother, 17–46, 51, 54, 56, 58, 59, 61, 64, 67–69, 71, 80, 94, 98, 99, 106, 111, 112, 121, 127, 128, 131, 134, 141, 157
Movimento Popular Nacional de Libertação de Angola, Popular and National Movement for the Liberation of Angola (MPLA), 185
Mozambique, 23, 45, 51, 70, 85, 119, 185–188
Multiple births, 37

Multiracial, 1n1, 15, 82, 96–99, 113, 120, 150, 170, 174, 178
Muslim, 18, 46, 47, 52, 53, 58, 62, 71, 103, 113–115, 119, 127

N
Namibia, 115, 164, 166
Natal Colony, 79, 82, 108, 162
National Service (Tanzania), 181, 182
National Union of Ghanaian Students, 180
Ndebele, Njabulo S., 193
Newborn, 17, 18, 34
New System, 117, 118
Niger, 26
Nigeria, 2, 9, 26, 91, 101, 102, 112, 123, 124, 152, 169, 171
Nkrumah, Kwame, 180, 183
Noble Savage, 87
Nongqawuse, 158–160
North America, 83
Nyakyusa, 24, 25
Nyasaland, 98, 134, 143–146
Nyerere, Julius, 152, 153, 182, 183

O
Operation Vijana, 181
Oral history, 12, 142
Oral tradition, 12, 13, 18, 20, 35
Orphan, 56, 158
Ovamboland, 164
Oyo, 38, 53, 83

P
Palm oil, 83, 142
Pandemic, 191
Parent, 1, 11, 15, 18, 21, 23, 30–33, 36–39, 44, 47, 55, 58, 60, 61, 64, 71, 74–77, 79–82, 87, 89, 90, 93, 95, 97, 99–104, 110, 111, 114, 115, 118, 120, 123–129, 131, 133, 141–144, 146, 149, 152, 155, 157, 165, 167, 169, 173, 176, 186
Partition, 48, 82–86, 103, 110
Pathfinders, 152
Patriarchs, 138, 139, 144, 148, 158, 160, 162, 165–167
Pawn, 28, 47, 51, 52, 58–60, 63, 77, 133, 134
Pawning, 14, 15, 29, 46, 48, 51–53, 58–60, 68, 75–77, 85, 134, 138, 139, 146, 184
Pawnship, 8, 29, 47, 51, 58–60
Pedi, 25, 34–37, 134, 135
Pitje, Godfrey, 7, 25, 34, 35, 134, 135
Placenta, 33
Plantation agriculture, 66, 143
Plantation slavery, 49
Play, 3, 15, 31, 35, 36, 39, 42, 88, 97, 128, 131–154
Poll tax, 162
Polygyny, 25, 29
Pondoland, 34, 144, 145, 164
Porter Reformatory, 170
Porters, 86, 134, 142, 146, 170, 185, 186
Portugal, 62, 185
Poverty, 45, 97, 118, 125, 130, 141, 149, 153, 154, 186, 191
Precolonial era, 11, 23, 25, 43, 133, 136, 158, 160, 166, 173, 194
Pregnancy, 33, 125, 151, 173
Primary school, 102, 114, 116, 129
Pro-natalism, 95
Protest, 2, 68, 90, 124, 158, 171, 176–183, 188, 189
Protestant, 84, 85, 111
Puberty, 25, 26, 38, 92, 105, 159, 194
Pubescent, 39, 62
Pupil, 47, 108, 111, 114, 120, 122–129, 176, 178

R
Race, 1n1, 3, 4, 6, 7, 9, 79–100, 109, 127, 192, 194, 195
Racism, 87
Rape, 67, 73, 188
Rebellion, 6, 16, 67, 73, 84, 90, 109, 154, 157, 158, 160, 162, 165
Reformatories, 12, 169, 171, 172, 189
Refugee, 185

INDEX 215

Resistência Nacional Moçambicana, Mozambique National Resistance (RENAMO), 185
Réunion, 69
Rhenish Missionary Society, 115
Rhodesia, 85, 97, 185
Roman Catholic Church, 120
Rwanda, 22

S
Sahara, 18, 21, 22, 46, 48, 53, 55, 194
Sahel, 18, 22, 86
Saint-Louis (Senegal), 74, 85, 112, 113
Save the Children Fund (SCF), 94, 148
School, 4, 6, 12, 15, 47, 74, 79–82, 88, 92–94, 97, 101–130, 132, 139, 146, 149–153, 158, 163–166, 168, 169, 172, 173, 176–180, 183, 194
Schooling, 15, 93, 95, 97, 100–130, 144, 145, 161, 171, 173, 174
Scientific racism, 84, 89, 100
Scouting, 152, 153
Scramble for Africa, 48, 84
Secondary school, 162
Second World War, 76, 86, 95, 101, 119, 123, 162, 166, 167, 170, 171, 174, 185
Sellasie, Haile, 107
Senegal, 18, 60, 74, 85, 106, 112, 113, 115, 127, 182, 183, 188
Servants, 15, 26, 47, 56, 61, 62, 67, 69, 71, 74, 134, 140, 144, 150, 167, 169, 184
Settler colony, 100, 117–119, 125
Sex, 8, 24, 25, 33, 35, 38–40, 62, 94, 98, 106, 125, 150–152, 170, 173, 186, 187
Shaka Zulu, 42
Sibling, 24, 45, 64, 66, 102, 134, 145, 184
Sierra Leone, 51, 60, 66, 120, 183, 186, 187, 189
Slavery, 7, 8, 13, 29, 45–60, 63–66, 68, 70, 73–78, 86–89, 117, 138, 140
Slave trade, 46, 52, 53, 55, 58, 65, 66, 70, 77, 78, 83, 87, 89, 100
Social death, 49

Socialisation, 7, 25, 28, 31, 35–37, 44, 103, 133, 134, 145, 149, 164, 168, 169, 172, 173
Somalia, 23, 167
Somali Youth League, 167
South Africa, 1n1, 2, 23, 25, 33, 34, 40, 53, 84, 85, 105, 118–120, 127, 140, 141, 143, 144, 151, 152, 164, 166, 177–179, 185
South African Students' Organisation (SASO), 178
South African War, 118, 184
Southern Africa, 1n1, 19–21, 23, 96, 97, 143, 161
Southern Rhodesia, 84, 97, 125, 137
South Sudan, 27
South West Africa, 115–117
Soweto uprising, 179
Stick fighting, 41, 42, 136, 172
Stowe, Harriet Beecher, 86, 87, 89
Student, 1, 10, 30, 102, 107, 114, 121, 122, 124, 126, 129, 140, 176–183
Subculture, 175, 176
Sundiata, 17, 18, 20, 30–32, 40
Swahili, 54, 71
Swahili coast, 70, 71

T
Tanganyika, 84, 152, 169, 181
Tanzania, 8, 21, 24, 25, 27, 41, 45, 72, 84, 107, 181, 182
Tanzania African National Union (TANU), 181
Tanzania African National Union Youth League, 181
Taxation, 73, 77, 182
Taxes, 63, 76, 85, 86, 162
Tea, 143, 146, 150
Teenager, 6, 16, 149, 150, 181
Tigray, 2
Tobacco, 143, 152
Toddler, 3, 31
Tradition, 12, 13, 18, 20, 35, 37, 40, 43, 94, 121, 123, 129, 143, 156, 158, 164, 178, 180
Trans-atlantic slave trade, 3, 14, 48, 49, 53, 87, 173
Transkei, 144

Tsotsi, 174, 175
Tutelle, 74, 75
Twins, 33, 37, 38

U

Uganda, 27, 32, 86, 90, 128, 152, 162, 163, 183, 186
Uncle Tom's Cabin, 86
Unfreedom, 45–78
União Nacional para a Independência Total de Angola, National Union for the Total Independence of Angola (UNITA), 185, 186
United African Students Revolutionary Front, 182
United States of America, 6, 60, 61, 86, 88, 91, 127, 149, 176
University, 4, 102, 103, 123, 128, 129, 166, 176–178, 181–183
Urbanisation, 3, 7, 150, 163, 168–176, 189

V

Village, 17, 22–25, 28, 30, 31, 45, 101, 102, 104, 111, 112, 114, 132, 144, 156
Violence, 2, 9, 10, 16, 50, 51, 57, 62, 65, 68, 86, 90, 126, 130, 149, 155–189
Vocational training, 103, 107, 109, 112, 182
Voice, 11–14, 102

W

Wage labour, 47, 73, 88, 145, 161, 163, 168, 169, 181
Wages, 16, 93, 119, 131, 132, 138, 139, 143–145, 148, 154, 161, 162
Waithood, 192–194
War, 2, 21, 35, 41, 52, 60, 68, 71, 84, 136, 159, 183–188
Wayfarers, 152
Wealth in people, 14, 23–30
Wean, 32, 35

West Africa, 15, 18, 21, 22, 30, 38, 42, 46, 49, 53, 62, 63, 75, 84, 86, 96, 106, 182
Wheatley, Phillis, 60, 61, 65, 66, 77
Wife, 17, 26, 31, 33, 40, 45, 56, 58, 59, 111, 112, 131, 139
Wilson, Godfrey, 7, 8, 164
Wilson, Monica, 7, 8, 24, 25, 164
Work, 3, 4, 6, 7, 10, 12, 14, 15, 20, 29, 32, 36, 44, 47, 49–52, 54, 59, 61, 62, 69, 71, 73, 74, 79, 81, 86, 88, 90, 91, 94, 97, 101, 105, 109, 111–113, 115, 116, 120, 131–154, 158, 160, 161, 163, 166–171, 173, 176, 178, 180, 182, 185, 189, 194

X

Xhosa, 23, 33, 39–42, 136, 144, 145, 159, 160

Y

Yao, 45, 46, 54, 68, 143, 160
Yoruba, 22, 36–38, 59, 60, 83
Young people, 2, 3, 6–10, 12, 13, 15, 16, 24, 25, 27, 30, 31, 36, 38–40, 43, 44, 47, 48, 53–55, 65, 82, 89, 91, 96, 100, 103–105, 113, 124, 133, 136, 138, 144–146, 148–154, 157, 158, 160, 162–174, 176, 179–185, 188, 189, 192–194
Youth bulge, 191, 192
Youth culture, 150, 154, 165, 168, 169, 174
Youth politics, 158

Z

Zaire, 148–150, 177
Zambia, 16, 84, 131, 132, 143, 153
Zanzibar, 46, 53–55, 68–71, 127
Zimbabwe, 84, 97, 125, 137, 185
Zondo, Andrew, 1–3, 6
Zulu, 23, 42, 43, 79–82, 84, 92, 99, 100, 108, 136, 162

GPSR Compliance
The European Union's (EU) General Product Safety Regulation (GPSR) is a set of rules that requires consumer products to be safe and our obligations to ensure this.

If you have any concerns about our products, you can contact us on

ProductSafety@springernature.com

In case Publisher is established outside the EU, the EU authorized representative is:

Springer Nature Customer Service Center GmbH
Europaplatz 3
69115 Heidelberg, Germany

www.ingramcontent.com/pod-product-compliance
Lightning Source LLC
LaVergne TN
LVHW020329260326
834688LV00037B/940